THE PRINCIPAL'S GUIDE TO
SCHOOL
BUDGETING

SECOND EDITION

Dedicated to Louise Moser and Xavier Barrera,
who helped shape us into effective school leaders.

—the Boys

THE PRINCIPAL'S GUIDE TO
SCHOOL BUDGETING

SECOND EDITION

RICHARD D. SORENSON
LLOYD MILTON GOLDSMITH

CORWIN
A SAGE Company

CORWIN
A SAGE Company

FOR INFORMATION:

Corwin
A SAGE Company
2455 Teller Road
Thousand Oaks, California 91320
(800) 233-9936
www.corwin.com

SAGE Publications Ltd.
1 Oliver's Yard
55 City Road
London, EC1Y 1SP
United Kingdom

SAGE Publications India Pvt. Ltd.
B 1/I 1 Mohan Cooperative Industrial Area
Mathura Road, New Delhi 110 044
India

SAGE Publications Asia-Pacific Pte. Ltd.
3 Church Street
#10–04 Samsung Hub
Singapore 049483

Acquisitions Editor: Arnis Burvikovs
Associate Editor: Desirée A. Bartlett
Editorial Assistant: Kimberly Greenberg
Permissions Editor: Karen Ehrmann
Production Editor: Veronica Stapleton
Copy Editor: Kim Husband
Typesetter: Hurix Systems Pvt. Ltd.
Proofreader: Dennis W. Webb
Indexer: Gloria Tierney
Cover Designer: Scott Van Atta

Printed in the United States of America

Library of Congress Cataloging-in-Publication Data

Sorenson, Richard D.

The principal's guide to school budgeting / Richard D. Sorenson, Lloyd Milton Goldsmith. — Second edition.

pages cm

Includes bibliographical references and index.

ISBN 978-1-4522-5547-7 (pbk. : alk. paper)

1. School budgets—United States. I. Title.

LB2830.2.S67 2013

371.2'060973—dc23

2012038231

This book is printed on acid-free paper.

13 14 15 16 10 9 8 7 6 5 4 3 2

Contents

Preface

Reform movements are continuously redefining effective practice in school administration and initiatives such as state deregulation, district decentralization, school restructuring, and other organizational modifications and transformations. These ever-changing practices, to include the reauthorization of the No Child Left Behind Act (2011), bring into question the roles and expectations associated with being a modern-day school leader, especially in an era of economic downturn and fiscal restraint. How will the next generation of educational leaders be prepared for the "real world" of school administration?

This newly revised, second edition of *The Principal's Guide to School Budgeting* is purposefully written for practicing and aspiring public and private school administrators who want to enhance their instructional, technical, and managerial skills not only as the school's leader but also as the school's visionary, planning coordinator, and budgeting manager. The authors provide the reader with an essential understanding of the interwoven relationship between two independent yet distinctly connected accountability systems—academic and fiscal.

School leaders—from a financial and budgetary perspective—are responsible for understanding the equity issues and fiscal consequences associated with school budgeting as well as the relationship between educational goal development and resource allocation management. The authors provide school leaders with an overview of school budgeting practices within a collaborative decision-making context. Using school-oriented situations and the national standards for administrators as they relate to school leadership and budgeting, the reader acquires the necessary skills to plan and develop a budget;

allocate, expend, and monitor funds; manage and evaluate budget reports; and prepare school action or improvement plans aligned with a fiscal accountability system.

To enhance the book's usefulness as a desk resource, it has been purposely organized into brief, single-topic-focused chapters. Each chapter begins with an appropriate quote and general overview and includes numerous visuals, tables, and relevant activities such as utilizing accounting codes, projecting student populations, conducting a needs assessment, implementing a budget calendar, and building, defending, and amending a budget. For example:

- Chapter 1, Understanding the Budgeting Process, examines the delineation between school finance and school budgeting, the basics of school finance, sources of school funding, codification processes as related to budgeting, and essential steps to budgetary success. This chapter also examines budgeting in times of economic downturn and fiscal conservatism. Specifically, the section of the chapter provides the reader with recommendations for school leaders in coping with budgeting in hard times.

- Chapter 2, The Budget–Vision Relationship and the National Standards, presents and reviews the Interstate School Leaders Licensure Consortium (ISLLC) standards in relation to the correlation between budget, vision, and planning, knowledge, and skills necessary to be an effective school leader, and the three keys to ethics in school leadership.

- Chapter 3, Culture, Data, and Celebrating Success, reflects upon the importance of school culture, data-driven decision making, and types of data and assessment as related to academic planning and school budgeting as well as the importance of celebrating success.

- Chapter 4, A Model for Integrating Vision, Planning, and Budgeting, showcases an eight-component model related to budget and vision implementation and concludes with a real-life planning metaphor that correlates with the elements of an educational action plan.

- Chapter 5, Effective and Efficient Budgeting Practices, examines the budget plan, expenditure accountability and control, budgetary systems, and accounting and auditing procedures. The reauthorization of the No Child Left Behind Act (2011) is examined in relation to the numerous dictates, such as high-quality teachers and schools in need of assistance, each of which are central to the act and, just as important from a budgetary perspective, cost money—money that school districts often do not have.

- Chapter 6, Building the School Budget, reflects upon the budgeting process and those responsible for building the budget, coding applications, the concept of projecting student enrollment, and major budgeting issues and considerations. This chapter also contains three student-centered case studies, including a major case study: *The Budget Development Project.*

Special features of the book include:

- Discussion questions
- Case Study applications and problems
- Experiential exercises
- Budgeting Checklist for administrators
- Selected templates and forms
- References and resources

School budgeting is a daunting process for many school leaders because most are not bookkeepers, accountants, or financial planners. Many have received minimal training in the budgeting process. This process involves not only computerized accounting procedures and programs but also vision and goal development, instructional planning, and decision making. This can intimidate even the best educational leaders due to their lack of understanding of school-based budgeting and its integrative approaches. Such can explain the willingness of some leaders to ignore, avoid, or pass on certain budgetary and planning responsibilities to others. For these reasons alone, the newly revised *The Principal's Guide to School Budgeting* has been written by two former school administrators with a combined 75 years of experience in the public school arena and who, moreover, have extensive practical experience working with site-based decision-making committees in writing instructional goals and objectives, in the development of school and district budgets, and in defending instructional and budget outcomes to superintendents and school boards.

The Principal's Guide to School Budgeting, second edition, is not designed to be an exhaustive study of the budget and planning subject, nor is it designed to merely provide a basic understanding of the topic. Instead, the contents provide the necessary information and tools needed to incorporate the ideas set forth into real school applications. As a result, readers will be able to take the integrated budget, vision, and planning concepts presented and incorporate them in a practical and relevant manner in their own school settings.

Note: The authors have made every effort in this book to provide accurate and up-to-date Internet information. However, the Internet and electronically posted information are continuously changing. Therefore, it is inevitable that some of the Internet websites listed within this text may change or become obsolete.

Acknowledgments

We would like to express our appreciation to several individuals who contributed to the development of our book, both the first and second editions of *The Principal's Guide to School Budgeting*. So many people have influenced our lives and careers as school administrators and university professors. To those special individuals and friends, we publicly extend our respect and gratitude. A special acknowledgment is extended to the fine folks at Corwin, especially Arnis Burvikovs, our editor, and Lizzie Brenkus, our first editor, both of whom believed in us and took our written project and helped us fulfill another goal in our professional lives. Also, we are so appreciative of the guidance and help we received from Kimberly Greenberg, our editorial assistant.

First, I would like to thank my spouse and children: Donna, my loving wife and best friend of 37 years, and the mother of my two adult children—Lisa (a kindergarten teacher) and Ryan (a physical therapy student). Of course, I would be remiss in not recognizing our fine son-in-law, Sam (a petroleum engineer), and our first grandchild, Savannah Grace (You bring a smile to my face each time I see or think of you!). Hook Em Horns, kiddos!

Second, this book has been strengthened by the contributions of my dear friend and former colleague—Alice Frick, school finance wizard extraordinaire—and two very special research assistants: Mary F. Sholtis (second edition) and Adriana E. Spencer (first edition). These three individuals—Alice, Mary, and Adriana—provided me with invaluable advice and assistance. Mary and Adriana did exceptional research for me. They actively and accurately followed my credo: "Dig, and dig deep!" Thank you, ladies!

Finally, for allowing me to try out all of my budgeting "stuff," a special note of appreciation is extended to all of the graduate students in the Department of Educational Leadership and Foundations at the University of Texas at El Paso. Serving you has been an honor and a privilege.

—RDS

I would like to thank Mary, my patient wife and confidant, for having patience with me through this process. I want to thank my colleagues, Dr. Donnie Snider, Dr. Karen Maxwell, and Dr. Bruce Scott, for their invaluable support and advice. A special thanks to my colleagues on the Texas Council of Professors of Educational Administration Executive Board for their friendship and support. Finally, thanks to Bob and Montie Spaulding for being spiritual advisors to me for most of my life, helping me to keep first things first.

—LMG

About the Authors

Richard D. Sorenson is the director of the Principal Preparation Program and department chairperson in the Educational Leadership and Foundations Department at the University of Texas at El Paso. He earned his EdD from Texas A&M University at Corpus Christi in the area of educational leadership. Dr. Sorenson served public schools for 25 years as a social studies teacher, principal, and associate superintendent for human resources (personnel). Currently, Dr. Sorenson works with graduate students at UTEP in the area of school-based budgeting, personnel, educational law, and leadership development. He was named the University of Texas at El Paso College of Education Professor of the Year (2005), and he is an active writer with numerous professional journal publications. Dr. Sorenson has also authored textbooks, teacher resource guides, and workbooks in the area of the elementary and secondary social studies curricula. He conducts workshops at the state and national levels on topics such as instructional leadership and effective teaching practices, and he has been actively involved in numerous professional organizations, including the Texas Elementary Principals and Supervisors Association (TEPSA), the Texas Association of Secondary School Principals (TASSP), for which he conducts annual new-principal academy seminars, and the Texas Council for the Social Studies (TCSS). Dr. Sorenson's research interest is in the area of the school principalship, specifically the examination of conditions and factors that inhibit and discourage lead teachers from entering school administration.

He has been married to his wife, Donna, for the past 37 years, and has two children, Lisa and Ryan, a wonderful son-in-law, Sam, and one grandchild, Savannah Grace—all of whom are the pride and joy of his life. Of course, the Sorenson family remains a lover of pugs, most notably one Little Bit (wanna go?) and Olive (wanna snack?) too!

Lloyd Milton Goldsmith earned his EdD in educational leadership from Baylor University. He is a professor in the Graduate Studies in Education Department at Abilene Christian University, where he also serves as the Director of the Principal Preparation Program. Dr. Goldsmith teaches school budgeting and instructional leadership and supervises practicum experiences. He served public schools for 29 years as an elementary science teacher, middle school assistant principal, and elementary school principal. He and a fellow chemistry professor are in their 11th year codirecting a program facilitating high school chemistry teachers in developing effective instructional strategies. Dr. Goldsmith has served on several state committees for the Texas Education Agency. He is the president of the Texas Council of Professors of Educational Administration. His research interests relate to effective principal practices and practicum design. Dr. Goldsmith enjoys teaching in his church's inner-city outreach ministry, where he helps equip those living in poverty to better handle life's challenges. He is active in Kiwanis International, serving as a volunteer at a local elementary school. Dr. Goldsmith has been married to his wife, Mary, for the past 26 years and has three adult children—Abigail, Eleanor, and Nelson. Abigail and son-in-law Andrew recently made him a grandfather with the birth of Luke Walling Harmon. Llola, his chocolate lab, is royally spoiled and walks the good doctor daily. Life is good. Eleanor is nearing completion of her elementary education degree with ESL and bilingual certification. Nelson is a sophomore accounting and finance major and avid bass fisherman.

Introduction

Budgeting and accounting intimidate many individuals, whether it is at work or at home. In this book, the reader examines numerous budgeting processes and connects each to the school's vision as well as the national Interstate School Leaders Licensure Consortium (ISLLC) standards. Other factors such as culture, data, and celebrating success are also considered.

The reader is introduced to a budget model that integrates visioning, planning, and budgeting. Effective and efficient budgeting processes are explored, as is building a school budget.

However, before delving into school budgeting, the authors encourage you, the reader, to complete the *Gladys Weatherspoon Case Study* located in Resource B. This case study is about an aging mother who can no longer continue to live independently. The reader, acting in the role of one of Gladys's adult children, must review the situation to determine what must be done given Gladys's situation and her financial resources. The resources are not as much as desired and will have to be managed efficiently to meet Gladys's individual needs.

This case study is realistic, and many if not most will face this situation at some point in life. All learners gain a deeper understanding of lesson concepts when a personal connection is involved. Completing the Weatherspoon case study will help the reader better understand the factors and issues involved in school budgeting.

Go to Resource B and complete this case study. It will be even better if completed as a group project.

Chapter 1

Understanding the Budgeting Process

A budget will not work unless you do!

—Anonymous

The Basics of School Budgeting

School leaders must devote a vast amount of time and energy to school funding and budgeting issues in any era, but especially in eras of fiscal conservatism and economic downturn. Those leaders who fail to do so commit a terrible disservice to their schools and, more important, to their students. Why is budgeting so essential beyond the stated reason? First and foremost, the budgeting process enables school leaders to develop an understanding of the need for strong organizational skills, technical competence, and the collaborative process to include trust development. Numerous studies have documented the importance of strong organizational skills to an individual's success and effectiveness as a leader. Hughes, Ginnett, and Curphy (2009) reveal that technical competence concerns the knowledge base and particular behaviors that one can bring to successfully completing a task. School leaders generally acquire technical competence, specifically in relation to the budgetary process, through formal education or training but more often than not from on-the-job experiences (Yukl, 2010). Thus, one can readily note that one of the primary purposes of this book is to serve as a school leader's guide to appropriate and effective school-based budgeting.

Knowing how to properly develop a school budget and recognizing why budgeting and accounting procedures are an integral part of an instructional program are keys to understanding why goal development and instructional planning are significantly impacted by the budgeting process. Appropriation of public funds for a school is ensured by adopting a budget that includes all estimated revenues and proposed expenditures for a 12-month fiscal year. Budget accounts in most states are reported electronically under a Fiscal Education Information Management System (FEIMS). The FEIMS process will be examined in greater detail in Chapter 5. Therefore, the adoption of a district budget by the local school board provides the legal authorization for school leaders to expend public funds.

The nationally recognized Governmental Accounting Standards Board (GASB) prescribes that budgets for public education entities be reported on the basis of a standard operating accounting code structure (National Center for Education Statistics, 2009a). An example of a state's operating accounting code structure is shown by fund, function, object, sub-object, organization, fiscal year, and program intent code in Table 1.1. Most states require that a standard operating accounting code structure be adopted by every school district. A major purpose of the accounting code structure is to ensure that the sequence of codes is uniformly applied to all school districts to further account for the appropriation and expenditure of public funds (Governmental Accounting Standards Board, 2011). This aspect of the budgeting process will be further explored in Chapter 5.

Table 1.1   Example of a State's Operating Accounting Code Structure

199 — 11 — 6399.00 — 001 — Insert Current Year — 11						
1	**2**	**3**	**4**	**5**	**6**	**7**

1 = Fund Code. *How will the expenditure be financed?*

School district accounting systems are organized and operated on a fund basis. A fund is an accounting entity with a self-balancing set of accounts recording financial resources and liabilities. There are more than 500 different types of fund codes, and examples include: General Fund, Bilingual

Education, Special Education, Title I, Vocational Education, and so forth.

2 = Function Code. *Why is the expenditure being made?*

The function code is an accounting entity that is applied to expenditures and expenses and identifies the purpose of any school district transaction. There are at least 27 different types of function codes; examples include: Instruction, School Leadership, Guidance Counseling, Health Services, and so forth.

3 = Object Code. *What is being purchased?*

The object code is an accounting entity identifying the nature and object of an account, a transaction, or a source. There are more than 35 different types of object codes and examples include: Payroll, Professional and Contracted Services, Supplies and Materials, Capital Outlay, and so forth.

4 = Subobject Code. *For which department or grade level is the purchase being made?*

The subobject code is an accounting entity that is often utilized to delineate, as an example, secondary-level departments.

5 = Organization Code. *What unit is making the purchase?*

The organization code is an accounting entity that identifies the organization, that is, High School, Middle School, Elementary School, Superintendent's office, and so forth. The activity, not the location, defines the organization within a school district. There are more than 900 organization codes. For example, expenditures for a high school might be classified as 001, as the organization codes for high school campuses are generally identified as 001 through 040. Middle School organization codes are typically stipulated as 041 through 100. Elementary schools fall into the organization code range of 101 through 698.

6 = Fiscal Year Code. *During what year is the purchase being made?*

The fiscal year code identifies the fiscal year of any budgetary transaction. For example, during the 2019–2020 fiscal year of a school district, the numeral 20 would denote the fiscal year.

7 = Program Intent Code. *To what student group is the instructional purchase or service being directed?*

The program intent code is used to designate the rationale of a program that is provided to students. These codes are used to account for the cost of instruction and other services that are directed toward a particular need of a specific set of students. There are approximately a dozen program intent codes; examples include: Basic Educational Services, Gifted and Talented, Career and Technology, Special Education, Bilingual Education, Title I Services, and so forth.

NOTE: The reference numbers used in Table 1.1 were presented by the National Center for Education Statistics (2009a) and the Governmental Accounting Standards Board (2011). These codes are representative numbers often assigned to state operating accounting code structures.

School leaders, typically early in their careers, realize that setting goals, establishing measurable objectives, developing action plans, incorporating the entire learning community in a collaborative or participatory process, developing trust, acting with integrity, and making student enrollment projections are essential components in the development and implementation of an effective school budget. Said qualities further ensure effective and strong school leadership (Sorenson & Goldsmith, 2009; Sorenson, Goldsmith, Méndez, & Maxwell, 2011). School administrators must recognize that it is not mere coincidence that the budget planning and development process coincides with the instructional or school action planning process. Both processes are essential to the overall success of any school or, for that matter, any school administrator (Brimley, Verstegen, & Garfield, 2012). These two processes must be developed in an integrated approach to achieve the maximum benefits for schools and students (see Chapter 4). A school budget must have as its foundation the academic or action plan that details all of the educational programs and initiatives of a school. Such plans must be consistent with the school's vision or mission (Sorenson & Goldsmith, 2007). Each program, initiative, and/or activity within an academic or action plan dictates how appropriate budgetary decision making, as related to funding appropriations and levels, will occur and how it will ultimately impact student achievement.

Breaking the Budgeting Myths

Many instructional leaders begin their careers with several mythical notions related to the budgetary process. The reason for such thinking may simply relate to the role of leader. Numerous myths are readily associated with leadership and have been documented in related research (Hughes, et al., 2009). For example, one leadership myth that is most applicable to the budgetary process stipulates: *Leaders are born, not made.* While certain natural talents or characteristics may provide some individuals with advantages over others, one's training and experiences can play a crucial role in the development of leadership abilities, traits, and skills. This is especially true when one considers that most school leaders have limited knowledge about finance and budgeting but quickly realize that they must build upon their minimal skills. Interestingly, several school-based budgeting myths quickly come to mind. These myths often serve to further complicate the budgeting process and can, in fact, serve to disengage a school leader from monitoring and managing an important, if not a critical, aspect of the education business—the school budget. Listed below are 10 myths often experienced by and associated with school leaders and the school-based budgeting process (Sorenson, 2010; Sorenson & Goldsmith, 2004; Sorenson & Goldsmith, 2007).

1. School leaders must have an analytical mindset.

2. School leaders must have an accounting background or degree.

3. Budgeting, like any fiscal accounting procedure, is too difficult.

4. Educators are "right brained" and, as a result, would rather create than compute.

5. Budgeting is for the site-based decision-making team to figure out.

6. Physical school-site inventories have little to do with the budgeting process.

7. Instruction and curriculum are more important.

8. School leaders simply do not have the time to meet the demands and dictates associated with the school budget.

9. Central administration retains most of the money anyway.

10. District business managers or comptrollers do not care about or understand the fiscal needs of individual schools.

Few factors pose a greater obstacle to the school leader than unsubstantiated and self-limiting beliefs or myths about the budgeting process. It must be argued that by acknowledging and then avoiding these myths, the school leader is provided with the basis for better understanding, developing, and handling a school budget. While the 10 myths are unfortunately prevalent in the world of school administration, recognition of said myths also provides school leaders—particularly novice administrators—with insights that allow for the development of those essential skills to successfully emerge as effective managers of school-based budgets. Being able to recognize and analyze your own experiences in terms of the budgeting myths may be one of the single greatest contributions that this text can provide. Remember, a budget will not work unless you do!

Delineating Between School Finance and School Budgeting

School business is big business. Many school districts across the nation are by far the largest enterprises in their communities in terms of revenues, expenditures, employment, and capital assets. Unfortunately, school leaders often fail to understand the basis for funding public schools and, as a result, become victims of their own demise by failing to recognize the financial challenges that are frequently associated with being a fiscal leader in a big business. School leaders often fail to understand the fundamentals associated with school budgeting. In far too many instances, school leaders possess limited background, experience, or expertise with the budgeting process as related to the fiscal management of schools. This dilemma is further complicated by the fact that school leaders have an inadequate understanding of the basic delineation between school finance and school budgeting.

School finance is regulated by state and federal legislation, as well as by the courts. All of these have initiated, by law, stringent policies and procedures to infuse greater accountability through the development of financial plans and reports as related to a process that records, classifies, and summarizes fiscal transactions and provides for an accounting of the monetary operations and activities of a school district (Baker, Green, & Richards, 2008). School finance is most assuredly a concern for superintendents, district business managers, and school board members because the adequacy and equity of state and federal funding is the fiscal lifeline of a school district. However, this book is not about school finance. This read will be from the perspective of the school leader who must be dedicated to better understanding and appreciating the interrelationship of the school-based budgeting and academic planning processes.

While many school leaders are focused on increasing revenue for their schools in an era of increased mandates and state and federal funding constraints, other school leaders are focused on a much more timely and relevant question: Are schools allocating, budgeting, and spending their money intelligently, notably during times of fiscal constraint and conservative funding (Cavanagh & Hollingsworth, 2011; Thompson, Wood, & Crampton, 2008)? A recent review by the National Conference of State Legislatures (2012) reveals that states face a total budget gap of $4.4 billion, up approximately $2 billion from the pre–Great Recession fiscal year 2006. While this figure sends chills up and down the spines of school officials across the nation, this truth readily relates to the fact that Congress has, at the time of this publication, signaled the closing of the federal pocketbook to states. In Texas, for example, the state legislature in 2011 planned to cut statewide education funding for schools by $9.8 billion over the fiscal year 2012–2013 biennium as a result of the federal funding deficit. Fortunately for Texas school districts, after significant public uproar, the Republican-held state legislature rescinded the excessive cuts and the action failed (National Conference of State Legislators, 2012).

There is, however, some good news: tax receipts are on the upswing in numerous states during the post–Great Recession era. The overall fiscal outlook for school systems across the nation, based on the National Conference of State Legislature State Budget Update (2012), is either positive (seven states) or cautiously optimistic (23 states). Unfortunately, 20 states remain concerned about their overall fiscal outlook and, thus, continue to struggle to regain economic stability. Relative to the "concerned" outlook, state tax collections continue to be below (about 12%) where they were prior to 2008. On another positive note, no state is pessimistic about the future fiscal outlook for school systems.

Budgeting in Times of Economic Downturn and Fiscal Constraint

The funding of schools has always been a difficult prospect. Ever-increasing inflation rates from the 1970s to the present date have only aggravated the funding of public schools. More recently, inflation actually became deflationary—the economy became terribly depressed with the onslaught of the Great Recession. By mid-2009, inflation leveled, but only to a low of –2.10% (Stokes, 2011). As a result,

LEADING, BUDGETING, AND SURVIVING IN TOUGH TIMES: A TRUE STORY

"You're home early," said Anna, Tim's wife, as he walked into the kitchen one evening in the midst of a recent economic downturn. The economic collapse had negatively affected so many. Anna asked, "Everything okay, babe?"

"It's been a tough day," said Tim, principal at Bud E. Ebsen Elementary School. "One of the associate superintendents from central was on campus. She's called 'The Hatchet,' because she's got a skill for carving up and cutting out personnel—making our district a lean, mean, workforce machine! She's making significant cuts in personnel and in other aspects of our school and district budgets, to include instructional programs and curricular initiatives."

"So you…are you part of the personnel cuts?"

"No," Tim exclaimed. "But my fate may be actually worse. She demoted Eliot Nesselbaum, Director of Elementary School Curriculum and Instruction, to assistant principal at Fess Parker Elementary School. They're going to cut his old position from the budget, and The Hatchet has asked me to take over his responsibilities."

"Oh, my gosh," Anna gasped, stunned by the news! "So, who's going to help you, Tim?"

Tim took a deep breath. "Me."

Anna let out a muffled sigh. "Just you, Tim, and no one to help you? They expect you to do two jobs and be paid for one?"

"Yep, you've got it," said Tim. "However, I do get to keep my assistant principal, although I'm still searching for someone to replace Helen Milsteen, who went over to Camino Heights Middle School as the new principal. I'm just hoping The Hatchet doesn't decide to cut the AP position from my campus! Anna, times are tough. I think I'm lucky to have a job or at least to keep the one I've got, even if I have to take on more responsibilities!"

Tim walked across the kitchen toward the sofa in the living area and then turned back, looking at his wife, saying, "Well, Anna, like I said, I'm glad to have work during these tough economic times. What I'm really concerned about is how to make up for all the budget deficits on campus. What am I supposed to do? What am I supposed to tell my faculty and staff? How can we survive as a team?"

Anna replied: "Maybe they'll give you a pay raise, Tim. You know, to make up for the extra work you'll have to do with your job and all the new responsibilities—don't you think?"

(Continued)

(Continued)

Pause and Consider

- Educators experienced the tough economic times associated with the Great Recession. Now, pause and consider the following: What innovative practices and/or practical approaches to campus budgeting could be initiated at your school during an era of fiscal conservatism (a time of budget shortfalls and funding restrictions)?
- Need a few ideas? Read the remainder of this section: *Budgeting in Times of Economic Downturn and Fiscal Constraint.*

school districts found that with the drop in housing prices and property valuations, a lingering decrease in property tax revenues, and community job losses, drastic budgetary measures were necessary.

Between 2008 and 2011, most school districts had to make budgetary cuts that, in far too many instances, directly affected faculty and staff and, just as important, students and student achievement, to include:

- Laying off teachers
- Initiating hiring freezes
- Increasing class size
- Cutting extracurricular programs or limiting activities
- Eliminating summer school
- Cutting instructional programs such as the arts and fine arts
- Eliminating field trips
- Reducing or eliminating teacher and staff stipends and/or bonuses
- Closing older/economically burdensome schools
- Implementing changes in benefits, that is, higher health care deductibles
- Introducing energy/utility savings initiatives
- Cutting professional development for teachers and staff

Now that the cutbacks have been confronted, what are school leaders to do when it comes to budgeting in hard times? Here are a few key considerations:

- Communicate with faculty and staff how an economic crisis affects schools, most notably the budgetary process, and how it can be reasonably and effectively addressed.

- Establish budget advisory teams and develop site-based guidelines and practices, to include regularly scheduled budget and campus decision-making meetings.
- Collaboratively conduct a cost analysis of all campus-based programs and initiatives. Can certain "expensive" programs be replaced with similar "inexpensive" programs?
- Ensure purchases are extended to the lowest bidder.
- Conduct a needs assessment to include an intensive data-analysis process.
- Develop and analyze a campus action or improvement plan with specific goals, objectives, strategies, action implementations, staff responsibilities, timelines, resource (human/material/fiscal) identifications, and formative as well as summative evaluative measures.
- Align the school budget with the campus action or improvement plan.
- Develop a priority-setting process and strictly fund the greatest of instructional priorities.
- Accumulate an expenditure history: Examine how campus funding, over a period of 3 to 5 years, has been expended, on what, and why.
- Appoint a budget manager (principal, assistant principal, secretary, clerk) who at predetermined intervals reviews and assesses the campus budget and provides reports to the site-based team.
- Address student achievement by asking the pressing questions:
  - What is the most efficient method(s) of organizing our instructional programs and student-centered initiatives?
  - How can we better schedule classes, and not at the expense of students?
  - What are specific and effective methods of presenting instruction in the differing subject areas?
  - What classes are crucial for all graduates?
  - What is the value of programs such as prekindergarten, dropout-prevention initiatives, and the support of late graduates?
  - What class-size capacity can be reached without negatively impacting teaching and learning?
  - How can teacher quality, student learning, and instructional methodology be redefined in an era of technological norms and advancements?
  - What are the short-term and long-term impacts of budgetary cuts on student achievement?

- o What does the research reveal regarding current instructional programs and initiatives, and are we still doing the same old things the same old ways? Can improvements come with certain budgetary cutbacks?
- o What are other school districts and other schools doing to be more instructionally innovative yet cost effective?
- o What additional or innovative fundraising efforts, at least for the short term, can be implemented?
- o How can a school team communicate with state and federal legislators and provide them with a clear understanding of local conditions?

- Create an environment, a culture of constancy of purpose for continual improvement in all areas: services, products, and resource allocations. Note that every "nonnegotiable" must become "negotiable" whereby evaluative measures are initiated at least once a year.
- Carefully monitor enrollment trends. Conduct at the campus level the Cohort Survival Method process (see Chapter 6).
- Implement attendance incentive plans.
- Limit copier and paper usage.
- Carefully monitor and limit overtime.
- Reduce energy consumption.
- Limit travel expenses—especially out of state.
- Seek grant and foundation funding dollars.
- Permit district personnel and campus "experts" to provide quality staff development.
- Utilize "benchmarking" procedures as a method of identifying and monitoring student progress and achievement, thus reducing the purchase of unnecessary materials, as well as tutorial expenditures for students not in need of academic interventions.
- Develop community partnerships (Adopt-A-School, Friends of Education, etc.).
- Develop a materials center, an instructional resource center, where teaching and learning materials are stored for teacher/ student use. Material centers reduce cost duplications, create material check-out systems, serve as inventory depositories, better facilitate the sharing of materials, and reduce pilferage.
- Learn to say "no"—a small word with large implications, especially in economically difficult times!

Fiscal crises in schools are nothing new! The authors of this text have witnessed numerous economic downturns and their effects on schools—from the high-inflation era of the 1970s to the oil industry collapse in the 1980s to the disintegration of tax bases in the 1990s to the Great Recession in the first decade of the 21st century. In response, the adage "this too shall pass" is appropriate. However, it is important to keep in mind that until the current or any future era of economic downturn lapses, effective school leaders must maintain a single and most essential visionary perspective: Students—first and foremost, no matter the budgetary funding!

Allocation—The Key to the Budgetary Process

School budgeting is directly related to the allocation of those specified and, far too often, scarce sources of state and federal funding. To coin a financial term, the "bottom line" to adequately and effectively delineating between school finance and school budgeting can be summed up by one simple word, *allocation.* Allocation is the key to understanding the school budgeting process. Allocation, as well as efficient funding, especially during economic downturns, is not only important to state public education systems, the amount of money schools receive for budgetary purposes is critical to continued student success and achievement (Thompson et al., 2008).

Nevertheless, school leaders must realize and understand that the school budgeting process is much more than the technical skill associated with the term *allocation.* Exceptional school leaders recognize that effective budgeting must be an integrated approach incorporating team planning, visionary leadership, and data analysis to establish instructional priorities for necessary funding. This integrated approach to school budgeting is explored in greater detail in Chapters 4 and 5.

Sources of School Funding

The key to understanding sources of school funding is to realize that expenditures correlated with student educational needs are affected by whether federal, state, and local governments appropriately share in the responsibility for supporting schools (Brimley et al., 2012; Poston, 2011). Naturally, adequate and equitable funding during any fiscal era (upswing or downturn) becomes a critical issue not only with educators but with politicians and taxpayers as well. The reason why appropriate, adequate, and equitable funding is a contested issue in public education is related to the fact that our Founding Fathers failed to provide any arrangements for education in the federal constitution. As a result, the funding of schools has become the responsibility of individual states, whether by design or by default, and in most instances not by choice. By placing the responsibility for public education funding in the hands of individual states, our nation has become, in reality, 51 systems of education and, more notably, 51 sources of school funding (Brimley et al., 2012; Swanson & King, 1997; Verstegen & Jordan, 2008).

Education is the largest single budgetary component of state and local governments (National Center for Education Statistics, 2009). School districts receive nearly all of their funding for instruction, either directly or indirectly, from federal, state, and local governments, although the majority of this funding comes from local and state revenues as revealed in Table 1.2. While school districts depend, and most certainly place special emphasis, on the amount of federal funds received, the percentage of federal support for schools is relatively insignificant in relation to state and local funding. For example, many states provide well over 50% of school district funding. As further noted in Table 1.2, federal funding typically amounts to less than 10 to 15% of a district's funding dollars, with local revenue coming close to or exceeding that of the state funding allotments (National Center for Education Statistics, 2009).

Table 1.2   Percentages of Revenues by State for Education

State	Local Revenue	State Revenue	Federal Revenue
US	44.0	46.9	9.2
AL	29.6	55.5	9.0
AK	24.0	57.0	12.3
AR	32.4	58.2	11.7
AZ	39.5	47.8	7.8
CA	31.2	59.2	13.8
CO	49.0	42.8	8.2
CT	55.5	38.2	6.9
DE	29.7	61.8	7.7
DC	88.0	0.00	12.0
FL	52.3	42.1	15.3
GA	48.1	43.9	9.0
HI	3.7	87.4	15.5
ID	21.9	57.5	9.8
IL	65.4	31.8	7.5
IN	38.8	47.2	8.8
IA	45.0	45.8	10.3
KS	33.2	54.4	10.9
KY	30.6	56.7	10.6
LA	38.2	47.5	19.0

(Continued)

Table 1.2   (Continued)

State	Local Revenue	State Revenue	Federal Revenue
MA	56.3	42.7	6.5
MD	54.0	37.7	6.3
ME	51.1	41.0	11.0
MI	33.5	60.1	8.8
MN	14.9	69.6	8.6
MO	58.8	34.1	10.3
MS	30.7	54.0	16.0
MT	39.5	45.2	12.8
NE	53.6	31.3	7.8
NH	59.1	39.2	5.6
NJ	62.1	43.5	3.2
NM	16.4	70.0	13.0
NV	58.7	27.1	7.9
NC	43.7	62.7	8.0
ND	50.1	37.0	10.6
NY	46.7	43.0	8.3
OH	46.4	44.0	8.5
OK	34.7	53.4	11.8
OR	39.5	48.8	9.6
PA	55.1	36.0	6.2
RI	50.4	38.6	8.8
SC	40.1	45.3	9.1
SD	51.5	33.5	16.3
TN	42.9	43.2	11.7
TX	45.7	35.9	17.9
UT	36.5	55.0	12.2
VA	53.4	40.6	6.2
VT	5.4	85.0	7.8
WA	28.3	60.7	8.5
WI	44.4	50.8	6.2
WV	27.1	60.6	13.3
WY	33.8	51.8	6.1

SOURCES: National Center for Education Statistics [Online]. Retrieved February 14, 2012, from http://nces.ed.gov. Also from *Rankings and Estimates: Rankings of the States 2010*, National Education Association (2010), retrieved February 14, 2012, from http://www.nea.org/assets/docs/010rankings.pdf

NOTE: The totals for each row may not equal 100% due to rounding or due to states receiving intermediate revenue for education. Intermediate revenue is defined as receipts from county or regional governments that are typically quite small or frequently nonexistent in most states.

Naturally, a prerequisite for understanding the budgetary process is a keen realization of where the money comes from—the sources of money received to operate school districts. In financial circles, the appropriate terms are *revenue, income,* and *fiduciary* funding (Bannock, Baxter, & Davis, 2011). The flip side of the "money received" coin is *expenditure,* or "money spent." Income sources will be examined in greater detail later in this chapter. However, to better understand the relationship between revenue and expenditure, Figure 1.1 reveals, on a per-pupil basis, the revenue and expenditures of Texas schools during the fiscal year 2012–2013. The revenue amounts displayed in Figure 1.1 combine state aid and property tax levy figures from state agencies with the amounts in the budget for other sources of school revenue.

Notice in Figure 1.1 that the revenue figures are based on a funding starting point, an allocation simply known, from a school finance perspective, as the *basic allotment.* The basic allotment to school districts

Figure 1.1   Revenue and Expenditures Per Pupil, Texas School Budgets, 2012–2013

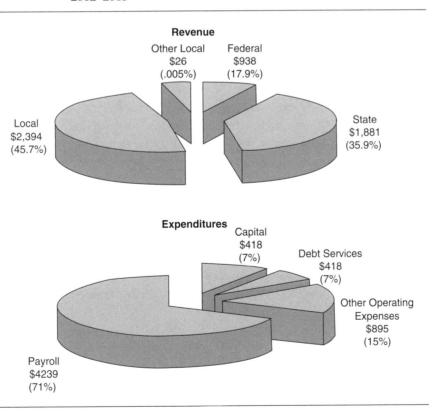

SOURCES: Figures utilized in this report were provided by the Property Tax Division of the Texas Comptroller's Office (2012), the Texas Education Agency (2012a), and the Texas Taxpayers and Research Association (2012).

can be further adjusted incrementally with "adjustment allotments" such as:

- *Cost of education index*—a funding "multiplier" designed to compensate districts for geographic (rural schools) and cost (the percentage of economically disadvantaged students) differences beyond the control of the local school system.
- *Small district adjustment*—small school systems are more expensive to operate due to diseconomies of scale. Districts, for example, with 1,600 or fewer students in average daily attendance could receive an increase in funding.
- *Impact aid*—districts can receive additional funding for each student who has a parent serving in the military on active duty.
- *Other "weighted" allotments*—for example, special education (districts could possibly be entitled to up to five times more funding for a student with special needs), bilingual education (possibly an additional 10% for English language learners [ELLs]), compensatory education (potential funding of 20% or more to pay for intensive or accelerated instructional services [tutoring, for example] for students who are performing below grade level or are at risk of dropping out of school), and so on.

Revenue is obtained primarily from tax collection and the sale of bonds. The tax-collection funds provide the majority of money received and money expended for the instructional and operational aspects of a school district. Bond sales provide revenue necessary for the construction of new school facilities.

Income is a particular funding category that is representative of funds received from the sale of goods and services. A perfect example of income funding is the district food services program. Since income can be generated from the sale of food items in the school cafeteria, district administrators must develop budgets that project sales and anticipate expenditures, and then they must implement and monitor a budget.

The fiduciary category refers to funds that are received from donations and thus must be managed by or entrusted to a school district in the most legal and ethical manner possible. While these dollars are important, such funds are generally not critical to the instructional operation of a school district. However, these same dollars may be very significant to a school that needs additional dollars to finance school-related initiatives and activities not normally funded by a school district. A perfect example of fiduciary receipts are monies generated from fundraisers and collected by student clubs, campus organizations, graduating classes, or booster clubs; as a result, the school district must agree to be the depository of these funds and must ensure that the funds are expended appropriately (Vail, 1999).

Expenditures are exactly that—money spent. Whenever money is spent, the expenditure must be charged against a revenue account and source. School leaders will invariably note that within their budget software listings or on their budget spreadsheets, the accounting term *encumbered* appears. Encumbered or encumbrance, by definition, is by no means the same as expenditure. However, both terms maintain a compelling correlation in terms of the budgetary process. For example, when a specified school account is used to initiate a purchase order, the funds are immediately set aside or encumbered, indicating that the dollars for products or services ordered have been committed, held back, set aside, or *encumbered*. At this point, a school leader can expect the purchase order to be processed, and when the goods are received, a payment will be submitted. When the payment has been issued, an expenditure of district dollars has occurred.

The expenditure of funds must always be accounted for, and thus a school leader may complain from time to time about the numerous business department forms that have to be completed, such as purchase orders, requisitions, travel reimbursements, amendments and transfers, and vouchers, all of which are examples of the paperwork commonly associated with district expenditures. Completing these forms may seem to be a nuisance, but they ensure fiscal accountability, and each may very well be the necessary documentation to keep a school leader out of a legal entanglement (Walsh, Kemerer, & Maniotis, 2009). Mutter and Parker (2004) in their book, *School Money Matters: A Handbook for Principals,* note that financial forms and accompanying safeguards are "designed to meet three important school financial objectives: (1) to protect school staff from suspicion of theft or laxness, (2) to protect school assets, and (3) to fulfill the stewardship responsibility for public funds expected by the general public" (p. 1). When fiscal accountability is ignored, for whatever

VERONICA'S PROBLEM

Veronica, an accounting clerk, was often embarrassed and angered by the numerous telephone calls she received at work from creditors who were demanding money for her husband's excessive expenditures. These accumulated debts arose from her husband's business. Veronica was just as responsible as her husband for these extensive debts, since both she and her husband resided in a community property state. His debts were her debts. Their financial predicament had reached a level of desperation, and Veronica knew something had to be done.

One day at work, Veronica was seen slipping a vendor check into her purse by Jenny, a friend and colleague. Jenny had a moral and ethical obligation to report Veronica's fraudulent actions. However, Jenny was reluctant to do so because her identity as a "whistleblower" might be revealed. Some months later, a company-hired Certified Public Accountant (CPA) took basic steps to prevent organizational fraud. The CPA soon learned from Jenny of the embezzlement scheme that Veronica was regularly playing out at the office.

Veronica subsequently confessed that she was processing certain invoices twice. When she was in need of cash, Veronica would make a copy of the invoice before stamping the original. The two were almost indistinguishable. Next, she would process the original invoice, send it on for approval, and then process the "copied" invoice several days later. The same invoice was paid twice. When the vendor realized the overpayment, it would send a refund check that always landed on Veronica's desk. Veronica pocketed the check and, in turn, her husband forged an endorsement and subsequently deposited the check in his business account. The whole fraudulent scheme occurred over a 2-year period, and more than $200,000 was embezzled. Veronica was ultimately indicted and convicted (Wells, 2002).

reason, the end result is less than attractive—much less. For example, consider Veronica's problem, a "no way out" situation involving an accounting clerk.

Veronica's problem is an obvious example of how school-based budgeting is much more than a technical or managerial skill and process. One must understand that the budgeting process constantly overlaps into the arena of certain behaviors—visionary, integrity, fairness, trustworthiness, legal and ethical, for example. These behavioral concepts, along with their impact on school-based budgeting, will be explored in more detail in Chapter 2.

Recapping, district revenue funds are generated by and large through taxes assessed on the general public and on for-profit businesses. As noted earlier in the chapter, school districts receive the vast majority of their revenue for instruction from federal, state, and local governments. Let's now examine specific sources of generated revenue or income for school districts.

Federal Sources of Income

Federal revenue comes in the form of different and distinct sources of transfer payments known as *general, categorical,* and *block grants* aid. General and categorical aid, the major source of federal income for education, significantly impacts and expands the capabilities of school districts to enhance student achievement (Brimley et al., 2012).

General aid flows from federal and state governments with few limitations to local school districts. General aid provides the largest proportion of financial support for school operations. Local school boards and district administrators largely determine how such income will be allocated to educational programs and other related expenditures.

Categorical aid is a source of funding to school districts that links funding to specific objectives of the government in support of specified programs such as special education, gifted and talented education, career and technology education (formerly vocational education), and compensatory education. Unlike general aid, categorical aid must be utilized for certain groups of students (e.g., those with disabilities), a specific purpose (e.g., pupil transportation), or a particular project (e.g., construction of a school facility). Most often, categorical aid calls for annual applications, documentation of expenditures, and frequent program evaluations and audits. Categorical aid was once the predominant form of federal income to states and school districts. However, other forms of federal aid now serve as district income supplements, with fewer restrictions at the local level. In recent years, much of the categorical aid has been absorbed into block grants to reduce the local paperwork and personnel productivity burdens associated with federal funds to education (Bannock et al., 2011).

Block grants aid provides funding for a wide range of services, with federal requirements for planning, implementing, and assessing programs being much less stringent than those associated with categorical aid. Block grants provide for local funding based on the number of students rather than through a competitive application process that identifies particular educational needs. Block grants provide local districts greater latitude and further give district administrators more discretion in program designs. As a result, local school boards and district administrators typically prefer block grants because they minimize governmental scrutiny and control, and they further provide for more opportunities for district officials to meet local priorities (Brewer & Achilles, 2008).

The largest of the block grant programs is Title I funding, which reaches 11 million disadvantaged students, with minority students accounting for two-thirds of the Title I participants (Institute of Education Sciences, 2012). Title I monies, in the form of block grants, go directly to school districts and schools where they are most needed and fund, for example, extra teachers and programs such as *Success for All*—all of which help students master reading, writing, and mathematics (Borman, Slavin, Cheung, Chamberlain, Madden, & Chambers, 2007). Over the years, block grant funding has served to focus on and improve proven programs that have turned around entire schools and even school districts. A perfect example is Asa Mercer Middle School, where student achievement in this diverse, poor Seattle, Washington, school district—that once languished as one of the worst schools in the city—recently made significant improvements in the areas of science, mathematics, and reading test scores (Rosenthal, 2011).

Federal aid has certainly served to promote equity and equality in education over the last 40 to 45 years and has generally improved the quality of education for all students. However, the "strings attached" or restrictions and regulations that generally accompany such financial aid have often been considered nothing more than unwarranted intervention by the "feds" into "local" affairs. As opposed to promoting efficiency in funding, the federal dollars and attached stipulations have often stifled local school officials' efforts in addressing student needs and community considerations for better schools (Guthrie, Springer, Rolle, & Houck, 2007).

State Sources of Income

Most states have—as their source of income—property taxes, sales taxes, or income taxes. These income sources determine the amount of state funding for school districts. This revenue allotment is then typically distributed to the differing school districts across a state by means of a *state-aid formula* (Texas Taxpayers and Research Association, 2012). These funding formulas are generally driven by student enrollment, and again, this aid comes primarily from assessed taxes. While property taxation remains the major source of local revenue for many schools across the nation, the local tax base is typically insufficient to support a school district. Therefore, most states have developed state-aid formulas as the basis for infusing some fundamental element of equity from district to district within a state. State-aid formulas are the result of legislative choice and litigation force (Schimmel, Stellman, & Fisher, 2010).

The purpose of state aid formulas is to counterbalance disparities in educational equity and opportunity that would most certainly be present if school districts depended solely on the local tax base (Baker et al., 2008). An example of such a disparity is illustrated below.

Another example is often evident in states with large urban centers that face vast disparities in their tax base due to ever-growing suburbs and the related citizenry and corporation flight to the nearby bedroom communities.

Most states develop foundation programs to facilitate the state-aid formulas. These programs are the mechanism by which the equalization of resources from district to district can occur. Foundation programs allow for the difference in the cost of a school program and the amount each school district must contribute from local taxation (Thompson et al., 2008). Today, very complex state-aid formulas advance the foundation programs, and such formulas are generally related to a fictitious

PORT GREGORY vs. NUECESTOWN: A CASE OF EDUCATIONAL DISPARITY?

The Port Gregory school system is located along a state coastline near a major seaport. This school system is the recipient of tax dollars generated by several major petrochemical corporations. These taxable entities generate significant per-pupil wealth on the basis of taxable property. A second school system, Nuecestown Public Schools, similar in size and population but located further inland, is solely dependent on the agribusiness industry, and thus this district receives only limited revenue from its economically depressed tax base.

Pause and Consider

- What type of funding mechanism might help alleviate the disparity between the two school systems identified in the scenario above?
- How is the financing of school systems in your state equalized?
- What has historically been the result of funding inequities of public schools in your state?

"weighted student" consideration. After the foundation program cost is determined by formula, financing is equalized by determining the local share for each district and then the remainder is funded by state aid. State aid for individual school districts equals the foundation program cost minus the local share. However, it is worth noting that state aid formulas have come under intense scrutiny in recent years, and to date, legal challenges related to formula funding continue to come before the United States Supreme Court. For example, the issue of equity in relation to educational opportunities for all students regardless of socioeconomic background and/or ethnicity continues to be a critical issue before the courts, both state and federal, as well as state legislatures. Inequities have long plagued public schools, particularly in the area of financing educational facilities with minimal funding reforms and state-led efforts. This is not to say that the courts have completely ignored equity in public school financing. Consideration by the courts is most certainly revealed in several recent court cases in which lawsuits have demanded that states provide adequate and equitable educational facilities. Unfortunately, the operative term and process utilized in response to these legal entanglements has most often been nothing more than *adequate*. Court cases from Texas (*San Antonio Independent School District v. Rodriguez*, 1973; *Edgewood v. Kirby*, 1986; and *West Orange Cove CISD v. Neeley*, 2007), California (*Serrano v. Priest*, 1971), Ohio (*DeRolph v. State of Ohio*, 2000), New Jersey (*Abbott v. Burke*, 1990), New Mexico (*Alamogordo v. Morgan*, 1995), West Virginia (*Pauley v. Bailey*, 1994), and Tennessee (*Small Schools*, 1988) serve to exemplify just a few decisions that have impacted, often minimally, equitable facilities and funding for all students (Alexander & Alexander, 2011; Brimley, Verstegen, & Garfield, 2012). An excellent source relative to school finance reform is *School Law: Cases and Concepts* (2011) by Michael W. LaMorte. See Chapter 7—"School Finance and School Choice Issues" (pp. 375–403).

Local Sources of Income

The majority of school districts in the United States obtain their locally generated income from at least one of the following sources: *ad valorem* (property) taxes, *sales* taxes, *income* taxes, or *sumptuary* (sin) taxes.

Property tax is the most common source of income for school districts. Typically, a tax is levied on property such as land and buildings owned by individuals and businesses. Generally, a property tax is determined on the basis of a percentage of the true market value of each piece of property assessed. These assessments are rarely accurate since local assessors either over- or underassess the value of the property. Typically, the assessed value of the property is adjusted to an agreed-upon percentage of the market value when it is sold (Baker et al., 2008; Brimley et al., 2012).

Property taxation remains a largely complicated and particularly controversial source of local income for school districts because numerous complexities are associated with the assessment process. Homestead exemptions, tax abatements, legal entanglements, tax-payer associations, and underassessments of property all serve to erode the "true" tax base for individual school districts. However, property taxation continues to be the most stable income base as well as a dependable source of income for school districts (Hylbert, 2002).

Another form of taxation that serves as a revenue source for many school districts is the *sales tax,* which is quite popular in many states. This tax is assessed on the price of a good or service when it is purchased by a consumer. The seller of the merchandise or service collects the sales tax dollars, which are included in the purchase price, and transfers the amount of the sales tax to the state comptroller offices. Since this tax is based on sales, its yield is quite elastic. As a result, a sales tax as a form of revenue for school districts is only as stable as the economy (Haveman & Sexton, 2008).

Some school districts acquire their local source of income from a state *income tax* that is levied on corporations and/or individuals. Income taxation is the most widely accepted form of taxation for schools, and it is considered the most equitable of any source of taxation. Over the years, several states have initiated income taxation as a source of funding education. In a majority of states, the taxing of income is considered the most appropriate mechanism for property tax relief. In addition, income taxation provides a high revenue yield and creates minimal social and economic disruption (Brimley et al., 2012).

Very few school districts derive income from *sumptuary taxes* on items such as tobacco, alcohol, and gambling. This type of taxation is somewhat different than income and property taxes because it is based on "sin" sales. Due to this dependency, the tax yield is quite elastic and thus, it—much like a sales tax—is only as stable as the economy. Also, the tobacco and alcohol industries extensively lobby state legislators, and, as a result, this type of taxation has not necessarily served as a viable taxing alternative (Owings & Kaplan, 2006).

Another source of educational revenue can be dollars received from a lottery—an assessment on legalized gambling. Many individuals believe that the proceeds from a state lottery system provide great sums of income for education. Nothing is further from the truth. This argument has been used for years by proponents of the legalization of state lotteries. The individuals most susceptible to the promises of a lottery are those in the lower income bracket, which further makes the proceeds from this form of state income regressive (Brimley et al., 2012). There is no evidence that any state lottery has significantly supported or benefited any school district or, for that matter, public education in general (Jones & Amalfitano, 1994). More recent studies conducted by Garrett (2001) and Erekson, DeShano, Platt, and Zeigert (2002) found that increased lottery revenues failed to provide any discernible increase in public school funding and, moreover, revealed that as lottery revenues increase, less state funding is appropriated to public schools. In fact, it was Richard S. "Kinky" Friedman, American Texas country singer, songwriter, novelist, humorist, and politician, who has said of the Texas lottery: "It's a shell game, instead of facing issues directly…for example, to pay for education, legalized gambling will produce $6 billion to $8 billion a year. That's why you see this Texas campaign from the lottery that claims the money goes to education. Why the campaign? Because every Texan knows it's a lie" (Negron, 2006).

Now that we have explored several of the possible sources of income for school districts, it becomes apparent that wherever the funding is derived, allocations to individual schools at the district level are made, and thus school leaders have as one of their many responsibilities the task of developing a budget. Developing a school budget can be an arduous undertaking, but it can be completed with some sense of ease and satisfaction when a school leader is able to utilize specific steps or methods to effectively and efficiently plan for a successful school budget.

Ten Steps to Budgeting Success

There are 10 important steps to successful and effective budgeting. These steps are identified below with brief descriptors explaining why each step is critical to a school leader's success in developing, implementing, and evaluating a budget.

1. Determine the Allotment

Before deciding what educationally related expenditures to make, it is important to know the specified funding allotment that has been appropriated within each budgetary category. Furthermore, certain budgetary allotments can only be used for a variety of specified services and expenditures at the school level. As a result, some funds are more restrictive than others. These restricted funds are often associated with Title I, Bilingual Education, and Special Education dollars and programs, for example. Restricted funds are examined in greater detail in Chapter 6.

2. Identify Fixed Expenditures

Recognize and note those expenditures that do not vary from year to year. Set aside the necessary funds in the amount of the fixed expenditures before building the school budget.

3. Involve All Stakeholders

Whether at school or home, everyone should be involved in the budgetary decision-making process. By involving as many stakeholders as possible, a school leader can more effectively ensure ultimate "buy-

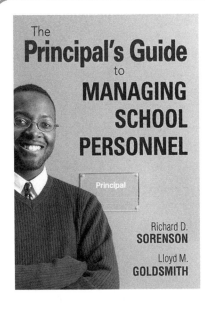

The Principal's Guide to Managing School Personnel (2009) is an effective source and reliable desk reference for practicing or prospective school leaders who desire to learn more about collaboratively working with school personnel. While each of the eight chapters within this text serve as excellent guides for school principals when interacting with campus personnel, Chapter 3: Personnel and the Principal (pp. 47–68); Chapter 4: Personnel and Communication (pp. 69–84); and Chapter 5: Personnel and Conflict Resolution (pp. 85–101), provide essential guidance, necessary information, and an examination of human resource skills critical to the successful principal–personnel relationship.

in" as related to the school budget and funded programs and initiatives. Stakeholders include, for example, faculty and staff, parents, students, community members, and any other interested individuals. When all stakeholders are provided with the opportunity for input, with their particular issues being given noteworthy consideration, "buy-in" is more likely, and any plans, preparations, or budgetary considerations are less susceptible to interference or possible sabotage by a disgruntled member of the learning community. The collaborative involvement process as related to stakeholders is further examined in Chapter 6.

4. Identify Potential Expenditures

The effective school leader reviews past budgetary records to better identify and predict future expenditures. Knowing which expenditures are necessary and imperative, a school administrator will help faculty and staff avoid making impulsive purchases.

5. Cut Back

Most newly created school budgets are overbudgeted. A school leader is responsible for examining all potential expenditures and must determine where cutbacks can occur. Remember, cutting back too severely can build discontent among the faculty. School budgets that are continually out of balance lead to greater fiscal sacrifices and may very well lead to a financial point of no return. Cut back as necessary and be aware that budgeting is an exercise in self-discipline for all parties. A simple yet effective way to cut back involves implementing a thorough physical inventory. School administrators should do more than just go through the motions when completing a physical inventory. Such an inventory will identify areas where unnecessary purchases can be avoided. Consider the following: Why continue to purchase supplies such as dry-erase markers, staples, paperclips, and the like when these items can be found in abundance in a classroom or office closet or central warehouse?

While cutting back is important in the school business, the creative school administrator is always seeking "windfalls." Additional funding sources are available to those administrators who are willing to put forth the time and effort to seek financial assistance. For example, one school in a property-poor district utilized the campus leaders, site-based team members, and the parent–teacher organization to canvas the community seeking adopt-a-school partners. A partnership with a large retail corporation proved extremely successful. The school was able to acquire not only essential supplies and merchandise for student use and consumption, the corporation also provided funding for computers and other important resources that otherwise would not have been available to either students or staff. Therefore, instead of operating according to the adage *Show me the money*, adopt a more useful motto: *I'll find the money!* Two excellent sources for finding, raising, and attracting extra dollars for a school or school system are *Fiscal Fitness for School Administrators* by Robert D. Ramsey (2001) and *Achieving Excellence in Fundraising* by Eugene Tempel, Timothy Seiler, and Eva Aldrich, editors (2011).

6. Avoid Continued Debts

The effective budget manager knows exactly what funds are out of balance and where debt is or has accumulated. Many school leaders fail to list and total their debts during the course of the fiscal year and thus wait until the end of the school year to make necessary budget revisions to amend for such shortsighted calculations. This is a poor practice. Some states and school districts do not allow individual school sites to acquire debts on a monthly or annual basis. Such a policy is not only worthwhile but wise. Nevertheless, debt reduction is readily achieved by avoiding unnecessary purchases. Consider the following example: Recall the old, wise advice that was shared with you and your spouse when first married: "Most unhappiness is caused by giving up what you want most for what you want at the moment!" Life as a school leader is stressful enough without further complicating matters by overspending at the expense of the school budget, if not the student population. Remember, the most important word to use as a school administrator, specifically in connection with the school budget, could be *no*—especially when it comes to unwise or inappropriate spending!

7. Develop a Plan

Any budget—school, home, or business—should be based on a plan. From a school perspective, an educationally centered action or improvement plan must be developed to target and prioritize instructional goals and objectives along with school programs and activities. In addition, a second plan of action (school budget plan) is designed to identify budgetary priorities, focusing on appropriations and expenditures. Furthermore, such a plan is designed to determine what programs and activities match the budgetary allotments for the school. Campus-improvement plan and budget-plan development are further examined in Chapters 4, 5, and 6.

8. Set Goals

Many would insist that "setting goals" should be first and foremost on any list of budgetary considerations. No argument here. However, it is important that the effective school leader do all the preliminary work of determining what funding is available before determining how to spend the fiscal resources. Nevertheless, setting goals (whether management or instructional) is the one fundamental step that all self-disciplined administrators utilize and the one step that most are—unfortunately—inclined to skip. As the budgetary process is developed and established, it is imperative that consideration be given to those issues, demands, and dictates—simply put: those purchases that are valued as necessities or absolutes. Again, by involving all stakeholders, goals can be identified and set. But remember, setting goals takes more than money; it takes time, effort, determination, and considerable thought and preparation. How does a school leader, working in collaboration with a learning community, set goals? Listed below are a few essential considerations.

1. Establish priorities—ascertain what is instructionally important.

2. Decide what can wait until later in the budget cycle or until the next school year.

3. Assess what is important today but will not be tomorrow.

4. Determine what priorities are meaningful compared to those that are mandated.

5. Submit various proposed budgets (by department, grade level, etc.) to the site-based committee that serves in part to determine if the allocated dollars within each budget correlate with the established goals of the school.

Finally, remember that goals can and will change. Therefore, as the school leader and budget manager, it is imperative that you, in collaboration with the school's decision-making team, regularly assess and evaluate each budgetary goal and make any necessary changes as the school year progresses.

9. Evaluate the Budget

After a plan has been developed, it must be put into action. Take time; meet at least once a month with the decision-making team to evaluate the budget process to better determine if the established goals and the budgeted dollars are equitable and compatible.

Planned budgeting and goal evaluation go hand in hand. Always seek answers to the following questions:

1. Is the budget within the allotted limits, or do adjustments (transfers and amendments) need to be made on the basis of alternative need or vision change?

2. Is progress being made toward the established goals?

3. Are purchases coinciding with planned goals?

4. Has the budget process been successful when compared with the established plan and goals?

5. What improvements can be made in the future?

10. Abide by the Budget

Abiding by the budget means living by the budget. A school leader must set the example in all areas of instructional leadership for others to follow. This is most certainly true in relation to the school budget. "Time on task" is an old adage in our business, but nothing rings more true in terms of the school budget and the necessity for the instructional leader to monitor, evaluate, and abide by the budget and the accompanying action or improvement plan.

Final Thoughts

School leaders must invest the necessary time and energy to deal with the funds appropriated as well as the learning community. Wise budgeting will bring a sense of accomplishment and even fulfillment—most notably when the instructional program improves and student achievement excels. However, before budgeting, plan. Planning is defined in this context as meaning the development of a vision, the establishment of goals, the determination of objectives, and the initiation of strategies for school implementation. Such is critical if a leader envisions and expects a continuing effort to increase student achievement. Each of these planning indicators is an essential element in the development of an effective budget, using an integrated and collaborative approach to budgeting.

A budget is not a once-a-year event, something developed and never examined again. A budget must be abided by, reviewed, and amended on a regular basis as the needs of its academic counterpart change. This requires ongoing evaluation and revision. Nothing in life is perfect, and the same holds true for school budgets. Academic goals—while imperative to the budgeting process—must, from time to time, be reorganized and adjusted. Action planning and goal development, academic improvement, and budget management must be integrated if school leaders intend to bring about educational excellence and increased student achievement. Certain standards as analyzed in Chapter 2 must be emphasized and incorporated by the school leader if the budgeting process is to meet with success. Abide by the budget; implement necessary changes, and always follow up with ongoing evaluation. Allow self-discipline, trustworthiness, transparency, integrity, and collaboration to be guiding factors in budgetary decision making. Finally, remember: An integrated budget and academic action plan will not work unless you do!

Discussion Questions

1. Consider each of the local sources of income that support school districts. What are the advantages and disadvantages of each in relation to equity, yield, and taxpayer acceptance?

2. Why is it important to integrate the school budget and the academic or action plan? How can the budget and academic planning processes be integrated?

3. Which of the budgeting myths pose a more fundamental obstacle to the school administrator in relation to the development of a campus budget? Why?

4. What might be considered a serious risk factor that a school administrator could face in relation to fiduciary receipts?

5. What are the commonalities and differences of the three federal sources of district income?

6. Should any one of the 10 steps to budgeting success be considered more important than the others? Which one and why?

7. To better understand the percentage of revenues, as exemplified in Figure 1.1, contact the official state education website (see Resource D) as well as the school business administrator or superintendent of schools to determine the sources of income for the school district.

Case Study Application: Fiscal Issues and the New Principal

The application of a case study as related to campus visioning, planning, and budgeting will be presented at the conclusion of each chapter in this book to provide applicable and relevant workplace scenarios so the reader can apply, in a practical manner, the knowledge acquired through textual readings.

Part I: "Boy, Do I Have a Lot to Learn!"

Dr. Ryan Paulson, new principal at Mountain View Middle School, arrived at Vista Ridge Independent School District from a neighboring state. While Dr. Paulson certainly knew and understood certain aspects of the fiscal and budgetary processes in his former state, he realized that he needed a refresher course in budgeting, especially as related to the fiscal issues he might face in his new state and school district.

Dr. Paulson decided to stop by the administrative offices of Vista Ridge Independent School District and visit with the superintendent, Dr. Mildred Dunn, as well as the associate superintendent for school finance, Dr. Gene Corley. Certainly, these two individuals could bring him up to speed on the fiscal expectations of his new state and school district. As good fortune would have it, the first two individuals he encountered, as he stepped into the main offices, were Dr. Dunn and Dr. Corley. Dr. Corley, a most gregarious individual, was the first to see the new principal and hollered out at him: "Hey, hot-shot, did you get to eat some of that good barbeque that I told you about?" Dr. Paulson responded that he had not yet had the opportunity, but he was looking forward to getting over to Elginton for a tasty plate of sausage and ribs. Dr. Dunn then spoke up and asked what was on the young man's mind.

"Well, since you've inquired," replied Dr. Paulson, "I need some guidance about the state's fiscal policies and the district's budgeting practices." Dr. Dunn suggested that all three step into Dr. Corley's office for, as she put it, "a quick review of School Budgeting 101."

"School budgeting and finance, in this era of change, economic downturn, and fiscal restraint, is a real juggling act," noted Dr. Dunn. "However, let's start with the basics and get you on the right track before school starts," suggested the superintendent. Thus began an afternoon of one learning experience after another. By the conclusion of the meeting, Dr. Paulson had come to realize that costly wars, an economy hit hard by the Great Recession, and federal and state accountability standards, mandates, and funding cuts, as well as numerous other conditions, had negatively influenced the ability of both the state and local districts to raise tax revenues to meet the demands of educating today's students. These challenges most notably and negatively reflected on each school's list of priorities and each district's ability to finance them.

The bottom line of the first meeting among the three parties revolved around the realization that education must be viewed as an investment in human capital. Resource allocations to public schools are the responsibility not only of the federal and state governments but of the local school district as well. Moreover, funding the rapidly increasing costs of education is an ongoing challenge for schools, and such funding is becoming more frequently associated with accountability expectations and standards at all levels—local, state, and federal.

A most interesting point made by Dr. Dunn related to the proposition that educational services and funding must be provided with equality, but could it be provided equitably?

"Wow," thought Dr. Paulson to himself, "Does anyone have an answer to that question?"

Furthermore, Dr. Paulson recognized that even though the cost of education continues to increase annually, this burden is eased when one realizes that while the cost of public schooling involves money, mostly in salaries, much of the cost is readily returned to the marketplace, thus benefiting the economy, consumers, local households, individual citizens, and, most important, local students. This meeting reminded Dr. Paulson of a fact that had been drilled into his head by a former professor in his principal certification program at Union State University: "While the cost of education may be high, the defining and measuring result must always be quality in learning."

Finally, Dr. Paulson had been directed to the state's website regarding operating accounting codes and structures. It was essential that he quickly learn the proper budgetary coding procedures as dictated by the state's education agency. He had already memorized the website address and was now ready to adapt to the new coding structure and fiscal practices associated with his new school system and campus budget. As he left the district's administrative offices he could not help but think: "Boy, do I have a lot to learn!"

Application Questions

1. What is meant by the following terms: *adequacy, equality, equitable, human capital, quality?*

2. How is the theoretical concept, "education must be viewed as an investment in human capital," realized in your community? Provide concrete examples.

3. Can educational services and funding be provided with equality and equity? Support your answer.

4. What is meant by the quote: "While the cost of education may be high, the defining and measuring result must always be quality in learning?" How does this proposition relate to the concept of vision development?

5. Contact your business department administrator or school super-intendent or state finance person to obtain a copy of the state's Operating Accounting Code structure. How is this structure similar to or different from the example utilized in Chapter 1?

Part II: "Well, It's My Money!"

Dr. Ryan Paulson, now into his second semester as principal at Mountain View Middle School, had just developed—in collaboration with his site-based decision-making team—the campus budget for the next school year. He had learned much since that initial meeting with Dr. Dunn and Dr. Corley the preceding July, but, as is always the case, much more was yet to be realized. The budget for Mountain View Middle School included funds to retain three special education aides who assisted with the inclusion program. These aides worked with special-needs students who warranted considerable assistance and who required significant class time to complete the assigned academic tasks.

When the budget was submitted to Olga Bitters—the associate superin-tendent for secondary instruction—for approval, she cut the aide positions and transferred the funds to the appropriate account for the purchasing of e-tablets for students in the gifted and talented program. These tablets were state of the art, remarkably thin and lightweight, with two cameras, one for face-to-face interactive communication and the other for video recording. Dr. Paulson realized the importance of purchasing the tablets for students, and he understood the importance of superior technology in the hands of the gifted and talented students. However, he thought that the school district should fund such items. He further believed that the functioning of the special-needs students in the inclusion program would suffer by the budgetary reduction of the three special education aide posi-tions. He was quite irritated by the recent turn of budgetary events and he knew he must address the situation, and soon. Additionally, he thought to himself: "Well, it's my money and I should be able to spend it how I please!"

Application Questions

1. Regarding his concerns about the transfer of funds as made by the Associate Superintendent of Secondary Instruction, how should Dr. Paulson address this budgetary issue and decision-making con-sideration? How is this particular issue related to a trio of concepts: integrity, fairness, and ethics?

2. What are the potential implications as related to the decision made by the associate superintendent in relation to the site-based decision-making team? the school community?

3. Identify the possible repercussions as related to the special education department. What legal issues must be considered as related to the removal of the special education paraprofessionals, as well as the maintenance of services to the students, in light of Individual Education Plans (IEPs) and associated stipulations? Can funds that were originally designated for the special education paraprofessional be transferred and used to purchase e-tablets? If such action is legal, is it fair or ethical? Support your conclusions.

4. Immediately after the budget changes are made public, Dr. Paulson receives several telephone calls from the parents of a number of the students in the inclusion program. These parents are disturbed about the effects on the learning environment in their children's classes as a result of the loss of the aides. How can Dr. Paulson best respond to these parents?

5. What did Dr. Paulson infer by stating, "Well, it's my money and I should be able to spend it how I please"? Could such a statement be justified in relation to the Ten Steps to Budgeting Success? Support your answer.

Chapter 2

The Budget–Vision Relationship and the National Standards

You do not lead by hitting people over the head—that's assault, not leadership.

—Dwight David Eisenhower (Thinkexist, 2012)

School leaders face the challenge of improving student academic achievement in a time of contracting resources and a host of other challenges, including:

- Maximizing scarce resources
- Making budget adjustments without adversely impacting student achievement
- Fiscal efficiency
- Stretching human capital
- Serving an increasingly poor student population
- Providing individual instruction more quickly and cheaply
- Using funding as a lever to spur innovation

- Aligning goals and strategies with funding
- Providing teachers and principals what they need, how they need it, when they need it
- Meeting the high expectations held by top-performing nations in reading and mathematics
- Increasing parental involvement (The Center for Public Education, 2009)

Innovative and courageous leadership combined with fresh ideas enables educators to conquer these and other challenges in schools. School leaders would do well to remember a leadership lesson from General Eisenhower, who led the American armed forces to victory in Europe in World War II. As a military officer, he realized that assault was not leadership. General Eisenhower's advice is worth remembering in the heat of budget battles.

School budgeting. School vision. These are two issues that school leaders must confront on a daily basis. The relationship between school budgeting and vision is as intertwined as is love with marriage. In both cases, you can't have one without the other (Iger, 1998). These two forces, budget and vision, come with their own accountability systems. The former is fiscal; the latter is academic. State and federal legislation continues to raise the ante for success in both of these systems by creating new measures designed to add increased external accountability for improving student achievement. The No Child Left Behind Act of 2011 continues student academic performance accountability, adequate yearly progress, and a focus on improving teacher and principal quality at a local level. This law requires core subject teachers to meet specific competency and education requirements, increased accountability for student academic performance, adequate yearly progress, campus and district report cards, and employing and training highly qualified teachers using scientifically based practices (Texas Education Agency [TEA], 2012b). Technology gives rise to greater and more complicated accounting procedures. Leaders can become overwhelmed when trying to make sense of a sea of data being spewed from a variety of sources. With all of these and other demands, what is a school leader to do? A different approach to the situation is required. Lead; don't assault.

School budgeting is more than spreadsheets, reports, tracking the expenditure of funds, and the completing of a myriad of accounting forms. It is easy to get caught up in the accounting dimension of budgeting and neglect its companion—vision. It is the integration of vision within the school budgeting process that transforms school budgeting from merely number crunching to purpose-driven expenditures supporting academic success for all students. An articulated and shared vision creates an environment necessary for planning academic success to flourish for all students.

Principals must rethink their approach to school budgeting. School budgeting must not be thought of as merely an accounting responsibility. Leaders must leave the primary accounting responsibility to CPAs and the business office. These folks must be allowed to provide the technical expertise and support necessary to meet the regulatory requirements associated with state and federal fiscal accountability standards. Principal leadership skills must carry the school budgeting process to the next level. This is achieved by integrating the school vision with the budgeting and academic processes for the purpose of achieving academic success for all students.

Imagine a train heading down a track, as depicted in Figure 2.1. The train is the school. The locomotive represents the school leader. This individual leads the local motivation to create a shared vision for the school. The remaining cars are the school's vision and budget and planning process. The movement of the train down the track is the school year. Like the locomotive, the leader is key to moving the school "down the track." Bringing the cars of vision, budget, and planning is essential—so essential, in fact, that they are recognized and supported in the Interstate School Leaders Licensure Consortium (ISLLC) standards.

The National ISLLC Standards

The Interstate School Leaders Licensure Consortium (ISLLC) standards are a logical place to commence a discussion of the relationship between leaders and school budgeting. Sometimes in the heat of the battle of school budgeting, planning and the ISLLC standards can appear distant to the leader. That should not be the case.

A brief examination of the ISLLC standards provides an overview of the authors' assertion that the ISLLC standards address budget issues and do indeed speak loudly to leaders engaged in the budgeting process. The lofty goals of the standards *are* connected to the reality of leading schools. The 2008 ISLLC standards and their accompanying functions can be downloaded at http://www.ccsso.org/Resources/Publications/Educational_Leadership_Policy_Standards_ISLLC_2008_as_Adopted_by_the_National_Policy_Board_for_Educational_Administration.html.

The Council of Chief State School Officers (CCSSO), a national organization of state-level education leaders, created the ISLLC standards (Murphy & Shipman, 1998; Shipman, Topps, & Murphy,

Figure 2.1   The Integrated Budget Train

> The school leader is in the locomotive leading the cars of vision, planning, and budgeting."Yes you can! Yes you can! Yes you can!"comes rolling back from the locomotive for all to hear.

SOURCE: Kathy Myrick, illustrator.

1998). This consortium spent years developing a set of standards that codify the skills effective principals possess. These standards, revised in 2008, remind leaders that improving teaching and learning is a central responsibility of those in leadership positions. The standards demand active, not passive, leadership. The standards assume that leaders are collaborative and inclusive in leading their schools. Finally, the standards do not subscribe to any particular theory of leadership. No one leadership theory has proven to be adequate to be franchised as *the* leadership theory for school administrators. The necessary skills and characteristics of leadership must still be developed and fostered in school leaders (National Policy Board for Educational Administration, 2002).

Steven Covey (2004), in his book *The Seven Habits of Highly Effective People,* encouraged leaders to "begin with the end in mind." In essence, that is exactly what the ISLLC standards call on school leaders to do when in each standard the charge is to "promote the success of every student." *Every* means all students, 100%. Who wants a child or grand-child not to meet with academic success? Can school leaders walk down a school's hallways and look at students and determine which ones they do not want to meet with success? What moral choice do school leaders have but to "promote the success of every student"? This "every student" dimension of the national standards demands a train trip to Utopia for planning big and promoting success. It requires another visit to two long-time friends—school budgeting and vision—and an examination of their often-overlooked relationship in the planning process.

Table 2.1   Monikers for the ISLLC Standards for School Leaders

Standard 1	Vision
Standard 2	Learning
Standard 3	Environment
Standard 4	Community
Standard 5	Ethics
Standard 6	Global

To facilitate an examination of the ISLLC standards, the authors assigned a moniker to each standard, condensing the underlying principle of the ISLLC standard into one word (see Table 2.1). This moniker provides a "mental shoulder tapping" of the underlying concept behind the standard, which is typically referenced numerically.

The ISLLC standards are examined through a school budgeting lens in an effort to explore how the national leadership standards address the school budgeting process. This examination provides school leaders with some guiding principles for school budgeting.

Initially a leader might be criticized for taking this Utopian train trip. Critics will accuse the leader of not living in the real world. School leaders will suffer through the criticism and cynicism of these sarcastic and skeptical voices because of our understanding that every student meeting with success is by its very nature a Utopian goal. Visiting Utopia will provide us with a perfect vision for our schools. It is imperative to begin with this perfect vision. To begin planning for academic success for every student with a vision that is less than ideal dooms a leader and team in the quest for academic success for all children.

Shifts in Knowledge and Skills

Any visit to Utopia begins with an examination of three paradigm shifts identified by Scott Thomas, past executive secretary of the National Policy Board for Educational Administration (NPBEA). In writing an introductory rationale for the ISLLC standards, Thomas identified five broad based shifts in the knowledge and skills required of educational leaders today compared to the traditional knowledge base (NPBEA, 2002). It is significant that the underlying premise of this book—integrating budgeting and vision—is at the center of three of the five shifts identified by Thomas.

From Technical Skills to Interpersonal Skills

This "shift" for school leaders is all about the vision thing. Thomas advances the idea that gaining a common vision for a school involves interpersonal skills rather than technical skills. In order to gain a common vision, principals must generate a learning culture, work with staff in improving instruction, be collaborative, and identify and solve problems, all the while addressing ethnic and gender differences (NPBEA, 2002). As the American society has become more pluralistic, more groups with greater diversity have evolved, and thus leaders must work to sculpt a common vision for schools. Blumberg and Greenfield noted as far back as 1986 that principals who were effective in advancing a school vision were competent in three skills: (1) articulating a vision for schools and openly exchanging views with others about accomplishments; (2) persuading teachers and others in the school community to internalize or incorporate the vision into their daily conduct; and (3) encouraging teachers and others to make personal sacrifices toward its realization. All three of these skills are interpersonal skills. Lunenburg and Irby (2006) noted the importance of building confidence in stakeholders that the vision could be accomplished.

From Director to Consensus Builder and Motivator

The second broad shift identified by Thomas involves changing from director to consensus builder and motivator. Thomas recognized that involving as many stakeholders as possible in the decision-making process improved the quality of the decision as well as the motivation for ensuring the successful implementation of the decision (NPBEA, 2002). Once again, Blumberg and Greenfield (1986) reinforced these ideas in their research almost three decades ago. They found that schools that make meaningful progress toward accomplishing the school vision have principals who (1) are effective in exchanging ideas about the vision with others; (2) regularly encourage sacrifices on behalf of that vision; and (3) work with teachers who freely accept and share the campus vision. Yesteryear's research applies today, as Lunenburg and Irby (2006) stress the need for principals to stay with the vision to provide direction and purpose and keep the vision in front of all stakeholders.

From Resource Allocation to Accountability

Finally, Thomas identifies a broad shift in resource allocation to accountability for learning processes and results. This shift demands that school budgeting, vision, and planning be an integrated process. Thomas asserts that principals can no longer allocate resources that are not tied to measurable objectives. He further professes that the increased emphasis on improving student achievement must focus on accountability (NPBEA, 2002).

Thomas's broad shifts in knowledge and skills are requirements of today's educational leaders. The authors advance the proposition that the school budgeting process and the vision process must be integrated and synchronized in order for schools to be successful in improving student academic performance.

Examining the ISLLC Standards Through a Budget–Vision Lens

While in Utopia devising a plan for academic success for every student, give primary consideration to the interrelationship between school budgeting and vision. While neither of these concepts is new, it could be argued that school leaders have not given due consideration to the significance of the symbiotic relationship they have on the academic success of students and schools. It is important to consider budgeting and vision simultaneously in the planning process in order to increase our understanding of their influence on each other and the fulfillment of the national standard's clarion call for "academic success for all students." It is imperative that the discussion of school budgeting and vision begin with an examination of each ISLLC standard. It is also essential that this examination of the standards be accomplished through a school budgeting and vision lens.

ISLLC Standard 1—The Vision Standard[1]

An education leader promotes the success of every student by facilitating the development, articulation, implementation, and stewardship of a vision of learning that is shared and supported by all stakeholders.

---

[1] These standards are reprinted with permission from *Interstate School Leaders Licensure Consortium (ISLLC) Standards for School Leaders*. (2008). Washington, DC: Council of Chief State School Officers. The Interstate School Leaders Licensure Consortium (ISLLC) Standards were developed by the Council of Chief School Officers (CCSSO) and member states. The ISLLC standards may be downloaded from the Council's website at http://www.ccsso. org/Resources/Publications/Educational_Leadership_Policy_Standards_ ISLLC_2008_as_Adopted_by_the_National_Policy_Board_for_Educational_ Administration.html.

Standard 1, like each of the standards, includes the phrase *success of every student*. This phrase requires a leader to approach budgeting and vision with the expectation that every student will meet with success, not just those students who come to school prepared and nurtured by their families, but also those who come to us with little nurturing and minimal preparation. Leaders might do well to stop and reread the previous statement and allow the significance of it to sink in. "Success of every student" does not allow leaders to rationalize or explain away their responsibility to have every student meet with success.

Budgeting, vision, and academic success are intertwined with each other in the planning process. They are not isolated variables operating independently in a school's culture. When leaders accept this coupling of budgeting and vision and understand their combined effect on academic achievement, then budgeting expands from a fiscal responsibility to a fiscal-vision opportunity that in turn drives planning for academic success for all students. Regardless of what a leader may think about the provisions or requirements of the No Child Left Behind Act of 2011, its intent is noble in that, like the national standards, it seeks the Utopian goal of success for every student.

Standard 1 is at the very core of this book's purpose in that it calls for the melding of vision with budget and planning. Not only must a school leader facilitate the development, articulation, and implementation of a school vision, the leader must also be a steward of that vision. Stewardship is the administration and management of the financial affairs of another. A school leader ensures that the resources of the school are allocated in a manner that supports the school's vision. The school's budget does not belong to the principal. It belongs to all the school's stakeholders. It belongs to the public who sacrificed through the payment of taxes to provide the revenues for the budget. It does not belong only to the principal. Chapter 3 contains a further examination of this standard.

ISLLC Standard 2—The Learning Standard

An education leader promotes the success of every student by advocating, nurturing, and sustaining a school culture and instructional program conducive to student learning and staff professional growth.

Standard 2 is a key element in growing the integrated budget–vision–planning process. It is noteworthy that this standard immediately follows Standard 1, which establishes the importance of having a school vision. Once the vision is collaboratively developed, the work is just beginning. Leaders must advocate, nurture, and sustain a school culture conducive to student learning and staff professional growth. It is the responsibility of the school leader to nurture and develop the school culture (Hoy & Miskel, 2012). This is a responsibility that cannot and must not be delegated. It is within the school's culture that the traditions, values, and beliefs of the various stakeholders are manifested (Deal & Peterson, 2009). School leaders must seize the opportunity to define and shape the school's culture. Leaders must be certain not to lead with reckless behavior. It is important to get everyone on board. If principals see the importance of an integrated budget-planning process and the faculty, staff, and other stakeholders fail to see its importance, then the process will fail. Failure is not an option.

What is valued by leaders will, through time and labor, be valued in the school's culture. If principals value the importance of integrating school vision with the budget and planning process and advocate and nurture the integrated budget–vision–planning process, it will become part of the school's culture. Principals are likely to hear someone say, "At this school we put our money where our mouth is." A principal would translate this comment as an affirmation that: At this school (*at this school*) the stakeholders understand (*we put*) that the budget (*our money*) is aligned with the vision (*where our mouth is*).

Resources must be aligned with the school's vision during the planning process if the school's culture and instructional program are to be conducive to student learning and staff development. Anything less than aligning the budget with the vision bastardizes the process. This standard will be revisited in greater depth in Chapter 3 and Chapter 5.

ISLLC Standard 3—The Environment Standard

An education leader promotes the success of every student by ensuring management of the organization, operation, and resources for a safe, efficient, and effective learning environment.

One attribute of successful school management is the skillful handling of resources—thus the budget connection is established in Standard 3. Resources are not limited to but include both internal and external funding, time, personnel, equipment, and facilities.

Leaders are required to manage resources for a safe, efficient, and effective learning environment. The importance of a safe learning environment to student success is reiterated in the pioneering effective schools research of Ron Edmonds and his colleagues (Taylor, 2002). The funding dimension of a safe learning environment requires that we properly budget for essential safety materials and services.

An efficient learning environment is one that functions to achieve a desired result without waste. Dollars dedicated to education are difficult to come by. It is imperative that the budgeting process be integrated with the goals and objectives of the campus to obtain optimum results. Schools can no longer afford the luxury of keeping ineffective programs, pet projects, or any other distraction that drains precious resources from the implementation of its shared vision.

An effective learning environment is one in which intended goals and objectives are achieved. Leaders and teams can possess the greatest of intentions and passion, but if the collaborative development of goals and objectives and budgeting of resources to those goals and objectives does not occur, then it is impossible to create an effective campuswide learning environment.

ISLLC Standard 4—The Community Standard

An education leader promotes the success of every student by collaborating with faculty and community members, responding to diverse community interests and needs, and mobilizing community resources.

Mobilizing community resources, the final phrase in Standard 4, establishes the budget–vision link. When school leaders mobilize, they not only organize the fiscal resources, they organize all stakeholders, readying them for action to achieve essential goals and objectives.

It is essential that all stakeholders possess ownership of the school's action plan and recognize the importance of allocating community resources to achieve the desired results that are in line with the school's vision. Remember, the community is literally investing its resources in its children and is expecting a return on its investment in the form of educated, enlightened, and productive individuals. When schools fail to produce this product, the community resources must be reallocated to address this failure in the form of welfare, juvenile detention, and adult prison programs. The failure of schools to meet student needs creates a domino effect that is felt throughout the community. Failure to meet the campus goals for students creates an intensely competitive environment for the community resources, as other public institutions vying for the same limited public resources must meet the shortcomings of school programs.

An example of added costs to the public when education is not successful is found in the prison system. The 2003 Literacy Behind Bars Survey revealed that 41% of prisoners in state and federal prisons had their high school diploma or equivalent. This compares to 85 to 88% of the general population. This survey, the most comprehensive assessment of educational backgrounds of prisoners in 10 years, also reported overall prison inmates with GED/high school equivalency certificates had higher literacy scores than those with high school diplomas (Greenberg, Duleavy, & Kutner, 2007).

Keeping a person in prison costs more than two and a half times the amount it takes to educate a child. The average per-pupil expenditure for students in U.S. public elementary and secondary schools in 2008–2009 was $12,250. Utah at $7,954 spent the least per pupil in educating children. New York spent $20,645 per student, making it the largest spender per pupil (U.S. Census Bureau, 2009). The Vera Institute for Justice reported that in 2010, the average cost to taxpayers to keep a prisoner incarcerated was $31,116 (Henrichson & Delaney, 2012).

The cost to the public for unsuccessful schools is also reflected in the median earning of adults based on educational attainment. The U.S. Labor Department, Bureau of Labor Statistics reports the more educated a person, the greater the person's income is likely to be. Conversely, the earlier a person drops out of school, the lower the person's income is likely to be. This relationship between educational attainment and income is shown in Table 2.2 (Bureau of Labor Statistics, 2011). The cost to society for students not meeting with academic success is staggering. Assuming a 40-year work career and not adjusting for inflation, the worker with a bachelor's degree or higher will earn $1,235,520 more in a work career than the student who left school with less than a high school education.

Table 2.2   Earnings According to Education Attainment

Educational Attainment for Adults Age 25 and Over	Median Annual Earnings 2010
Less than a high school diploma	$ 23,088
High school diploma	$ 32,552
Some college, no degree	$ 37,024
Associate degree	$ 39,884
Bachelor's degree	$ 53,976

SOURCE: Bureau of Labor Statistics ("Education Pays," 2011).

When schools fail to achieve the national standards' call for academic success for every student, then schools can expect other systems to compete with them for public resources. It is imperative that students meet with academic success so that not only do they become greater producers for society, but also the need for other institutions such as prisons and welfare programs is lessened; this, in turn, increases the availability of funds to enrich the services provided by public education.

ISLLC Standard 5—The Ethics Standard

An educational leader promotes the success of every student by acting with integrity, fairness, and in an ethical manner.

Standard 5 is a reminder that character does in fact count. Principals must examine personal motives and their treatment of others, as well as how they carry out their personal and professional missions. Then leaders must decide what they are not willing to do in order to achieve personal and school goals (see Chapter 7).

Integrity, fairness, and ethical behavior are a trio of concepts that school leaders struggle to define. Former U.S. Supreme Court Justice Potter Stewart, commenting in the *Jacobellis v. Ohio* case concerning the issue of pornography, stated he could not attempt to define pornography and yet acknowledged, "But I know it when I see it" (Linder, n.d.). Like Stewart, educators know integrity, fairness, and ethical behavior when observed but struggle to define this trio of terms.

This trio can be analyzed utilizing the works of Plato, John Locke, Immanuel Kant, Niccolo Machiavelli, and others, but that might seem detached from the day-to-day challenges school leaders face. Leaders must depend on their personal judgment and experiences in determining how to react to given situations. Possibly the readers should take time from their busy schedules to consider integrity, fairness, and ethical behavior. After all, the "in-the-face" demands of academic accountability, student discipline, per-pupil expenditure, and a host of other demands provide for a variety of excuses for bypassing an examination of these terms. Cooper (1998) suggests that school leaders often make administrative decisions using rationality and systematic reflection in a piecemeal fashion. Cooper asserts leaders are ad hoc problem solvers, not comprehensive moral philosophers who only resort to the next level of generality and abstraction when a repertoire of practical moral rules fails to assist in reaching a decision. Sound familiar?

Examining Three Key Terms—The Trio

It is important to examine Standard 5 in the light of budgeting and vision and pay close attention to the three key terms found in this standard—*integrity, fairness*, and *ethical manner* (see Table 2.3).

Integrity. Integrity, the first of the trio of ethical terms, is an important dimension of leadership. Leaders who value integrity are not only interested in results but are also interested in relationships. This is easily illustrated in the world of high-stakes student assessment. Each year, educators are under increasing pressure to meet a mandated level of academic performance for their students. The consequences for not achieving these defined goals are increasing. The temptation from a variety of schemes for school leaders to manipulate these data is also increasing.

Principals must not only consider integrity within the sphere of academic goals. They must also consider the integrity of our relationships with all of the school's stakeholders. It is essential that leaders earn the trust of all stakeholders to be successful. For integrity to exist, leaders must show genuine concern for others and their personal goals. When concern and integrity exist, trust flourishes and further empowers the leader to lead the school toward fulfilling its shared vision.

Stories abound in which school leaders succumb to temptation and misrepresent themselves, inappropriately use school funds, or manipulate data. When this is discovered, these leaders lose their reputation and effectiveness along with their dignity. It takes a lifetime to build a good reputation and only a minute to lose it. A superintendent from a school of 33,000 students retired from her job with 3 years remaining on her contract as a result of a controversy associated with recommending a contract to be offered to a firm for the delivery of services to the school district. At issue was her failure to advise the board that she had worked as a consultant for several years for the firm (Borja, 2005). Chapter 5 contains a further examination of the integrity issue from the perspective of a leader's reputation.

Table 2.3   Key Terms in ISLLC Standard 5—The Ethics Standard

Integrity	Soundness of and adherence to moral principle and character
Fairness	Free from bias, dishonesty, or injustice
Ethics	A system of moral principles

SOURCE: *The Random House Dictionary of the English Language* (Unabridged Edition).

High-stakes testing is a prime area for leaders to be tempted to cheat by manipulating data. Variables such as test security, student exemptions, and test preparation become factors. In one school district, eight elementary schools, including a Blue Ribbon campus, were being investigated because of unusual swings in the state test scores (Garza, 2005). In a highly publicized case, systematic cheating was uncovered in Atlanta's public school system. Forty-four schools and at least 178 educators including the superintendent were involved in this alleged cheating incidence (Severson, 2011). Cizek (1999) compiled a list of euphemisms that have been used by educators in attempts to soften the term *cheating*. Sadly, two of the more creative euphemisms were "falsely reporting success" and "achievement similarities not attributable to chance."

Samuel Johnson, one of the most quoted men from the 18th century, said, "Integrity without knowledge is weak and useless, and knowledge without integrity is dangerous and dreadful" ("The Samuel Johnson," 1751). Integrity alone will not allow a school leader to meet with success. Principals must understand every facet of a school and its students. We must have a command of the school's vision and its budget. If a leader lacks integrity, the school is at risk; doubt and fear will replace integrity. People will revert to the selfish nature of man, and the common good of the learning community will be forgotten.

Fairness. Once again, school leaders risk their effectiveness when they separate vision from the budget, especially when it comes to fairness. It is essential to consider both budget and vision as integral parts of the planning process to completely understand the complex nature of fairness.

Fairness, the second of the trio of key terms, does not mean ensuring that everyone gets the same amount of something or the same treatment. Fairness is when everyone receives what is needed in order to successfully accomplish his or her goals. Some students will need one cup of patience while others will require two, three, or even four cups of patience to reach their goals. Still others will need different resources dedicated to them to ensure their academic success. For example, students with learning disabilities might need greater resources in order to reach their instructional goals than those without disabilities.

When principals accept the fact that vision is what drives the budget and that shared vision is designed to help all students achieve their potential, then they begin to understand that fairness requires resources to be allocated on the basis of needs in order to obtain academic goals. Fairness is not dividing the financial pie into equal pieces. For example, the New Jersey School Board Association (NJSBA) reports that in 2006–2007, the New Jersey per-pupil expenditure for students in special education was $16,081 compared to $10,050 for general education (NJSBA, 2007). The financial pie was not divided into equal pieces. Instead, it was apportioned based on meeting the individual needs of students.

Schools perish when a lack of vision exists. When money is thrown at problems, human nature takes over to ensure "give me my fair share." This usually translates into "get all that I can get." In the absence of an understanding of the budget–vision relationship in the planning process, greed takes control and the good of the learning community is abandoned.

Unfortunately, fairness does not become a part of a school's social fabric overnight. It cannot be ordered or microwaved into existence. Instead, the leader must keep the budget–vision relationship in front of the team and make inroads into fairness as opportunities arise. Through persistence, fairness will become valued as part of the school's culture and will manifest itself in ethical behavior.

Ethical Behavior. Ethical behavior is the last of ISLLC Standard 5's trio of key terms. Ethical behavior is an essential part of the school leader's persona. Fairness, integrity, and equity are employed to best conduct the school's business. School leaders must act in an ethical manner when handling discipline problems, implementing state-mandated accountability testing, managing school budgets, consulting with parents, supervising faculty and staff, and in a host of other situations.

A continued examination of the national standards with regard to their implication on budgeting and vision reveals how appropriate it is to consider the principle of benefit maximization. This principle requires principals to make choices that provide the greatest good for the most people. When we are developing our school vision, the process must be one of inclusiveness. Shared vision is about meaningfully involving everyone, not just those with the greatest political clout or the loudest voices in the vision-development process. The principal must help craft and share a school vision that not only provides all of our students with the opportunity to meet with success but also a vision that is truly shared by all the stakeholders. The No Child Left Behind Act's name in itself codifies the call to create schools to meet the ISLLC's mantra of "promotes the success of every student."

The principle of benefit maximization also applies to the budgeting process. Budgets must provide the greatest good for the most students. This means that tough decisions must be made. Tough decisions are not always popular decisions. But tough decisions made with integrity, fairness, and in an ethical manner will propel schools toward the fulfillment of a school's vision. It is essential that the school budget be considered in tandem with the school vision.

The budget is an essential tool in turning the vision into reality. When the budget process is divorced from the vision process, the likelihood of the vision being fulfilled dramatically decreases. Bracey (2002) provides a vivid illustration of what can happen when the budget process and the academic vision process are divorced. In his book *The War Against America's Public Schools,* Bracey (2002) writes about a group of superintendents enthusiastically embracing a new efficiency model that changed them from scholars into managers. Bracey (2002) concludes his chiding of this particular efficiency model by writing, "Of course, one might wonder why, instead of studying ways to save money on toilet paper, superintendents didn't investigate why their charges dipped it in water and slung it at the walls" (p. 37).

Considering the toilet paper problem from a purely accounting perspective, focus is only on the financial cost associated with providing the toilet paper for student use and neglects the possible academic issues at play in the misuse of the toilet paper. By only considering the financial issue associated with the use or misuse of the toilet paper, leaders wipe out the opportunity to get to the academic bottom of the toilet paper cost problem in terms of its cost to the school's vision to have all students meet with academic success. By including the academic perspective in conjunction with the budget perspective, hence the budget–vision connection, the toilet paper problem is then also considered as a potential indication of an academic failure to meet the needs of all students. Bottom line: Budgeting and vision must be considered simultaneously if schools are to reach their goal of 100% student success.

A second principle to consider in the examination of ethics is the Golden Rule. Many might mistakenly limit the Golden Rule to the teachings of Jesus; however, there is some version of the Golden Rule in all of the major religions of the world. Table 2.4 provides a comparison of the Golden Rule in five of the world's major religions. The universal truth found in the Golden Rule is important to consider in our ethical treatment of others. It requires principals to treat all people with equal value. People are entitled to equal opportunity. Principals must value all people and respect their educational goals. People must not be considered as merely assets to be used to achieve the school vision.

Finally, leaders must respect individual rights to make their own choices. When including the Golden Rule as part of the code of ethics, principals are more apt to integrate the budget process with the vision. The end result: Leaders are less likely to see people as objects to be manipulated to achieve selfish purposes.

ISLLC Standard 6—The Global Standard

An educational leader promotes the success of every student by understanding, responding to, and influencing the political, social, economic, legal, and cultural context.

Principals must approach any discussion of this standard from a global perspective. Intellectually, it is important to acknowledge that schools do not operate in a vacuum. Yet not to get so caught up with the day-to-day demands of guiding a school, it is essential to never allow the big picture to slip under one's desk clutter. Standard 6 is a clarion call for leaders to understand their interconnectedness with each other and with the rest of the globe.

Table 2.4   Golden Rule in the World Religions

Religion	Golden Rule
Buddhism	Hurt not others in ways that you yourself would find hurtful. (Udana-Varga 5,1)
Christianity	All things whatsoever ye would that men should do to you, do ye so to them; for this is the law and the prophets. (Matthew 7:1)
Hinduism	This is the sum of duty; do naught unto others what you would not have them do unto you. (Mahabharata 5, 1517)
Islam	No one of you is a believer until he desires for his brother that which he desires for himself. (Sunah)
Judaism	What is hateful to you, do not do it to your fellowman. This is the entire Law; all the rest is commentary. (Talmud, Shabbat 3id)

SOURCE: (TeachingValues.com, 2012).

Schools are interlaced in a myriad of political, social, economic, legal, and cultural ways at the local, state, national, and international levels in an increasingly complex and interconnected world. Accelerated technological developments have created dramatic social, political, and economic changes. The connectivity infrastructure with its DSL lines, smart phones, wireless technology, and high-speed modems is linking the planet together via the Internet. This explosion in the instantaneous sharing of information has had the effect of shrinking the globe and bringing the global village concept into a reality. Marshall McLuhan, a Canadian scholar and communication theorist, coined the term *global village* and captured the impact of technology on lives when he said, "Ours is a brand-new world of allatonceness [all-at-onceness]. 'Time' has ceased, 'space' has vanished. We now live in a global village…a simultaneous happening" (McLuhan & Fiore, 2005, p. 63).

The American economy is part of a global economy, as witnessed by the outsourcing of American jobs overseas. Therefore, global events affect the economy; that, in turn, affects the amount of tax revenue that is available for public schools; that, in turn, impacts school budgets; and that, in turn, influences both the school planning and budgeting process. Wow! All of a sudden it is easy to feel like the end of a food chain (Figure 2.2)!

Figure 2.2   The Budgeting Food Chain

| World Economy | U.S. Economy | State Economy | School Revenue |

SOURCE: Kathy Myrick, illustrator.

All said and done, Standard 6 reminds principals that leading a school that promotes the success of every student is accomplished within a global context, one in which both national and international events impact the availability of funds for our school budget.

Final Thoughts

School budgeting and vision must be considered simultaneously in the planning process in order for schools to increase their likelihood of achieving the Utopian goal of "every student meeting with success." The ISLLC standards provide the guideposts necessary for school leaders to facilitate academic success for all.

The trick is for school leaders to incorporate the generalities of the national standards into practical steps to achieve the ideal of academic success for all students. This chapter at times might appear to be "Pollyannaish." Some of the examples and metaphors could illicit a "pie in the sky" reaction from you, the reader. However, it is important to begin the integrated budget planning process with a "pie in the sky" perspective. To do otherwise would immediately lower expectations to less than 100% of the students obtaining academic success. Achieving 99.9% is not good enough. If 99.9% were good enough, then 12 babies would be given to the wrong parents each day, two planes landing daily at O'Hare International Airport would be unsafe, and 291 pacemaker operations would be performed incorrectly this year (Godwords, n.d.).

HOW DO I INTRODUCE THEM?

Felix Navidad, principal of Mistletoe High School (MHS), wants to increase the role of shared leadership at MHS. He recently attended a workshop exploring the ISLLC standards. What he once thought was abstract and not connected with him or his faculty and staff became a motivational source for changing MHS into a more collaborative environment. Felix's challenge was how to introduce the faculty and staff to the ISLLC standards without them rolling their eyes and closing their minds. Felix knows the introduction of the ISLLC standards to his team is crucial for creating a positive, collaborative environment.

Pause and Consider

- How should Felix introduce the ISLLC standards to his faculty and staff?
- What should he definitely avoid when introducing the standards?

Covey (2004) encourages school leaders to begin with the end in mind. The end in mind is 100% of students meeting with the academic success called for in each of the national standards using an integrated approach to budgeting process. There are many forces working against school leaders in achieving this goal. In the remaining chapters, greater specificity is provided to help leaders and teams obtain the 100% expectation.

Discussion Questions

1. Which ISLLC standards do you think influence the budget–vision relationship the most in your situation? Why?

2. Do you agree or disagree with the authors' contention that we "must visit Utopia" in creating a vision for our schools, or is this just "fluff"? Support your response.

3. How have you witnessed the shift from technical skills to interpersonal skills?

4. How have you witnessed the shift from director to consensus builder and motivator?

5. How have you witnessed the shift from resource allocation to accountability?

6. What are your initial thoughts on the authors' contention that budgeting and vision must be integrated in the planning process in order to promote the success of all students?

7. How have you been a part of or witnessed a situation similar to the budget–vision disconnect toilet paper problem?

Case Study Application: Belle Plain Middle School

Belle Plain Middle School (BPMS) is composed of approximately 1,000 students in Grades 6 through 8. The school is 40% Anglo, 25% Hispanic, 25% African American, 5% Asian American, and 5% other. Of these students, 60% qualify for free or reduced lunch; 12% of the students are identified as limited English proficient; the campus mobility rate is 30%.

The facility is 25 years old and is in an average state of repair. The neighborhood around the school is composed of modest homes of a similar age to the school. Many homes are in good repair and evidence pride in ownership. Most of the nearby businesses are independently owned small businesses. There is the typical scattering of franchised fast-food restaurants.

The majority of parents of the students at BPMS are employed in blue-collar jobs. A recently constructed subdivision of upper-middle-class homes in the attendance zone has created the potential of changing the campus demographics. The supermajority of students who reside in the new subdivision are either being home-schooled or are enrolled in a private school 20 minutes away because of parent concerns about the academic integrity of Belle Plain Middle School. The parents from this subdivision who have enrolled their children in the school want to meet with the principal about becoming more involved in the school and in their children's education.

The BPMS faculty is divided into two groups. The Old Pros are those teachers who have an average experience of more than 15 years at the school. The Greenhorns are faculty and staff that have less than 5 years' experience at the school. The latter group has a high turnover rate. There is tension between the two faculty groups as well as a certain amount of distrust. The Old Pros perceive the Greenhorns as short on experience and long on idealism. The Greenhorns perceive the Old Pros as jaded and insensitive to the needs of the students. They also accuse the Old Pros of being unwilling to attempt innovative strategies to meet student needs because of professional bias.

A total of 65% of all students passed the state reading test. The passing rate for Hispanics and African Americans was 52%; limited-English-proficient students had a 47% passing rate on the state reading test. Percentages who passed the state mathematics test were: 71% of all students; 59% of the Hispanics passed the mathematics test; 61% of the African American students; and 53% of the limited-English-proficient students passed the mathematics test.

The percentage of students identified as needing special education services is 17% above the state average. The percentage of Hispanic students in special education is 53% higher than the Anglo rate.

You are the new principal on the campus. You are the third principal in 5 years. The selection process for hiring you was substantially different from that used with previous principals. The superintendent secured a search committee comprising parents, teachers, staff, and community members. A successful effort was made to involve individuals of all ethnic and socioeconomic groups. The superintendent screened the initial applicant list and submitted the names of five individuals for the committee to interview and make a recommendation to him. The two male and three female finalists were ethnically diverse. Like you, all of the finalists were from outside the school district.

The superintendent and board have set a priority of turning Belle Plain Middle School around. You have been promised a 12% increase in your campus budget for the next 3 years. The campus has also been allotted two additional faculty positions to be determined by you in a collaborative effort with the faculty and staff.

The previous two principals gave lip service to involving teachers and staff in making academic plans for the students. A campus academic improvement plan was developed each year but was never referred to during the school year. The previous principals usually made some modifications to the previous year's plan and ran it by the faculty for a quick vote before sending it to the superintendent.

Teachers have little or no knowledge about the campus budget. They are not aware of what financial resources are available to the campus. Currently, the primary way of securing financial resources is to ask the principal and wait until a response is received.

Three years ago, the parent–teacher organization was abandoned for lack of attendance. The superintendent has informed you that the two Hispanic board members receive frequent complaints that Hispanic parents do not feel welcome or valued on the campus. A recent parent survey compiled by the central administration indicates, among other things, that many of the Old Pros believe their students are not performing well because the children do not try hard enough and the parents do not care.

Application Questions

Consider the following questions. A suggestion: Download the 2008 ISLLC Standards to have access to each standard's functions. This will assist in developing deeper responses to each question as well as increasing your understanding of the ISLLC Standards.

1. How can you as the principal of Belle Plain Middle School promote the success of every student at Belle Plain Middle School by facilitating the development, articulation, implementation, and stewardship of a vision of learning that is shared and supported by all stakeholders?

2. How can you as the principal of Belle Plain Middle School promote the success of every student at Belle Plain Middle School by advocating, nurturing, and sustaining a school culture and instructional program conducive to student learning and staff professional growth?

3. How can you as principal of Belle Plain Middle School promote the success of every student by ensuring management of the organization, operation, and resources for a safe, efficient, effective learning environment?

4. How can you as principal of Belle Plain Middle School promote the success of every student by collaborating with faculty and community members, responding to the diverse community interests and needs, and mobilizing the community resources?

5. How can you as principal of Belle Plain Middle School promote the success of every student by acting with integrity, fairness, and in an ethical manner?

6. How can you as principal of Belle Plain Middle School promote the success of every student by understanding, responding to, and influencing the larger political, social, economic, legal, and cultural context?

7. What additional information would be beneficial in addressing the issues raised in the first six questions?

Chapter 3

Culture, Data, and Celebrating Success

Anyone could carve a goose were it not for the bones.

—T. S. Eliot, 1935, *Murder in the Cathedral*, p. 111

The trip to Utopia provided a clear view of the ideal world principals must seek for their schools. Unfortunately, no one lives in an ideal world. Instead, the world is filled with many challenges such as shortages of financial and physical resources, and schools serve an ever-growing and increasingly diverse student population. In an opinion column, George Will commented on the challenges of constructing the federal government budget when he penned, "'Anyone,' said T. S. Eliot, 'could carve a goose were it not for the bones.' Anyone could write a sensible federal budget, were it not for the bones—the sturdy skeleton of existing programs defended by muscular interests" (Will, 2005). The same can be said about the integrated school budget process. When school leaders become serious about aligning the school budget with the school vision, they can expect to encounter the sturdy skeletons of existing programs as they carve a budget aligned with the school's vision. The bones of programs near and dear to some stakeholders will not necessarily be germane to attaining the school's vision. Besides the bones of existing programs, school leaders can also expect bones of impaired vision from stakeholders who either do not understand or choose not to accept the academic success for all as exemplified in Ron Edmonds's remark uttered more than 30 years ago, "We can, whenever we want, successfully teach all children whose schooling is of interest to us. We already know more than we need to do that. Whether or not we do it must depend on how we feel about the fact that we haven't so far" (Edmonds, 1979, p. 56). The challenge for the principal and school stakeholders is growing a culture that supports the school's vision and mission. An examination of the importance of school culture, data, and celebrating success in the integrated budget model is in order

Culture

The importance of a school culture receptive to the integrated budget model purported in this book cannot be overemphasized. Wilkins and Patterson (1985) wrote: "Culture consists of the conclusions a group of people draws from its experience. An organization's [school's] culture consists largely of what people believe about what works and what does not" (p. 5). Integrating the budget and vision into a single process cannot flourish unless it is woven into the fabric of the school's culture. The integrated budget model requires a school culture receptive to collaboration. Schools, which possess a collegial spirit, share values, beliefs, and traditions and are more apt to spawn the required collaborative environment that in turn increases enthusiasm, energy, and motivation (Green, 2013; Lunenburg & Irby, 2006). This integration must be valued by the school's culture since it frequently influences people's opinions and behaviors while serving as the vehicle to turn dreams into reality.

School culture was touched upon in the examination of ISLLC Standard 2 in Chapter 2. This standard calls on education leaders to "promote the success of every student by advocating, nurturing, and sustaining a school culture and instructional program conducive to student learning and staff professional growth." This national standard warrants closer examination because the integrated budget process cannot exist with any degree of usefulness unless it is inculcated into the school's culture.

Reginald Green (2013) defined culture as "the shared values, beliefs, assumptions, rituals, traditions, norms, attitudes and behaviors of the faculty and staff. It is the tie that binds all elements of the school" (p. 92). The community is the school. Green's use of the adjective *shared* in defining culture is of importance when considering it with the ISLLC Standard 2 edict that education leaders *promote* a school culture. *Shared* is a WE thing. *Shared* implies that all stakeholders in the school possess common core values. *Promote* requires school leaders to take the initiative to advocate, nourish, and sustain the school culture in such a manner that meets the edict of Standard 2.

A brief examination of school culture's three elements—values, beliefs, and attitudes—makes a case for the integration of budget and vision a part of every school's culture. This examination is conducted within the ISLLC obligation to advocate, nourish, and sustain the school culture.

Values

Values are those ideals leaders hold near and dear. They are the ideals leaders deem important. Values shape the practice of teachers and staff (Nash, 1996). For the integrated budget approach to become inculcated within a school's culture, stakeholders must understand how this approach helps them fulfill their personal mission as well as the school's mission. It is essential for leaders to model their values (Shaw, 2012). Leaders advocate for the integrated budget approach to budgeting when they support it, plead its case, and assist the stakeholders in understanding it. Leaders nurture it by discussing it in formal and informal team meetings and by sharing it with parents and community members. Leaders sustain it by never allowing the integrated budget approach to be removed from the stakeholder's conscience.

Beliefs

Beliefs are what leaders hold to be true. The integrated relationship between budget, vision, and planning must become something stakeholders hold to be true. Gradually, through time and effort and by consistently keeping the integrated budget process at the center of school planning, events will unfold and stories will develop that will become part of the school's heritage. Some stories will be rooted in cherished accomplishments that occur through the integrated budgetary process. Rituals will manifest themselves as ceremonies. Deal and Kennedy (1982) purport that ceremonies are to culture what movies are to scripts. They afford the players an opportunity to act out their beliefs. Ceremonies become ongoing events that sustain the integrated budget approach in the school culture.

SAD SACK SCHOOL

Good, bad, or ugly, schools have a culture. The authors observed a school with a poisonous culture. A strong level of distrust existed among this school's stakeholders. Teachers didn't trust the principal. The principal didn't trust the teachers. Friction was high between professionals and paraprofessionals. No sense of community existed. The campus ran amuck. If there was a mission statement, it was likely "Take care of yourself." Throughout the campus, an air of failure and defeat prevailed. Distrust had replaced trust. Rumors replaced constructive conversation. Data were abused and used to abuse. The school was in a hopeless downward spiral.

This school did not set out to become what it had become. Undoubtedly the school at one time was quite different. It appeared that time, difficult problems, and tough situations combined with weak leadership and lacking a plan to address the school's challenges led to the poisonous culture. It was obvious that the stakeholders were not satisfied with their situation but they couldn't overcome their sense of helplessness and frustration. Their negativity generated more negativity, spinning into a bottomless downward spiral.

However, despite this desperate situation, glimmers of hope existed in a couple of areas within this school. This story illustrates the impact of an unhealthy culture on schools. The story also offers hope for those who are trapped in unhealthy cultures. This story is for those who are hunkered down in bunkers of positive thought in an unhealthy culture. Culture can be changed! Culture changes when hunkered-down groups purposefully seek change. Change agents identify the root causes of discontent and start addressing these root causes, gradually dismantling the negativity.

Attitudes

Attitudes are how leaders feel about things. Did a parent or caregiver ever tell you "Watch your attitude!"? This statement usually had "that" tone in it, letting you know your attitude was not appreciated for whatever reason. You learned as a child there were ways things were done around your home. In healthy homes, parents communicated with the family members to collaboratively develop a shared family culture respecting all of its members. In unhealthy homes, dysfunctional behavior had family members in contentious relationships. Eventually, some unhealthy families seek intervention to improve the family. Other unhealthy families never seek intervention and either dissolve or remain contentious.

Schools are a lot like families. Over time, a school's stakeholders realize that their school cannot function at its best unless they develop a healthy culture. The integrated budget approach is at the core of a healthy school's planning process. The more the integrated budget process is used in planning, the more deep-seated it becomes as part of the school's culture, and the organization's health improves. Deal and Peterson (1998) aptly observed that an attitude develops that this is the way things are done in the school, this is how we celebrate, and this is how we appreciate each other. It takes time for ideas like these to become part of the school's culture. Ebullient leaders never tire in their effort to advocate and nurture the budget–vision–planning relationship for it to be incorporated as a part of the culture. Leaders must never cease in their efforts; they must constantly strive to sustain them as part of the school's culture.

Data

Lorna Earl's school and data observation is quite astute: "We live in a culture that has come to value and depend on statistical information to inform our decisions. At the same time we are likely to misunderstand and misuse those statistics because we are 'statistically illiterate' and consequently have no idea what the numbers mean" (Earl, 1995, p. 62). Schools, at times, appear to be drowning in data. State testing data have a prominent role not only in state accountability policies but also in federal accountability policies. Celio and Harvey (2005), along with others, suggest schools are awash in data. Leaders must ensure that high-quality data are used in decision making. School leaders must work with school stakeholders in analyzing data, identifying solutions, and implementing those solutions. Time must be allocated for data gathering and analysis.

Data-Driven Decision Making

The Sorenson-Goldsmith Integrated Budget Model (Figure 4.1, p. 81) is introduced in the next chapter. The third and fourth components of this model involve data gathering and data analysis. Before getting the proverbial cart before the horse, the authors are compelled to call attention to data gathering and analysis before introducing their model. It's okay to look ahead and take a peek at the model in the next chapter.

Effective use of data changes a school's culture. Data expose bias and ignorance; they provide "Aha!" moments, as well as debunking ineffective practices. In short, data gathering and analysis are a catalyst for changing a school's culture for the good.

The authors have personal experience in using data to expose ineffective teaching practices. Ineffective practices, left alone and unchallenged, become encoded within the school's culture. To be fair, principals must not think that ineffective practices are deliberately adopted with the intent to harm or limit student achievement or potential. This said, whether ineffective instructional practices are unintentional or intentional, the results are the same—low performance for students *and* teachers, low expectations, and a drag on the school's culture.

Both authors had the opportunity to affect school culture by using data to end the practice of ability grouping into academically segregated classrooms. Providing our faculties with longitudinal as well as disaggregated student achievement data made it apparent to the stakeholders that this teaching practice was only widening the gap between the various subpopulations on their campuses. This data "Aha!" could not be refuted by anecdotal arguments offered by those clinging to this failed instructional strategy. The dismantling of ability groups began, albeit with strong resistance from a group dedicated to the ability-grouping mantra. A data decision-making culture planted a foothold in the school's culture.

As time passed (this type of change doesn't happen overnight), both campuses matured in incorporating data within the decision-making process. Stakeholders seeking additional data sources evidenced this. As the use of data-driven decisions increased on the campus, so did the level of teacher expectations for all students. No longer were faculty and staff content with whole-school academic performance data. There was an expectation for data to be disaggregated into the appropriate subpopulations. Data analysis sparked imaginations as interventions were formulated to improve the performance of subpopulations not meeting campus expectations.

As data gathering and analysis continued their mercurial rise in the school's culture, so did the concept of continuous incremental improvement. No longer would faculty, staff, parents, and community members be satisfied with maintaining the status quo. The school was now committed to continuous improvement.

One example of continuous improvement was in the area of student achievement. One teacher group that had been using data-driven decision making for several years was consistently witnessing its students' mastery on the state reading examination fall between the 90% to 100% passing rate. This teacher group took its data analysis to the next level. These teachers began examining not only *if* their students passed the reading exam, but also *how well* they passed the exam. This led to a higher self-imposed level of expectation for student achievement. The academic goal would no longer be limited to the state's mandated passing score on the exam but on how well the students scored above the state's required reading exam score. How sweet it is—incremental improvement.

This story is not over. The faculty and staff did not stop at this level of data analysis. They drilled their data analysis of student subpopulation performance down to the reading objective level. They even added an analysis of student wrong answers on the exam questions. This analysis determined where and how the teachers refined their delivery of instruction to help the students master the reading curriculum. When faculty, staff, parents and the community value data-driven decision making, watch out! The sky's the limit on where academic success will go at that school.

Barriers to the Use of Data

The previous data story had a happy ending. But happy endings don't happen without hard work. Barriers block data use in schools. Stakeholders must be diligent in their quest to gather and analyze data required in the third and fourth components of the Sorenson-Goldsmith Integrated Budget Model.

Edie L. Holcomb (2004) identifies six reasons why data are little used and why it is a challenge to motivate people to be data driven. Holcomb's data use barriers are:

- Lack of proper training in involving others in decision making and in the appropriate use of decision-making
- Lack of time
- Feast or famine—fearing that there are no data or panicking over too much: what are we going to do with all these data?
- Fear of evaluation—that the data are going to be used against individuals or schools
- Fear of exposure—the fear that even though your colleagues believe you are a good teacher, the data might expose you as a fraud
- Confusing a technical problem with a cultural problem

Principals and faculties all have witnessed Holcomb's data barriers and, like the authors, have personally experienced them.

Developing an awareness of these data barriers is necessary to address data concerns. Holcomb (2004) postulates: Collecting data for the sake of collecting data is an exercise in futility "unless it engages people by connecting to the deep and authentic passion for teaching and learning" (p. xxi).

How does a school break down its data barriers? Johnson (2002) effectively describes five stages in the change process for creating stakeholders valuing the incorporation of data gathering and analysis into the decision-making process. Briefly, those steps are:

1. *Building the Leadership and Data Teams.* A recognition develops that data must be used in the reform process. Training is provided on the skills needed to collect and analyze data.

2. *Killing the Myth/Building Dissatisfaction.* Data are used to reveal false beliefs about educational practices such as having low expectations for certain groups of students.

3. *Creating a Culture of Inquiry.* The school values provocative questioning and responses that use data to inspire the school change process.

4. *Creating a Vision and Plan for Your School.* This stage requires a long-term collaborative planning process that will result in positive change. It involves establishing priorities, allocating resources, and assigning responsibilities.

5. *Monitoring Progress.* Monitoring becomes a part of the school culture.

This concludes an early peek into the Sorenson-Goldsmith Integrated Budget Model (p. 81).

Both Holcomb's and Johnson's books are superior resources in providing the technical expertise necessary in implementing the third and fourth components of the Sorenson-Goldsmith Integrated Budget Model introduced in the next chapter. Data gathering and data analysis are challenging components of this model. Be patient with yourself and others as data skills are acquired and honed.

W. Edwards Deming believed that "Quality comes not from inspection but from improvement of the process" (Walton, 1986, p. 60). Leaders improve the process when they improve the quality of the data used in decision making. Good decision making is only as good as the data used in formulating the decisions. The challenge for school leaders today is to sift through mountains of information to construct informed decisions. The dilemma faced in this process is that schools are about the business of students, and students' needs cannot always be easily described, plotted, and analyzed on spread-sheets.

Federal legislation such as the No Child Left Behind Act of 2011 as well as state legislation aimed at increasing education accountability requires school leaders to use new data sources. Laffee (2002) writes, "The tools of education—intuition, teaching philosophy, personal experience—do not seem to be enough anymore. Virtually every state has put into place an assessment system intended to measure and validate student achievement and school performance" (p. 6). School leaders need to not only possess the three skills that Laffee references; they must go beyond them.

Data Types

Today's school leader must employ a variety of data types. Disaggregated data, longitudinal data, perception data, qualitative data, and quantitative data are five data types (see Table 3.1). Each data type provides its own unique assistance in developing an inte-grated budget.

Table 3.1   Types of Data

Data Type	Definition
Disaggregated	Data broken down by specific student subgroups such as current grade, race, previous achievements, gender, and socioeconomic status.
Longitudinal	Data measured consistently from year to year to track progress, growth, and change over time. True longitudinal studies eliminate any students who were not present and were not tested in each of the years of the study.
Perception	Data that inform educators about parent, student, and staff perceptions about the learning environment, which could also reveal areas in need of improvement.
Qualitative	Data based on information gathered from one-on-one interviews, focus groups, or general observations over time (as opposed to quantitative data).
Quantitative	Data based on "hard numbers" such as enrollment figures, dropout rates, and test scores (as opposed to qualitative data).

SOURCE: From Using Data to Improve Schools: What's Working by AASA, 2002.

Disaggregated Data

Disaggregated data are data broken down by specific student subgroups such as current grade, race, previous achievements, gender, and socioeconomic status. Disaggregated data provide leaders with an additional level of specificity needed to identify the academic needs of students. A fictitious academic example of the Langtry B. Jensen Middle School (LBJ) is provided to illustrate the importance of disaggregated data. Table 3.2 displays student achievement disaggregated by grade, race, and economic status. For the sake of brevity, we truncated the display to only 2 years of data and limited it to two narrow areas of the curriculum.

Instead of examining student achievement data from a whole-school population perspective, principals now have the opportunity to examine student academic performance by ethnicity as well as socioeconomic status. For example, when examining the first-year seventh-grade reading scores, it is noticed that the campus had a passing rate of 83%, which was 1% higher than the state passing rate of 82%. The initial reaction might be one of academic smugness, believing that we were performing above the state average in seventh-grade reading. But by employing disaggregated data, the leader and faculty recognize problems exist in the reading program. Whites passed at the rate of 93%, Hispanics at 77%, and the low-socioeconomic-status group at 72%. The 16 to 21 percentage points lower performance of the latter two subpopulations provides us with priority and academic direction as to where we need to intervene. The use of disaggregated data assisted the leader and the faculty in identifying an instructional delivery problem that would not have been identified had it not been for the use of disaggregated data.

Longitudinal Data

Longitudinal data are data measured consistently from year to year to track progress, growth, and change over time. True longitudinal studies eliminate any students who were not present and tested in each of the years of the study. Returning to Table 3.2, it becomes obvious that not only does it contain disaggregated data, it also contains longitudinal data. Once again, for the sake of brevity, this example contains only 2 years of data. In an actual school situation, we would want 5 or so years of data if at all possible. As we examined these data for both years, we identified significant improvement in several areas. One example is the sixth-grade mathematics scores for low-socioeconomic students. In the first year, 53% of the

Table 3.2 Langtry B. Jensen Middle School State Academic Performance

	State	District	Campus	African-American	Hispanic	White	Low SES
Met State Standard: Grade 6							
Reading							
Second Year	87	83	86	*	84	89	82
First Year	80	76	83		80	88	74
Mathematics							
Second Year	78	65	80	*	77	84	73
First Year	71	61	65		64	68	53
Met State Standard: Grade 7							
Reading							
Second Year	83	79	94	*	92	98	94
First Year	82	78	83		77	93	72
Mathematics							
Second Year	71	60	71	*	69	76	69
First Year	63	52	57		52	69	43
Met State Standard: Grade 8							
Reading							
Second Year	90	88	94	*	89	99	84
First Year	84	79	86		83	93	75
Mathematics							
Second Year	67	57	83	*	76	92	72
First Year	62	50	48		44	55	38

NOTE: All numbers are in percent.

* = Less Than 10 Students

students passed the mathematics test compared to 73% in the second year. This was an increase of 20 percentage points. Another way to examine these data is to return to the low-socioeconomic sixth-grade students' mathematics score in the first year of 53% and compare it to the low-socioeconomic seventh-grade students' mathematics scores of the second year that were 69%. By comparing the scores in this manner, the leader and team are following relatively the same group of students over a 2-year period. This analysis reveals a growth of 16 percentage points between the first and second year in this same-group comparison. Using sophisticated software, school leaders readily construct longitudinal comparisons of same groups from year to year, which, in turn, provides guidance to areas of curriculum and instruction requiring intervention.

Perception Data

Perception data are data that inform educators about parent, student, and staff perceptions regarding the learning environment, which could also reveal areas in need of improvement. An example of perception data collection is a parent survey conducted by the school planning committee at LBJ. Table 3.3 contains a summary of the responses to 3 of 35 questions in the LBJ Parent Survey. Parents were asked to respond to the questions by circling a number on a scale of 1 to 4 (1 = strongly agree, 2 = agree, 3 = disagree, 4 = strongly disagree). The results for 2 years are included in Table 3.3. It should be noted that 61% of the parents responded to the survey in the first year and 62% responded in the second year.

Since Table 3.3 contains more than 1 year of survey results, not only are there perception data, but there are also longitudinal and quantitative data. One observation that can be drawn from these data is that parents have a more positive perception of the mathematics program in the second year than they did in the first year. Go another step further and return to Table 3.2 and note that during this same time period, there was also a corresponding significant improvement in student performance in mathematics. Could these two data observations be linked?

Qualitative Data

Qualitative data are data based on information gathered from one-on-one interviews, focus groups, or general observations over time (as opposed to quantitative data). One example of qualitative data is when a school district brings in focus groups to discuss a

Table 3.3 L. B. Jensen Middle School Parent Survey Results (Abridged)

Question	Response	First Year, %	Second Year, %
If I were given a voucher and could enroll my child at any other middle school, I would still enroll my child at L. B. Jensen MS.	1	82	92
	2	2	2
	3	3	4
	4		2
The reading program at L. B. Jensen MS is a good program for my child.	1	77	89
	2	4	8
	3	7	3
	4	12	0
The mathematics program at L. B. Jensen MS is a good program for my child.	1	66	82
	2	4	3
	3	10	8
	4	20	7

controversial topic such as sex education. The district compiles the comments from the sessions and uses them in conjunction with information from other sources to revise its sex education program.

Quantitative Data

Quantitative data are data based on "hard numbers" such as enrollment figures, dropout rates, and test scores (as opposed to qualitative data). Referencing to Table 3.2, one realizes it contains the reporting of test scores. This means these data are quantitative data. Two earlier examinations revealed that the data in Table 3.2 were also disaggregated data as well as longitudinal data. Data can meet the definition of more than one data category.

Assessment

There are two basic types of assessment: formative and summative. Formative assessment is "assessment in which learning is measured at several points during a teaching/learning phase, with the primary intention of obtaining information to guide the further teaching or learning steps. Formative assessments include questioning, comments on a presentation or interviewing" (AASA, 2002, p. 68). An example of formative assessment is a pretest given in an academic area such as algebra, reading comprehension, or keyboarding skills. This information would then be used to drive the instructional strategy and the development of lesson plans.

The second type of assessment is summative. Summative assessment is "an assessment at the end of a period of education or training that sums up how a student has performed" (AASA, 2002, p. 70). An example of summative assessment is a benchmark test given in mathematics, reading, science, or other subjects to determine individual student mastery of taught objectives. Formative and summative assessment, when planned properly, can yield all five types of data discussed earlier. Formative and summative data used in conjunction with each other are invaluable in making program adjustments.

Acknowledging Opportunities for Growth and Development

Schools have grown in complexity and require sophisticated assessment and data analysis. The immediate cause of this phenomenon, according to Elmore (2002), is quite simple. A powerful idea dominating policy discourse about schools stipulates that students must be held to higher academic achievement expectations, and school leaders must be held accountable for ensuring that all students meet or exceed such expectations. This perspective and multiple others subsequently dictate "numerous, simultaneous, and systematic changes in organizing, teaching, and administering schools" (Hoy & Miskel, 2012, p. 292). Such emerging viewpoints, demands, and expectations have dictated the absolute need for school leaders to be active participants in continuous and varied professional-development opportunities. Data analysis is at the heart of this process.

For school leaders to be successful leaders—whether it be envisioning school reform initiatives, planning programmatic changes, developing a school budget, or advancing opportunities for increased student achievement—they must understand that the once-standard, one-shot in-service workshop model is no longer acceptable. What is known and what research supports is that professional development must be entrenched in practice, research-based, collaborative, standards-aligned, assessment-driven, and accountability-focused procedures—all of which serve to increase the capacity, knowledge, and skills of administrators to improve their leadership practices and performances (National Staff Development Council, 2001). Educators must recognize that student learning can only be enhanced by the professional growth and development of school leaders (Desimone , Porter, Garet, Yoon, & Brisman, 2002).

Staff development, like other facets of a school, must be data driven. Needs assessment surveys from the faculty analyzed in conjunction with data from other sources such as student achievement data increase the effectiveness of the training, resulting in increased performance of both the employees and the students.

An example of data-driven staff development occurred in a school having a high percentage of students who were not meeting with success in writing as measured by the state's assessment program. A review of the testing data by the site-based decision-making (SBDM) committee revealed that this problem was evident throughout all the assessed grades. The SBDM committee surveyed the teachers and discovered that the writing teachers felt inadequately trained to teach writing within the parameters of the curriculum and assessment program. The committee also discovered that writing was only a priority for the language arts teachers in the grades that were tested by the state. Other teachers felt no ownership in teaching writing across the curriculum.

The SBDM committee conducted a review of potential writing workshops and selected one they deemed most appropriate for their students based on an analysis of the disaggregated achievement data. The committee also surveyed teachers throughout the district and developed a writing-across-the-curriculum plan that was supported by the faculty.

The SBDM committee ensured these two strategies were incorporated in the school action plan. Funding was secured to bring in the writing consultants as well as to secure the required materials for the teachers. Likewise, the training received priority on the staff development calendar.

Referring to Figure 3.1, evidence of the alignment of the three elements of vision, planning, and budget exists. Vision manifested itself in the school's vision to have all students meet with academic success. Planning occurred through data gathering, data analysis, and the needs prioritization conducted by the school's SBDM committee. Budgeting was present through the commitment of fiscal resources, time, and personnel. The writing project definitely resided in the Success Zone. Data support this conclusion in that, 3 years later, the school's scores in writing made significant increases, going from significantly below state average to above state average.

UNDERGROUND RESISTANCE

The members of LBJ Middle School's SBDM committee have grown in their understanding of the use and importance of a variety of data sources in campus planning. Unfortunately, not everyone at LBJ shares their enthusiasm for increasing the use of data-driven decision making. LaKisha Galore and Stan Barrier are vocal in their effort to diminish data analysis at LBJ. Their mantra is, "You can find data to prove anything." Ms. Galore and Mr. Barrier are creating a growing pocket of resistance to data-based decision making.

Pause and Consider

- What, if anything, should be done to address Ms. Galore and Mr. Barrier's campaign against data-based decision making?
- What could the LBJ SBDM committee do proactively to carry data analysis to the next level at LBJ?

Celebrating Success

School leaders must not underestimate their impact on the school's culture. The leader establishes the tone for the school. In an era of increased outside accountability systems along with fiscal constraints, stakeholders in schools are experiencing tremendous stress. Teacher attrition is the largest single factor determining the shortage of qualified teachers in the United States (Dove, 2004). Stress manifests itself with employees taking "mental health" days in order to flee the many sources of stress in their lives. Leaders must be cognizant of this underlying current in their schools.

Complainers abound in today's society. At times, complainers revel in their venting and, in some instances, in intimidation of school employees. Educators often receive exponentially more complaints than they do compliments. Yet a major motivation for people entering this field is an intrinsic one—one of personal satisfaction for helping others (Ryan & Cooper, 2004). Everyone holds precious memories of those notes and conversations in which appreciation was given for efforts. There are times when every educator mentally recalls these celebrations of success to help us cope with a current stress-filled situation.

Ubben, Hughes, and Norris (2011) caution leaders not to underestimate the efficacy of public achievement awards. Effective organizations celebrate success. There are many terms of endearment for celebrating success; among them are *fradela*, *hullabaloo*, *hoopla*, *tadoo*, *wingding*, and *heehaw*. The school leader must be the Director of Hullabaloo. Leaders must set the tone of the school. Leaders cannot shuffle this obligation to anyone else. They must lead in the establishment of a culture that appreciates success.

Leadership in celebrating success manifests itself in any number of ways. It is only limited by one's imagination. Leaders lead celebrations at their schools for achieving goals by performing out-of-character acts such as kissing a pig, shaving their heads, sitting on the roof, dancing in a pink tutu, doing an Elvis impersonation, and riding a Harley-Davidson through the gym. These manifestations of success celebration often bring with them the side benefit of positive local media attention to schools. Sometimes leaders must let stakeholders have a little fun at the leader's expense. Leaders do this because they know a school culture with an atmosphere of love and support for stakeholders will accomplish miraculous transformations in student performance.

Celebrating success is not limited to public stunts. Celebrating success can also be private. A handwritten note of thanks is worth a million dollars to the recipient. Who doesn't treasure personal notes of gratitude? These notes are often tucked away and read again in moments of frustration or times of reminiscing. An eye-to-eye verbal compliment reaps a positive benefit to the recipient as well as to the giver. Compliments need not be lengthy; they only need to be sincere. As a sidebar, leaders must know how to model accepting a compliment. Principals should not try to brush away a compliment by saying things like "It was nothing." Instead, we must honor the compliment-giver and say something like, "Thank you so much. I appreciate you recognizing my work and the work of my colleagues."

Celebrating success manifests itself in many other ways: awards assemblies, bulletin boards, newsletter references, marquees, parking privileges, covering a class so a teacher can have a longer lunch, T-shirts, and any other positive ideas you possess.

Opportunities to celebrate success increase when the budget is aligned with the school's vision and planning. Figure 3.1 illustrates the alignment of these three factors—vision, planning, and budgeting. Overlapping circles represents these factors. The overlapping represents alignment of the processes. For example, the area where the budgeting circle and vision circle overlap is where the budgeting and vision processes are aligned. The areas where they do not overlap are opportunities for improving the alignment process.

Figure 3.1   Integrated Vision, Planning, and Budgeting

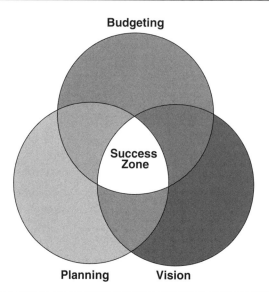

The area labeled Success Zone is where all three processes are aligned. The Success Zone is where leaders need to lead their schools. This is where the budget–vision–planning processes are fully aligned and integrated. The greater the alignment, the more the circles migrate toward the center of the figure and the larger the Success Zone becomes. Perfect alignment would manifest itself with all three circles stacked on top of each other with the Success Zone itself becoming a perfect circle.

When leaders lead their schools using the collaborative planning process to implement the integrated budget model, the size of the Success Zone will increase. This in turn leads schools to greater opportunities for success. Bathing schools in the celebration of success encourages the integration of budgeting, visioning, and planning. Schools just might reach Nirvana; that is, when their circles are completely stacked.

Celebration should be an all-inclusive process. Do not limit it to teachers and students. Include everyone—the custodians, bus drivers, cafeteria help, parent volunteers, and community members. A positive, optimistic, and supportive school culture increases energy and motivation, and this is contagious to all stakeholders (Deal & Peterson, 2009). Leaders encourage teachers to help their students celebrate success. Be the head cheerleader for your school—you might even get to wear the uniform! Leaders who do not celebrate success may find their goose cooked.

Final Thoughts

School cultures can change. Leaders must (1) involve all the stakeholders treating them with dignity and respect, (2) be results oriented while being data driven, (3) constantly monitor school culture, (4) see possibilities and not problems, (5) ensure that efforts are ongoing, and (6) see the value of all stakeholders. Schools are more likely to fulfill their mission when they put their money where their mouth is and align their budgets and commit their resources to the school's vision. The best way to make a school successful is to foster a culture in which the stakeholders have a shared vision of the school's purpose and future and they "take deliberate and collective action with them in mind" (Shaw, 2012, p. 184).

Discussion Questions

1. Consider three values you share with your school. How do you impact the school with those values?

2. How do attitudes of the various stakeholders at your school impact your school's culture? Provide positive and negative examples.

3. How do the school leaders affect school culture positively and negatively?

4. List your Top Ten data sources for building your campus budget. Why did these sources make the Top Ten list?

5. How can the effective use of data impact your school's culture?

6. How can the effective use of data impact your school's budgeting process?

7. How have you witnessed data being used in the decision-making process at your school? Was it used effective? Defend your response.

8. How would you use data on your campus in a way it is not currently being used? Why would you use it this way?

Case Study Application: L. B. Jensen Middle School

L. B. Jensen Middle School, a school of 540 students in Grades 6 through 8, is located in a southern border state less than 200 miles from the U.S.–Mexico border. It is 62% Hispanic and 38% Anglo. It is one of six middle schools in Kilnwood City. Juan Quervo is the principal. Although LBJ has always been predominantly Hispanic, Dr. Quervo is the first Hispanic to be named as the principal of LBJ in its 42 years of existence. Dr. Quervo has been enthusiastically accepted by all of the school's stakeholders. He is using this acceptance capital to make needed instructional changes to ensure that all children meet with academic success.

Table 3.2 contains 2 years accumulation of achievement data for LBJ. Table 3.3 contains a partial report on the responses to the parent survey for the last 2 school years. Use these data to respond to the following questions.

Application Questions

1. Using the data provided, identify at least two instructional concerns at LBJ. What types of data did you use to identify the concerns?

2. Using the data provided, what would you recommend to Dr. Quervo as the top instructional priority? Support your recommendation with data.

3. There was a noted increase in the positive perception of LBJ by the parents between the first year and the second year. Is there anything in the given data that might explain the recent upward swing in the campus's public perception? Support your response.

4. What data are not provided that you would like to have to be better informed about the needs and strengths of understanding LBJ?

5. What other data would be useful in determining the reason(s) for the improvement of the mathematics and reading scores?

Chapter 4

A Model for Integrating Vision, Planning, and Budgeting

Alice:	Would you please tell me which way I ought to go from here?
The Cat:	That depends a great deal on where you want to get to.
Alice:	I don't much care where—
The Cat:	Then it doesn't matter which way you go.
Alice:	—so long as I get somewhere.
The Cat:	Oh, you're sure to do that…if you only walk long enough.

—*Alice's Adventures in Wonderland* (1993, p. 40)
by Lewis Carroll

Alice and the Cat in Lewis Carroll's *Alice's Adventures in Wonderland* had a provocative conversation on visioning and planning. Alice is seeking direction on where she needs to go. The Cat replies he cannot help here unless she knows where she wants to go. Sadly, Alice doesn't know or even care where she goes. Alice's attitude allows the

Cat to tell her it makes no difference since she just wants to go somewhere. The Cat concludes the conversation by telling Alice to keep walking and she'll get somewhere.

Unfortunately, many schools are like Alice. They are going somewhere—anywhere. These schools appear not to care much where they go just as long as they go somewhere. In this chapter, a case is made that it *does* matter where a school goes and how it gets there. The Sorenson-Goldsmith Integrated Budget Model provides a purposeful map for a successful, meaningful school journey. Walking aimlessly might be acceptable to Alice, but it is not acceptable for our schools and our students.

In an earlier examination of the integration of the vision, budgeting, and planning processes, a school leader made the important delineation between school finance and school budgeting. Next, the budget relationship to ISLLC standards was completed. Finally, a closer examination of the budgeting and vision relationship with an emphasis on culture, climate, and data-driven decision making took place. Now it is time to allow these underlying principles to manifest themselves into a practical and workable budget model.

Figure 4.1 provides an illustration of such a model. It is necessary to consider each component of the Sorenson-Goldsmith Integrated Budget Model individually to ensure a thorough understanding of this model's integrative nature. This model employs many principles associated with the site-based decision-making (SBDM) process. The SBDM process, a collaborative process using stakeholders within the organization, is required in Colorado, Florida, Kentucky, North Carolina, and Texas in some form. It is also used in districts throughout the United States (Clover, Jones, Bailey, & Griffin, 2004). This process functions at either the campus or district level but is best when applied at both levels. The term *school* in the remainder of this chapter refers to either a campus or a district. The level of planning in which the Sorenson-Goldsmith model is utilized determines which definition of *school* is employed.

Sorenson-Goldsmith Integrated Budget Model

Leadership

Leadership is located at the top of the model, not to symbolize top-down leadership but rather to represent the relational leadership exhibited between a shepherd and the sheep. For centuries, shepherds have tended flocks in isolated areas. Shepherds assist in meeting a host

Figure 4.1   Sorenson-Goldsmith Integrated Budget Model

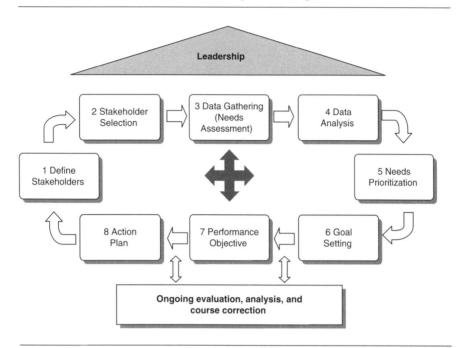

of needs of the sheep through service and openness, producing a trusting relationship. Shepherds feed their sheep, find water for them, and protect them from predators. If a sheep is lost, shepherds search for it. Shepherds know each lamb in their flock by name. Shepherds do not walk behind their sheep; they lead them. Likewise, the sheep recognizes the shepherd's voice and touch (Anderson, 1997). School leaders must provide this same relationship and communication as they assist and nurture their flocks using a collaborative planning process.

Rigid top-down leadership might initially produce positive results—but at a cost to the collaborative planning process. Decisions may be made in an orderly meeting run with firm control, but apathy and resentment may be the price to be paid (Yukl, 2010).

Communication is an essential leadership skill in working with the school planning committee. The school leader must communicate passion for the school's mission. The leader must kindle the imagination of all the stakeholders about what can be done to help the school achieve its vision and mission. A leader cannot be a visionary without being persuasive. The school planning committee must witness the leader's passion for the school.

Leaders must foster the crafting of a clear school vision, one resonating with all stakeholders. Leaders must inspire committee members to fulfill the school's vision. It is incumbent on leaders to provide stakeholders with opportunities to envision, understand, and experience the school's vision as they develop the school's action plan using this model. Vision is not free. It costs time, money, and energy. The components of this model will be individually examined in an effort to make the vision a reality.

Component 1: Defining Stakeholders

If the entire learning community is to share ownership of the site-based decision-making process, then it must commence by involving all stakeholders. Expected stakeholders include

- Teachers
- Staff members
- Other professionals
- Administrators
- Parents
- Community members
- Students

Every stakeholder is valuable to the collaborative planning process, for each stakeholder brings a unique perspective to the planning process.

Teachers are the stakeholders who have the most contact with students on a daily basis. Staff members refer to those who are noncertified employees. They include but are not limited to paraprofessionals, cafeteria workers, bus drivers, and custodians. Other professionals are degreed individuals such as counselors, nurses, and educational diagnosticians. Administrators include both campus and district administrators. Parents are those adults who have guardianship over the children who attend the public schools. Finally, community members are people who live in the community but who have no child in the public school system.

It is important to note that the majority of households in this country do not have children in the public schools, yet schools must seek and gain the support of these households if school funding and bonds are to be enacted into law. It is imperative that this group of stakeholders be represented in the campus planning process.

Component 2: Stakeholder Selection

An examination of state and local policies is appropriate to ensure compliance with any state laws or regulations in selecting stakeholders.

Local policies and administrative procedures must be put into place to determine the structure and authority of the school collaborative planning committee. Procedures should also be established defining the roles and responsibilities of the committee.

Committee Size and Structure

The size and structure of the collaborative planning committee must be considered. The authors believe teachers should comprise somewhere between a majority to a supermajority of the committee positions. The election and selection of committee members should be as simple as possible. While it might serve well to elect faculty and staff committee positions, it would be more efficient if other positions, such as parents and community members, were appointed. Once again, clear procedures must be in place.

Diversity

Careful consideration should be given to creating diversity on the committee in the selection of appointed committee members. Appointments should represent the community's diversity. Besides ethnic diversity, other populations should be represented. Parent representatives must also reflect the diversity of the student population. Among those populations to be considered are parents of children who

- Speak English as a second language
- Have special needs
- Have special gifts and talents
- Come from a variety of socioeconomic situations

There are several actions administrators should take to increase the diversity of the SBDM committee. Chief among those actions are

- Posting on the school's or district's websites
- Advertising in the local newspaper
- Securing public service announcements on local television and radio stations
- Seeking nominations from PTAs or PTOs
- Seeking nominations from local businesses
- Seeking nominations from community organizations such as the Chamber of Commerce or service organizations like the Kiwanis Club

Members who are nominated must be willing to serve and invest time in the school's planning process. This is not the time for arm-twisting. An unwilling volunteer will likely lead to an empty seat and a missed opportunity for diverse representation.

The administrator or selection committee that finalizes the selection of the school planning committee members must deliberate conscientiously over the nominations. It is paramount that the intent of ISLLC Standard 5, the ethics standard, bathes this process. Some questions to consider include

- Does this individual have the time to attend committee meetings?
- Will this individual be willing to attend site-based training on the committee?
- Does this individual demonstrate the capacity to consider all sides of an issue?

Committee Member Training

Committee members need training to understand their role in the collaborative decision-making process. McCloskey, Mikow-Porto, and Bingham (1998) reveal that frequently, principals and faculty members have not been trained adequately to meet with success in the collaborative planning process. The committee needs designated areas to examine budgeting, curriculum, staffing patterns, staff development, and school organization if it is to improve school performance (Odden & Wohlstetter, 1995). These areas must be clearly defined in the training process. Training prevents misunderstandings about the committee's function and authority.

Committee members benefit from training in team-building skills. Committee members must develop their listening skills, understand other cultures, and know how to use conflict-resolution skills. Finally, training must be provided in the collection and interpretation of data. The committee must be convinced of the merits of using data as the basis for creating change in the school (Earl & Katz, 2005).

Staggering the Terms

Consideration must be given to staggering committee members' terms. This technique ensures stability and experience over time. If members serve 2-year terms, then at least 50% of the school planning committee would be experienced members at any given time. Three-year staggered terms allows for two-thirds of the committee to be experienced members with institutional memory. This strengthens the process as well as assists the one-third that is starting to serve on the committee.

Component 3: Data Gathering (Needs Assessment)

A head start on discussing data gathering occurred in Chapter 3. Like businesses, schools are expected to verify their performance with solid data. The No Child Left Behind Act added new responsibilities for schools to gather, collect, and analyze data from a wide range of sources. Federal law requires state education agencies to report student performance by income, English fluency, migrant status, race, gender, and disability. The increased pressure for external accountability heightened the need for schools to be data driven (Creighton, 2006; Harris, 2004; Laffee, 2002; Mandinach & Jackson, 2012). A school's program success is dependent on how efficiently data are collected on measuring the change being implemented in the school (Fullan & Steigelbauer, 1991; Learning Point Associates, 2004).

Needs assessment requires the school planning committee to ponder, "How well is our school doing in meeting our school-improvement-plan goals?" The answer to this question goes beyond the hunches and feelings of committee members. No longer can schools simply proclaim, "We had a great year. Our students made tremendous progress." The answer to this question requires the committee to gather data from an array of sources in order to complete a comprehensive assessment of the school. The more data collected from a broad range of sources, the greater the likelihood that the committee will accurately respond to the posed question.

Philip Streifer, a superintendent, accurately described data collection when he said, "Data collection is a messy, messy business. It is done in different formats, some electronically, sometimes on cards or paper; often it's incomplete. Teachers collect it differently and not everybody has the same access to it, which means not everybody is going to be on the same page" (Laffee, 2002, p. 7). Data originate from a wide array of sources. A partial list for collecting school data includes

- Student achievement test results
- Campus and district websites
- State education agencies' websites
- Attendance data (student and faculty)
- Dropout data
- School budget reports
- Parent surveys

- Student surveys
- Faculty surveys
- Focus groups
- Volunteer logs
- Transfer requests (student and faculty)
- Retention data
- Failure reports
- Discipline data
- Facilities reports
- Organizational description (mission, vision, values)
- Staff development needs
- Staffing patterns
- Accident reports
- Extracurricular data
- Special populations data
- Mobility rate
- Unusual events on the campus (i.e., death of a student, fire, shooting, etc.)
- Any other information useful in measuring the school's performance

As data are gathered in an ongoing process, a school profile emerges. This profile reflects the school's operating environment, key educational programs, resource allocation, and other facets of the school. Once data are gathered, the committee must sift through them to derive meaning from the sea of numbers and reports. Needs assessment never ends. Schools constantly gather data. Data gathered must go to the next step—data analysis. After all, what good does it do to gather data and not analyze it?

Component 4: Data Analysis

A discussion of measurement, analysis, and data management as keys to improving student performance began in Chapter 3. Data analysis takes needs assessment or data gathering one step further. Data analysis provides the crucial linkage between data examination and the development of effective strategies. In this process, the school planning committee interprets probable causal factors. These factors can be anything from a high dropout rate to a low attendance rate to low academic performance in specific curriculum areas.

In the simplest terms, the Sorenson-Goldsmith Model component is the "brain center" for aligning the school's delivery of instruction and related services to meet individual student needs. This component addresses knowledge management and the basic performance-related data and comparative data, as well as how such data are analyzed and used to optimize the school's performance.

Individual facts and isolated data do not typically provide an effective basis for establishing organizational priorities. The model's data analysis component emphasizes the need for an alignment between analysis and school performance. This alignment ensures relevancy in decision making, thus precluding decisions made using irrelevant data, statistical outliers, or personal prejudices.

Collecting data without analyzing them is an exercise in futility. Data analysis can be a daunting task for the school planning committee, particularly for the nonschool employee members as they face the infamous "stack of stuff." This is where the school leader provides much-needed assistance and assurance, particularly to the nonschool committee members. The leader ensures that committee educator members do not freely throw around acronyms and educational jargon at the expense of the noneducator members' comprehension of the data. Educators may inadvertently speak in shorthand by saying things like "LEP (limited English proficient), AYP (adequate yearly progress), IDEA (Individuals With Disabilities Education Act), Title 1, or two deviations below the norm." Remember, this lingo is foreign to most nonschool committee members. The school leader must be sensitive to this issue and be certain the dialogue remains inclusive to all committee members.

Data must be disaggregated to obtain the level of specificity required to ensure all students meet with success. Data disaggregation requires data differentiation by subpopulations. Examples of subpopulations include race, gender, and economic status.

One example of data desegregation is found in student achievement data. To better illustrate desegregation of student data, we will examine an abridged report on student achievement in fifth-grade mathematics at the fictitious Fort Chadbourne Elementary School (FCES) identified in Table 4.1.

In reviewing these data, several observations can be made about the mathematics achievement of students at Fort Chadbourne Elementary School. The Low SES score refers to students who are of low socioeconomic status. Low socioeconomic status is typically defined as being eligible to participate in the federal free or reduced-price lunch program.

Before reading the following list of the authors' observations about FCES, stop and construct a mental or physical list of observations

Table 4.1   Fort Chadbourne Elementary School State Academic
                  Performance Report

Fifth-Grade Mathematics

5th Math	% Passing							
	State	*Campus*	*Anglo*	*Hispanic*	*Black*	*Low SES*	*Male*	*Female*
Second year	88	87	94	81	78	68	91	85
First year	84	86	94	77	69	57	87	81

based on a data analysis of the FCES performance report in Table 4.1. Compare the findings of the data analysis with the authors' observations.

- The campus performed above state average last year and below state average this year.
- The Anglo subpopulation performed the highest in both years.
- The Hispanic subpopulation performed second highest in both years.
- The Hispanic subpopulation increased its performance by four points in the current year.
- The black subpopulation performed the lowest of the three sub-populations both years.
- The black population had the greatest increase in performance (nine points) of the three ethnic groups.
- The gap in achievement between the three ethnic groups is narrowing.
- The lowest-performing subpopulation of any is the low-SES group.
- Students who were in the low-SES group made the greatest gains of any subpopulation.
- Males outperformed females each year.
- Males and females each improved their performance by six points.
- The profile of the most at-risk student at FCES based on these data is a black female student who is on free or reduced-price lunch.

Hopefully after this brief analysis of abridged data, other questions are forming about FCES, questions requiring additional data gathering by the collaborative planning committee.

What additional questions would provide a better understanding of the issues at FCES based on the data? Stop and develop a list of questions about FCES based on these limited data. Considering the following, a partial list of questions that might come to a committee member's mind based on data presented in Table 4.1 includes

- What, if any, intervention was initiated that improved the performance of the Hispanic, black, and low-SES subpopulations?
- What was the performance of these same groups of students on the tested mathematics objectives?
- Did students perform poorly on the same math objectives each year?
- How did students at the lower grades perform on mathematics in comparison to the fifth-grade students?
- Are there problems on the same type of objectives between grade levels?
- How did this same group of students perform on the mathematics exam last year?
- Is the FCES mathematics curriculum aligned with the concepts assessed on the state exam?
- Do the same subpopulations have the lowest scores in other areas of the exam?
- What interventions were in last year's FCES school improvement plan? How effective were they?

This initial examination of the snippet of gathered data in Table 4.1 led to some obvious observations, which in turn led to a greater depth of questioning and a need for assimilating additional data. (This requires the committee to revisit Component 3—Data Gathering.) The analysis also led to the previous year's school plan and into the arena of school plans evaluation. Hopefully, a need for additional data was raised.

Had it been feasible to make the FCES example include more data than the student performance on mathematics at one grade level over a 2-year period, more questions would have been generated. These questions would likely be more specific and of greater instructional depth. With a broader array of data, a broader field of needs would be identified. Earl and Katz (2005) call to our attention that, "Data do not provide right answers or quick fixes, but data offer decision-makers an opportunity to view a phenomenon through a number of different lenses to put forward hypotheses to challenge beliefs, and to pose more questions" (p. 19). This leads to needs prioritization, the fifth component of the Sorenson-Goldsmith Integrated Budget Model.

Component 5: Needs Prioritization

After completing the data-driven process of identifying the school's needs, the school planning committee is frequently confronted with more needs than can be realistically addressed within the confines of both human and fiscal resources. At this point, the committee must determine which needs receive priority. Hopkins and West (1994) note that successful schools prioritize their needs and address a few at a time.

Data review is an integral part in prioritizing needs. Failure to use data knowledge effectively is costly to schools (Creighton, 2006; Yeagley, 2002). Loeb and Plank (2007) recommended training in data analysis at all levels in the education system. Educators must learn to use data to inform academic progress (Data Quality Campaign, 2009). Committee members must review the data at hand and reach consensus on what needs should receive top priority in order to propel the school toward the fulfilling of its mission. Fullan and Miles (1992) report that a cross-role group (i.e., school planning committee), a term they use to define a group with a variety of stakeholders, can assist in change. They observed, "different worlds collide, more learning occurs, and change is realistically managed" (Fullan & Miles, 1992, p. 752).

Conflict can arise while planners are attempting to reallocate resources. When needs are identified using a data-driven process, the identified needs immediately possess a stronger status than those identified from a purely partisan process.

Prioritizing limited resources for data-driven needs is no doubt a challenge for all involved. The school leader must approach the situation in a nonpartisan manner. This is a situation in which those skills and attributes embedded in ISLLC Standard 5, the ethics standard, are so important.

In the discussion of this standard in Chapter 3, fairness was examined. Fairness—to be free from bias, dishonesty, or injustice. Fairness necessitates that principals model to the planning team how to put the interests and needs of others above their own interests and needs. It also requires leaders and their teams to remember that to best meet the needs of students does not necessarily translate into equal distribution of the resources. Leaders need to allocate ample time for all to be heard and try to reach consensus. If the planning team approaches the situation with this mindset, then the chances dramatically increase for a successful resolution that can be supported by the majority.

Joey Cope, a practicing attorney and mediator, writes, "peace can always be present—even in the presence of conflict" (Sorenson & Goldsmith, 2009, p. 89). Cope offers what he calls "The Principal's Peace Primer" with eight platforms to assist principals in guiding the campus collaborative planning committee in *The Principal's Guide to Managing School Personnel* (2009).

But what if resolution cannot be achieved? Then the leader must make a decision. This should be done with great caution, for it has the potential to cause stakeholders to feel they really have no voice in the process and become disenfranchised. If the situation is particularly sensitive, the planning committee should consider bringing in a knowledgeable neutral party who possesses conflict-resolution skills to help them overcome their impasse. In the end, the process could draw the planning team closer together emotionally as well as missionally. Once the needs have been prioritized, the site-based committee is ready to start setting goals.

Component 6: Goal Setting

Goal setting is a crucial component in the integrated budget model. Goals unify stakeholders by providing meaning and purpose. Goals are broad statements of expected outcomes consistent with the mission, vision, and philosophy of the school. Goals must be driven by student-performance-based needs and must be consistent with the school's vision and mission statements (Oliva, 2005).

A school leader must be sensitive when beginning in earnest to develop data-driven goals. Data will reveal differences in performance. They point their digital fingers to strengths and weaknesses in the school. This makes some stakeholders uneasy. The collaborative committee process must not ignore where data are pointing, nor can it bury the facts. Academic integrity demands that the committee examine the actions dictated by the data and develop the appropriate goals.

The school planning committee must be involved in the goal-setting process because goals reflect the essence of the school's culture. When goals are assimilated into the school's culture, stakeholders are more motivated to achieve them and more likely to punish members who abandon them. In fact, goals can become so incorporated into the school's culture that they continue to exist through changes of administration (Gorton, Schneider, & Fisher, 1988). Maeroff (1994) asserted that results-driven goals motivate and engage effective teams. It is imperative that the collaborative planning committee assist stakeholders in making the connection between goals and improvement if there is to be a significant chance for improving the school.

The planning committee has gathered data, analyzed data, and prioritized needs. By this time in the planning process, each committee member should have a greater understanding of why things are the way they are at the school. Ubben, Hughes, and Norris (2011) provide four assumptions to guide a principal in working with the school planning committee on goal setting. They are

1. People at the working level tend to know the problems best.

2. The face-to-face work group is the best unit for diagnosis and change.

3. People will work hard to achieve objectives and goals they have helped develop.

4. Initiative and creativity are widely distributed in the population.

It is the leader's responsibility to keep the goals in front of the stakeholders. Goals must be distributed and displayed in a variety of forums such as PTA/PTO meetings and community service organization meetings. Goals must be reviewed at every faculty meeting, every grade level, or every department meeting. They must appear in faculty newsletters or emails; they must be posted on the school's website. They must be embedded in parent communications. In other words, they must be constantly kept in front of the stakeholders. Leithwood (1990), in describing goals cleverly wrote, "The glue that holds together the myriad actions and decisions of highly effective principals . . . [are] the goals that they and their staff [school planning committee] have developed for the school and a sense of what their schools need to look like and to do in order to accomplish those goals" (p. 85).

Component 7: Performance Objectives

Once goals congruent with the school's vision and mission are established through the collaborative planning process, performance-based objectives must be developed to provide increased definition to the course of action. Performance objectives identify specific, measurable, and expected outcomes for all student populations served. Performance objectives must be driven by student performance-based needs-assessment data. Table 4.2 contains two objectives. The first objective is not a performance objective. The second objective is a performance objective.

Table 4.2   A Comparison of a Nonperformance Objective
                  to a Performance Objective

Nonperformance Objective	Students will do well in mathematics this school year.
Performance Objective	Student scores in the state assessment exam on mathematics will increase by 5% in each of the ethnic subpopulations with an $N > 30$.

The first objective is not measurable because the students are asked to do "well" in mathematics this year. *Well* is a subjective term and can vary from individual to individual in definition. This objective is also vague in that it not only lacks specificity, it does not prescribe a method for completing the measurement.

The second objective is a performance objective for three reasons: (1) A data source for the assessment is identified—the state assessment exam; (2) a specific improvement of 5% is expected in each of the ethnic subpopulations; and (3) it adds specific accountability to subpopulations.

It is essential that all objectives in the school action plan be measurable if the school is to be data driven in its planning. When objectives are nonmeasurable, it is left up to each individual to employ personal feelings on whether the objective has been achieved. Ten different individuals could evaluate the objective 10 different ways.

Component 8: Action Plan

The action plan is the *living* document that serves as a guide for all stakeholders. Emphasis was added to the adjective *living* to call attention to the fact that the action plan is not static. (If it's static, it's likely to be dead.) The action plan is a living, breathing document. This point cannot be overemphasized. A quick review of the Sorenson-Goldsmith Model in Figure 4.1 reminds the principal and team that much effort is required to produce this meaningful document. The process began by defining and selecting the stakeholders to create the school planning committee. Gathering and analyzing data from a plethora of sources followed the creation of this committee. Next, needs prioritization allowed for the identification of the actions essential for the school to fulfill its mission. Goals and objectives were then put in place to create a step-by-step blueprint to turn the prioritized needs into prioritized fulfillments.

This entire process is chronicled in the action plan, where greater detail is added by including strategies and actions. But the process does not stop when the plan is put in writing and posted online. This is just the beginning of the action plan's function. At the base of the model in Figure 4.1 is a box with three terms—*ongoing evaluation*, *analysis*, and *course correction*. This foundational concept of the model demands that the action plan be a breathing document. *Ongoing* means that the process never ceases. Ongoing evaluation and analysis require continuous monitoring. This action manifests itself in ongoing course correction that results in editing marks appearing throughout the action plan.

A Planning Metaphor

Prior to boarding a flight in New York City to Los Angeles, the pilot has already filed a flight plan with the proper authorities. Once the plane departs New York, the pilot, copilot, and navigator continually reference the flight plan to ensure that the plane and its passengers meet the goal of the flight—to arrive in Los Angeles with all the passengers and the plane in safe condition. Despite the flight crew's effort in submitting a viable flight plan that, when implemented

---

KILLING TREES

Lost Pines Elementary School's campus action plan is posted somewhere on its website. The teachers were provided a hard copy of it. The principal and some other "district types" wrote it and asked the faculty to sign off on the plan. Plans were printed, distributed to all stakeholders, and placed somewhere. The action plan was required of all schools. But it didn't seem to be the effective tool that it was touted to be.

Pause and Consider

- Faculty and staff see no purpose in the campus action plan. Why do you think they fail to see the purpose in the campus action plan?
- Have you had a similar experience? If so, what were your thoughts about the campus action plan?
- Why is the campus action plan being ignored? What could be done to transform it into a living, breathing document?
- How does this scenario connect with the Lewis Carroll quote in this chapter's opening?

under static conditions, would allow the flight crew, passengers, and plane to meet its goal, events will occur during the flight that will require the crew to make course corrections in the flight plan.

As the plane approaches Missouri, it encounters severe thunderstorms. The pilot and crew consult and agree upon modifications to the plan so as to circumvent this unexpected weather event. Later, as the plane is approaching Nevada, a passenger becomes seriously ill. After a quick needs assessment of the situation, the crew decides to make an emergency landing in Las Vegas to secure the appropriate medical treatment for this passenger.

The plane leaves Las Vegas to finish the flight to LAX. Unfortunately, air traffic is stacked up and the plane is diverted to a holding pattern until space was available. After 45 minutes of circling Los Angeles, the plane makes a safe landing. The flight plan, along with the course corrections initiated by the flight crew, allowed everyone to celebrate the success of the plan by experiencing a safe arrival. But what about the passenger who was left in Las Vegas? This passenger received the appropriate medical treatment. The airline provided the passenger a ticket from Las Vegas to Los Angeles so he could reach his final destination. Granted, he did not reach it at the same time as the others. But through the appropriate accommodations, he achieved the goal of the original flight plan.

Several similarities exist between this flight and a school year. Like the flight crew, the school planning committee creates and files a flight plan, but it is called a school action plan. The plane's flight is representative of the implementation of the flight plan. Likewise, the school's activities during the school year represent the implementation of the school action plan. Both the plane and the school will encounter unanticipated events requiring its crews to revisit the original plan and incorporate the necessary changes to keep the plane or school on course to meet their goals. Failure to understand that no action plan is ever developed that does not require constant monitoring and adjustments dooms the flight or the school to failure.

This constant monitoring and implementation of change is represented two ways on the integrated budget model in Figure 4.1. First, it is represented by a pair of double-pointed arrows above the ongoing evaluation, analysis, and course correction box at the model's base. These arrows illustrate the need for constant monitoring of the action plan. Likewise, the quad arrow at the center of the model symbolizes constant monitoring. Constant monitoring and adjusting is at the center of the model's effectiveness. Visualize the quad arrow rotating while moving along a horizontal axis between the eight components. This visualization reminds everyone that the planning process must not only be constantly monitored but that it is also not a linear process.

Planning may progress from Component 1 through Component 8, but in the monitoring process, the committee can return to whatever component is necessary to make the appropriate course correction. For example, new data might be gathered (Component 3), which will be analyzed (Component 4), which will then necessitate action in Components 7 and 8.

This is exactly what happened in the New York-to-Los Angeles flight. The flight crew analyzed new data—a weather report. This analysis caused the crew to modify the flight plan to meet the goal of a safe flight. School leaders must ensure that action plans, which in reality are flight plans, are constantly monitored and appropriately adjusted.

The Elements of an Action Plan

It is time to construct a flight—that is, an action—plan. The process begins with an overview of the elements of a school action plan:

- Coversheet
- List of SBDM committee members
- School vision and mission statements
- School goals (if a campus plan, district goals should also be in place and cross-referenced where applicable)
- One action plan strategy page for each strategy

The coversheet design is an individual school's choice, as is the design of the listing of the school planning committee members and the vision and mission statements. It is important to include the vision and mission statements to keep them in front of all of the school's stakeholders, since they are at the core of the school's culture and climate. People are busy and are bombarded with information. Including these statements makes it convenient for the stakeholders to refresh their memories on these important statements.

The GOSA Relationship

Goals, objectives, strategies, and actions bring structure and detail to the planning process. These facets of planning are integrated on the action strategy pages in the school action plan. Understanding the relationship between these four planning facets is essential to understanding the school action plan. This relationship is illustrated in Figure 4.2.

Goals, the G in GOSA, were examined earlier in Component 6 of the Sorenson-Goldsmith Model. Measurable objectives, the O in GOSA, were explained in the discussion of Component 7 of the model.

The S in GOSA is strategy. A strategy is a statement that assigns resources to accomplish the goal and objective that it supports. Examples of resources include but are not limited to fiscal, information, employee, material, spatial, and technology.

Strategies can be broad initiatives that cover the breadth of a school. Examples include a math-manipulative program, a new tutorial design, or a dropout-prevention intervention. The strategy should be expected to significantly impact the performance of the targeted populations.

An example of a strategy statement is: implement a computerized reading lab targeting students who are reading one or more grade levels below their grade placement.

The A in GOSA is activity—a particular action that is required to implement a strategy. An example of an activity to be used in the strategy is: the director of technology will order 20 computers according to bid specifications.

Reading the GOSA elements in Figure 4.2 from the top to the bottom increases the specificity. The opposite occurs when they are read from the bottom to the top. The elements become increasingly general. This unique relationship allows the document to be examined on four different levels of detail. Reading only the goals and objectives

Figure 4.2   The GOSA Relationship

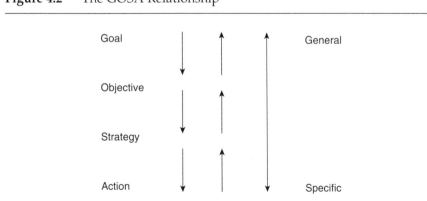

provides the reader with a quick general understanding of the school action plan. Reading all four levels provides the reader with the detail required for implementation of the goals and objectives.

An Example

Figure 4.3 is a completed strategy page from a school action plan. There is one goal on the page—all students will master the objectives of the mathematics curriculum. The goal is a broad statement supporting the school's mission of academic success for all students. It is also linked to student performance-based needs.

The objective is specific and measurable. It focuses on the mathematics goal and uses the results of the state assessment examination as its measure of mastery. Greater accountability is further achieved in that the objective is calling for a 5% increase in the performance of all identified student subpopulations.

The strategy, using the *Math Ace It* software program, assigns resources to support the goal and objective. Greater specificity of who, what, when, and where is provided with the inclusion of six specific action statements. For example, responsibilities are assigned to the principal, counselor, lab supervisor, and lead teacher. An accountability system is also in place for both formative and summative evaluation. The location of the evaluation data is even specified.

Finally, on this strategy page from a campus action plan, the integration of the budget with the vision and planning process is clearly in evidence (see Figure 4.3). Fiscal resources were budgeted, as evidenced by $18,500 in funds being assigned to this strategy, as well as personnel resources and facility resources. The allocated resources supported the school's vision of having all students master the mathematics curriculum. Planning is evidenced in the campus action plan through the strategy pages and minutes of the planning committee.

Table 4.3   Integration of Vision, Planning, and Budgeting in the Fort Chadbourne Elementary School

Strategy Page	
Budget	$18,500, personnel assigned, facility space assigned
Vision	Seeking mastery of mathematics by all students
Planning	Use of a planning team, page from the campus action plan

Figure 4.3   Strategy Page From the Fort Chadbourne Elementary School Campus Action Plan

Goal 1: All students will master the objectives of the mathematics curriculum.

Objective 1: Student mastery of the mathematics curriculum as measured by the state assessment exam will increase by 5% or more in each identified subpopulation.

Strategy 1: Students will use a diagnostic and instructionally managed *Math Ace It* software program to remediate specific mathematics objectives they are having difficulty in mastering.

Actions	Responsibility	Timeline (Start/End)	Resources (Human Material Fiscal)	Audit (Formative)	Reported/ Documented
1. Purchase *Math Ace It* software.	Principal	May 05/ July 05	$ 7,000	Purchase order	Principal's office
2. Provide faculty training on *Math Ace It* software.	Principal	August 05	Consultant, $ 1,500	Purchase order agenda	Principal's office
3. Provide math teachers with a list of identified students based on state assessment scores.	Counselor	August 05	Counselor	Student lists	Counselor's office
4. Assign students to three 30-minute sessions per week in the computer lab.	Lab supervisor	August 05/ Ongoing	Lab supervisor	Student lists	Computer lab
5. Provide teachers with progress reports on students.	Lab supervisor	2nd & 4th Fridays	Lab supervisor	Progress reports	Teacher files
6. Monthly planning meetings with the principal.	Lead teacher	4th Friday	Teachers	Agenda/ minutes	Lead Teacher
Evaluation (Summative): State Assessment reports, *Math Ace It* Reports					

GOSA Mapping

The school action plan is actually the integration and coordination of multiple GOSA relationships that are designed to fulfill the school planning committee's identified and prioritized school needs. A truncated illustration of this integrated GOSA design embedded in the school action plan is provided in Figure 4.4. Notice how specificity increases in Figure 4.4. Reading upward, generality increases. This is, in essence, a graphic depiction of the school action plan. How many action plan strategy pages would be used in the plan in Figure 4.4? Fourteen is the correct answer.

Final Thoughts

Implementing an integrated vision, planning, and budget model does not happen overnight. It requires a significant amount of commitment and labor from all stakeholders, but students as well as all other stakeholders will reap benefits in the long run. The transition to an integrated budget–vision–planning process evolves through four stages (see Figure 4.5.) The first stage, the Reactive Stage, is characterized by poorly defined goals and random strategies and activities designed to meet immediate needs. There is no coordination between the three factors, since they are headed in completely different directions. The second stage is the Transitive Stage. In this stage, there is evidence of a beginning of the alignment of goals, objectives, and strategies. Vision, planning, and budget are pointed in the same general directions. There are still deficiencies in planning and coordinating between the three elements. In the third stage, the Aligned Stage, alignment has been achieved between the budget, planning, and vision processes, but there is not integration among all elements. The final stage is the Integrated

Figure 4.4   GOSA Relationships Map

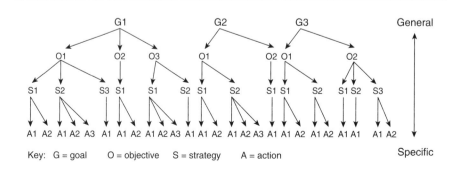

Key: G = goal   O = objective   S = strategy   A = action

Stage. By this time, an amalgam has been created using vision, planning, and budget. Collaboration and communication are now valued. Continuous evaluation and course correction are in place. The three elements are now one. They are all aiming toward the center, pointing toward success. Be patient with each other as you move through these four stages.

Schools need all stakeholders working together to ensure academic success for everyone. Roland Barth reminds educators, "I learned over and over again that the relationship among the adults in the schoolhouse has more impact on the quality and the character of the school—and on the accomplishments of youngsters—than any other factor" (Barth, 2001, p. 105). No family wants their child to be the student who does not meet with academic success. The construction of a school action integrating the school's vision with its budget greatly increases the likelihood of achieving the school's vision and mission.

It is up to the school leaders to keep the vision and the plan in front of the stakeholders. Remember, like the flight from New York

Figure 4.5   The Four Stages of the Implementation of the Sorenson-Goldsmith Integrated Budget Model

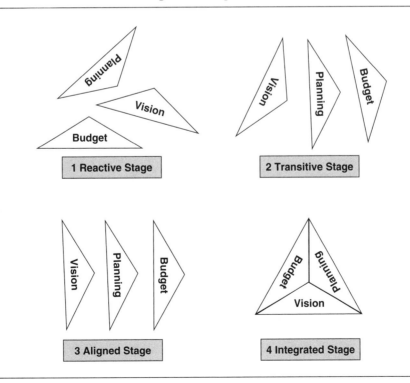

to Los Angeles, a school year will have situations requiring the school planning team to revisit the school action plan and make the necessary course adjustments throughout the school year. In the end, if everyone works collaboratively and commits to a well-constructed and managed plan, success happens.

P.S.

Odden and Archibald (2001) make an interesting point, "a reform goal is rarely accompanied by a 'fiscal note' which is legislative lingo for identifying the cost of achieving such a goal" (p. 2). Schools will never have enough resources to do everything for their students. The integrated budget model provides leaders with an opportunity to rearrange resources and use them in a more efficient manner. Stop and think about it: This is in reality an *increase* in revenue without asking more from the taxpayers.

Discussion Questions

1. What are the advantages of having procedures and policies in place to define the roles and responsibilities of the school planning committee?

2. What are the advantages of providing training to school planning committee members?

3. Describe four attributes of a data-driven school.

4. Data Analysis, the fourth component of the Sorenson-Goldsmith School Budgeting-Vision Implementation Model was referenced as the "brain center" of this model. What is the significance of this nickname for the fourth component of this model?

5. How is the quote at the beginning of the chapter relevant to this chapter?

6. Rewrite this nonmeasurable objective into a measurable objective: "More students will take AP courses next year." Defend your revision.

7. How does the Fullan and Miles quote, "different worlds collide, more learning occurs, and change is realistically managed" manifest itself in the needs prioritization step of the process?

8. How would the flight metaphor play out at your school?

9. In the Final Thoughts, the authors ask the readers to "be patient with each other." Why do you think they gave this advice?

Case Study Application: Shifting Paradigms With Changing Times

Note: This case study is designed to lead the reader through the Sorenson-Goldsmith Integrated Budget Model. In order to assist the reader in obtaining a global view of how this model functions, parts of the process are provided. The budget amounts are unrealistic but were kept small so the reader does not become bogged down in mathematics. Frequent references to Figure 4.1 can assist in observing the flow of the model through this case study.

Part 1: The Deal—Components
1 and 2 of the Integrated Budget Model

The Situation

Waterview is a prosperous suburb on Pecan Bay just south of the thriving seaport of Indianola. With a population of 25,000, Waterview has grown in the last 25 years from a sleepy coastal village to a thriving community where new industries and businesses continue to locate. Waterview is the county seat of Fannin County. Fannin Consolidated School District (FCSD) has 2 high schools, 4 middle schools, and 10 elementary schools. While the county's population has continued to decline for the past 20 years, Waterview is an exception. As a result of the population growth, two new middle schools and four new elementary schools have been built in Waterview in the past decade.

Two years ago, Dr. Ronald Scotts was named superintendent of FCSD. Dr. Scotts, a 48-year-old father of 13-year-old twin girls, moved with his wife Juanita from the upstate town of River City. While serving as the associate superintendent for finance, Dr. Scotts earned a reputation in River City as a strong and competent leader. The FCSD board hired Dr. Scotts to bring about change to the school system. Academic performance for the last 10 years was consistently mediocre. Routines had become the norm. The last innovation in the district was 10 years ago, and it was an automated substitute-teacher assignment system. The board with its three newly elected members wants FCSD to move from an attitude of mediocrity to one of excellence.

During his first year as superintendent, Dr. Scotts started a dialogue with the administrators about a decentralization plan for the school district. At the end of this year, before the principals started taking their vacations, Dr. Scotts announced that in the fall, he would provide an allocation of $25,000 to schools that wanted to receive training in a collaborative planning process. Principals would need to submit a plan outlining how the funding would be spent to train the faculty in the collaborative planning process. Dr. Scotts further told the principals that campuses with an operational campus planning committee would assume responsibility for the development, spending, and monitoring of the campus budget with the exception of salaries and maintenance and operations. With this newfound autonomy came accountability for the effective use of the budgeted funds.

Dr. Hector Avila and Ms. Abigail Grayson are in their second year at Pecan Bay High School. Dr. Avila had previously been a middle school principal in an urban district before being named principal at PBHS. He is the first Hispanic principal in the district. He has been well received by the community. Dr. Avila was hired to be a change agent at PBHS. Dr. Avila has the gift of being able to unite people behind a shared vision. Ms. Grayson had taught mathematics and served as the girls' basketball and softball coach at PBHS for the past 5 years. Ms. Grayson has a much-deserved reputation as an innovative classroom teacher who is willing to try new teaching strategies. Ms. Grayson attended mathematics training at a local university through a Teacher Quality Grant during the past two summers. Hector and Abigail like each other, and each one's talents complement the others.

After Dr. Scotts concluded his $25,000 challenge, Hector and Abigail immediately and aggressively spent 2 weeks on campus writing a proposal that was well documented by research and contained a detailed implementation plan based on the Sorenson-Goldsmith Integrated Budget Model. The two delivered the plan in person to Dr. Scotts, demonstrating their enthusiasm for the project. Dr. Scotts inwardly smiled and thanked the two for the proposal. Two weeks later, Pecan Bay High School became the first campus in FCSD to have its collaborative planning proposal approved.

During the first day of staff development in late summer, Abigail and Hector excitedly explained to the faculty their proposal using a PowerPoint presentation with coordinated handouts. The faculty was quiet. The principals were picking up on the body language that they were "bombing." Finally, Ed Feeney, a veteran teacher of 27 years at PBHS, broke the passive silence and asked, "Whose idea was this? Sounds like the superintendent wants us to do his work. I'm busy enough as it is." There was some applause. Latasha Jackson, a fourth-year drama teacher, asked, "Is this another one of those fads that goes through schools? I bet the state is up to this." Kelly Tyres, a paraprofessional commented, "No one ever asks us what we want. They just keep shoving stuff down our throat like the 'highly qualified' stuff from NCLB."

The two principals let the teachers go to lunch 30 minutes early (very popular) and went back to their offices, surprised and beaten. They kept repeatedly saying things to each other like, "Where did we go wrong?" and "I can't believe they are so negative," and "Where do we go from here?"

Thinking It Through

Hector and Abigail desperately need your assistance. Where did they go wrong? Where do they go from here? Hector and Abigail have a great proposal and are very capable administrators; yet they encountered strong resistance from the faculty. As that "other set of eyes," you need to stop at this point in the case study and write a step-by-step plan for these principals to win over the faculty. Some *Handy Hints* have been included to help you with this process.

Handy Hints

- Involve all stakeholders
- Talk mission and vision
- Communication
- Shared decision making
- Identify challenges
- Identify strengths
- Outside resources

You will discover that if you do this activity with several colleagues your intervention plan will be stronger than if you complete it by yourself.

Part II: The Needs—Components 3 through 5
of the Sorenson-Goldsmith Integrated Budget Model

Checking It Out

Thank you for your assistance in developing a step-by-step plan for assisting the PBHS faculty to reconsider and adopt the collaborative planning process! Your work is not done. Learning to use the collaborative process requires time and effort by all the school stakeholders. Read on and be prepared to provide assistance again as the process continues to unfold.

With the arrival of spring, the campus planning committee was established and the training completed. It is time to begin constructing PBHS's first-ever campus-based action plan with an integrated budget. The campus planning committee has been provided a data packet courtesy of Dr. Avila and Ms. Grayson. Data were gathered from a variety of sources. The principals spent countless hours gathering these data but only did so as a way to assist and encourage the committee in its inaugural year. The committee is free to gather any other data as it deems necessary. The two principals volunteered to assist the committee in data gathering. Dr. Scotts was pleased to inform the campus planning committee that PBHS would receive an additional allotment of $200,000 for the next school year. Nelson Clampett, the assistant superintendent of finance, trained the appropriate individuals on the district's budgeting software. Nelson is anxious to see his old alma mater meet with success. In fact, it was 17 years ago that he led the Fighting Squirrels baseball team to the state championship by pitching a no-hitter in the state championship game. Since that time, the school has not received any athletic or academic awards.

In order to assist the flow of this case study, the planning committee's work of data gathering and analysis (Components 3 and 4) has been completed for you. The committee spent several meetings analyzing the box of data provided by the principals. They requested additional data and were provided with all the data they requested.

Make a list of data that you would want to have if you were on the Fighting Squirrels campus planning team.

Thinking It Through

It is now time to proceed to Component 5 of the Sorenson-Goldsmith Integrated Budget Model. You must take the nonprioritized list of 10 identified needs by the PBHS planning committee and prioritize them. Remember, PBHS has an allocation of $200,000. The committee cannot exceed the budget allocation! Note that the identified needs will cost substantially more than the campus's allocation. It is time for the committee to make some tough

Table 4.4   PBHS Nonprioritized Identified Needs

Next Year

Your Priority	*Cost*	*Identified NEED*	*Committee Rationale*
	$20,000	• Copier contract	• Used by all departments • Basis of many academic assignments
	$30,000	• Reading intervention plan • $12,000 for software • $3,000 for training	• % freshmen reading below grade level is twice the state rate • % Hispanics reading below grade level is three times the state rate • Teacher survey shows reading issues number one on teacher concerns
	$40,000	• General supplies	• Meet basic office/classroom needs of paper, staplers, tape, etc.
	$6,000	• Special Olympics	• Add this program since these students are unable to participate in other extracurricular events • Parent advocacy group has made an appeal to the SBDM committee

Table 4.4   (Continued)

Your Priority	*Cost*	*Identified NEED*	*Committee Rationale*
	$30,000	• New band uniforms	• Current uniforms are 23 years old • Uniforms were water damaged and now have a mold problem
	$12,000	• Vernier instruments, other digital equipment	• Needed in advanced science and math classes • Essential to meet state curriculum requirements • Needed in Pre-AP, AP, and dual credit courses
	$17,000	• Professional travel	• New category • Teachers need to be able to expand their knowledge by attending professional development events • Number 4 need on the teacher survey
	$60,000	• Expanded technology in the library and computer center • $45,000 tech services • $5,000 printers • $10,000 supplies	• Students need access to Internet and other technology for AP, dual credit courses, research • Identified by teachers of advanced courses as a number-one priority
	$60,000	• 9th-grade school-within-a-school • $5,000 training • $35,000 facility upgrades • $20,000 curriculum materials	• High failure rate in freshmen classes • High referral rate to office • High absentee rate
	$7,000	• Spring athletic banquet • $5,000 honorarium for speaker • $2,000 catered meals for 200	• Boost enthusiasm for athletics • Increase school spirit

decisions. Assign your priority numbers to the needs using the column on the far left. Provide a written rationale to share with the faculty and administration to defend your needs prioritization.

Part III: The Action Plan—Components 6 Through 8 of the Sorenson-Goldsmith Integrated Budget Model

Now that you have prioritized the needs, it is time to construct an *abridged* action plan. For the purpose of this case study, you will only use the top two prioritized needs. As you proceed through this portion of the case study, it might be helpful to review the figures in Chapter 4 as well as the information in Components 6 through 8.

Using the number-one prioritized need, complete a strategy page to address the prioritized need. It may be necessary to use more than one strategy page due to space constraints. A clean copy of the strategy page is located in Resource A.

Repeat the process for the need you designated as the second priority. Once you have completed both priorities, review your pages. Are the goals, objectives, and strategies aligned and logical? Do the actions clearly define what was being done in order to implement the strategy? Are the resources, personnel, and evaluations in place?

Using your strategy pages, construct a GOSA map for your abridged action plan. Use the following scaffolding items to assist you in the construction of your GOSA map.

- How many different **g**oals did you have? _____ (Probably 1 or 2)
- How many different **o**bjectives did you have? _____ (Probably 1 or 2)
- How many **s**trategies did you have? _____ (Probably fewer than 5)
- How many **a**ctions did you have? _____ (Probably many more than the number of strategies)
- Review your GOSA map. Does it contain the same number of the different elements that you identified in the previous questions? If so, that is a strong indication that your mapping is on the right track.
- Using your strategy pages and your GOSA map, compare your actions to the strategies on the strategy pages to their counterpart on the map. Do they connect on the map as they do on the strategy pages? Repeat the process for the strategy–objective relationship and the objective–goal relationship. If they are aligned, this, along with a yes answer to the previous questions, indicates that you have successfully completed this final portion of the case study.

Chapter 5

Effective and Efficient Budgeting Practices

I find all this money a considerable burden!

—J. Paul Getty, American Industrialist
(Jonathan Lazear, 1992, p. 342, December 8)

The Budget Plan

J. Paul Getty (1882–1976), at one time the world's richest private citizen, no doubt found his extensive personal wealth to be a "considerable burden," as he was married and divorced five times, at great personal, professional, and financial expense. His monetary woes continued later into life as his 16-year-old grandson was kidnapped and held for ransom. J. Paul Getty refused to pay the ransom. Finally, after the kidnappers mutilated the grandson—his ear being delivered to a newspaper— J. Paul Getty decided to forfeit only a portion of the extorted demand, a maximum amount that was tax deductible. Getty then loaned the rest of the required extortion money to his son at 4% interest. The grandson was then released by the kidnappers but soon lapsed into permanent drug addiction, a consequence of the trauma suffered, which ultimately resulted in a stroke leaving him speechless, blind, and partially para- lyzed for the remainder of his life. Now, that said, it is not our wish or our intention for the school budgeting process to be nearly as complicated or problematic or even traumatic for the educational leader! In fact, our greatest desire is for the school administrator, as the budget manager, to find the practice of school budgeting to be efficient, effective, and far less complicated than one might assume. With this thought in mind, let's turn to the first rule of school budgeting: The secret for successful budgeting is three-part: visionary manifestation, constancy in planning, and an interminable linkage to school goals and objectives.

Theoretically, and most certainly appropriate in practice, the school academic action or improvement plan should be developed in tandem with the budget plan, which serves to identify the costs necessary to support the academic plan and instructional program. The budget plan is then converted into fund-oriented accounts (a school budget) as associated with the fiscal allotment provided to the school by the local district. The rationale for such planning makes sense because the obligation of any school administrator is to—first and foremost—plan for the specified needs of the students and not permit the available funds to dictate nor confine any aspect of a school's instructional program (Brimley, Verstegen, & Garfield, 2012). Unfortunately, and all too often, a lack of integrated budget and academic planning at the school or district level results in the selection and application of programs and services that are short sighted, insufficient, and ineffective in meeting the varied needs of the students served—resulting in wasted revenue and poor academic performance.

The purpose of the budget plan is to support the school's action or improvement plan and consolidate it into dollar appropriations. Basically, any action or improvement plan is worth nothing more than the paper it is written on unless it is integrated with the budget plan. Table 5.1 specifies the necessary steps that a school administrator and decision-making team should follow in relation to the budgetary process which includes training, planning, and development.

The budget plan must be developed with the following questions in mind:

1. Prior to any budget planning and development process, has the school leader provided professional development training that is essential to understanding how visioning and planning impact programmatic considerations and the school budget?

2. Has a needs assessment been conducted to address what impact programmatic initiatives—such as federal, state, and local—have on student achievement? (See the subsequent section on Adequate Funding in an Era of Accountability and Fiscal Constraint.)

Table 5.1   The Budgetary Process—Training, Assessing, Prioritizing, Goal
Setting, Objective Development, Monitoring, and Evaluation

1	2	3	4	5	6	7
Professional Development	Planning and Needs Assessment	Causal Barriers Identification	Prioritizing School-Based Needs	Goal Setting and Objective Development	Budget Development and Implementation	Budget Monitoring and Evaluation

8
◀ Have all stakeholders been actively engaged and involved? ▶

The budgetary process, from training to planning to goal setting and objective development to actual budget implementation, is a constant course of action that requires a principal to engage the decision-making team in a collaborative and problem-solving effort.

This table serves to illustrate how a principal can transform the budgetary process through a series of step-by-step essential elements that clarify the complexities associated with budget development, specifically as correlated with goal alignment and attainment.

Levin (2011) suggests that school leaders want to know which particular interventions are most promising for increasing student achievement and cost the least, because monetary resources are often in short supply. In other words, it is essential to ensure the effectiveness of school resources by incorporating methods that will promote an age-old adage: *Get the biggest bang for the buck!* This is what a needs assessment is all about.

3. Have student needs and academic achievement been addressed in the form of a school action or improvement plan that emphasizes goal development?

4. Following the needs assessment and goal-development process, have specific instructional as well as nonacademic programs been identified for implementation, improvement, or exclusion?

5. Have learning community representatives been provided with forms and figures that are indicative of previous budgetary allotments and expenditures for at least 1 prior year, preferably 3 to 5 years?

6. Has the learning community (specifically the teaching staff) been asked by school administration to submit requests for supplies, equipment, and facilities that are essential, if not critical, in meeting the academic needs of the students served and that are, further, necessary in relation to the dictates imposed on the school or district academic programs by state and federal mandates?

7. Have budgeted dollars been allocated to support the action plan, and have the budget manager and team regularly and collaboratively monitored and evaluated budgetary expenditures in relation to programmatic effectiveness and student academic gains? This is more than a "wish list" approach to instruction and school budgeting—this is an integrated-visionary process, through a needs-assessment process, that readily identifies priorities that are necessary for programmatic success.

8. Finally, have faculty, staff, students, parents, and community members been actively involved in the decision-making process leading to the development of the school action or improvement plan, as well as the campus budget?

These eight components represent sound budgeting theory, which better serves to ensure that the ideas and recommendations of the learning community are actively sought and incorporated into practice via the budgetary process.

Adequate Funding in an Era of Accountability and Fiscal Constraint

Recent education policy efforts at both the national and state levels have focused on standards-based reforms and assessments that place greater responsibility on school districts and, most notably, on campus principals to effect school change and improvement. Accountability mandates focus on aligning curriculum and assessments to rigorous academic standards, using high-stakes testing. This movement is at the center of state and federal accountability mandates. The reauthorization of the federal No Child Left Behind Act (NCLB) in 2011 is most reflective of such policy initiatives and, moreover, mandates that all teachers be of high quality, identifies schools in need of assistance, and, furthermore, provides educational options for students attending Title I schools that do not make adequate progress. Each of these dictates, central to NCLB, costs money—money that a school district frequently does not have, most notably during periods of economic downturn.

Current funding systems have yet to adequately link the availability of school funding and the educational needs and academic achievement of students. To date, while several strategies have been examined, critical funding has been limited in meeting the implementation efforts necessary to fulfill the federal guidelines associated with NCLB (Brimley et al., 2012; Glatthorn, Boschee, Whitehead, & Boschee, 2012). While states and districts are continually attempting to evaluate how schools are utilizing their funding resources to improve student outcomes, much work remains to be done to adequately ensure that school expenditures equate to student academic improvement. As a result, school leaders must continually contemplate and address the challenge of making every budgeted dollar stretch to meet mandated instructional initiatives, individual student needs, teacher requests, parent demands, district desires, and state expectations. No wonder a principal was recently heard to exclaim: "My budget is stretched so tight, it squeaks!"

Analyzing the School Action and Budget Plans

The school action or improvement plan, as previously examined in Chapter 4, serves as the vehicle that drives not only the instructional program but also the budget development process. Effective budgetary planning must allow for the school budget to be based upon the educational programs designated within the confines of an action or improvement plan. In other words, funding should be allocated to the educational programs as identified in priority order in the school action or improvement plan. There are numerous aspects or designators often associated with an action plan. In the state of Texas, for example, there are 13 components to be addressed within an action plan, as mandated by the Texas Education Agency (2012c). These 13 components comply with the reauthorized No Child Left Behind Act (2011). These 13 designators are identified as: (1) student performance, (2) special education, (3) violence prevention, (4) parental involvement, (5) professional development, (6) suicide prevention, (7) conflict resolution, (8) dyslexia treatment programs, (9) dropout reduction, (10) technology, (11) discipline management, (12) accelerated instruction, and (13) career education. While each of these components is mandated in one particular state, it is noteworthy to recognize that as a whole, they are quite representative of school planning issues that any state, district, or school might encounter.

Budget plans must be developed in tandem with an action or improvement plan. The budget plan serves effectively to (1) project all anticipated income, (2) identify all needed programs, and (3) project current and future average daily attendance or membership for the purpose of seeking a district allocation that will serve to meet the needs of all the students enrolled.

The purpose of the budget plan is to anticipate, project, and predict potential sources of income, program development, any financial deficit, and potential areas for budgetary reduction or additions. The development of the budget plan, much like that of the action plan, should be made in collaboration with a school's site-based decision-making team. This team, following the guidance of the school leader, is most often involved in decisions related to educational planning, curriculum development, instructional issues, staffing patterns, professional development, school organization, and, of course, budgeting.

Prior to developing the budget plan, the effective school administrator must insist on and ensure that a professional-development program has been initiated to train the learning community in the methods of generating and completing a needs assessment (see Table 5.2). A needs assessment and an information or quality analysis both effectively correlate with campus action or improvement planning procedures, as well as budget development processes. When utilized appropriately, a needs-assessment instrument and a quality analysis can do exactly what their names imply. Furthermore, each—working in tandem—can be the essential impetus for prioritizing school-based needs with the following caveat: students and the academic program are always in the forefront of any budgetary consideration.

Performing an Information Analysis

An information analysis, sometimes identified as a quality analysis, is a thorough examination of a campus action or improvement plan with implications associated with the campus budget-development process. Information analysis is a four-step process whereby certain campus underlying or problematic factors can be identified via a three-point assessment:

1. Establishing performance objectives;

2. Conducting a needs assessment; and

3. Scrutinizing an instructional problem (Sorenson & Cortez, 2010).

Information analysis must focus on a review and analysis of data, followed by the implementation of best-practice strategies. This is a principal-oriented and practice-based method of data scrutiny that guides a school leader and team in determining the problems or factors that are contributing to low student performance in particular subject areas for specific student populations (Sorenson, Goldsmith, Méndez, & Maxwell, 2011). Information analysis requires a principal, prior to developing a school budget, to seek "soft" or qualitative data and "hard" or quantitative data. Such data come from inside and outside the school or district. Consider the "What's a Principal to Do?" scenario, and reflect upon the four-step information analysis that follows as a means of determining how to solve the issue or problem.

WHAT'S A PRINCIPAL TO DO?

Whitten Van Horn is principal at Broadway School. He has a problem at school. A significant percentage of the students at Broadway School are struggling academically. Some are failing multiple classes. These students are English language learners (ELLs), and many are unable to read with comprehension or write in the English language with clarity. The ELL students are testing as English learners and are barely passing the English state exam. These students, however, have received passing grades in previous years. The ELL students seem bored, are often disengaged, and, based on their behaviors, are uninterested in school. Principal Van Horn thinks to himself: "What's a principal to do?"

Pause and Consider

- What is Principal Van Horn to do relative to the scenario presented? Need a helpful hint? See the next two sections—*Steps to Performing an Information Analysis* and *Conducting a Needs Assessment*.

Steps to Performing an Information Analysis

Step 1: Qualitative or Soft/Outside Data and Information

Principals and site-based decision-making teams must examine "soft/outside" data sources by

- Reviewing the research literature;
- Enlisting the support of district and professional facilitators who understand the problem at hand;
- Consulting educational research laboratories;
- Determining which best practices, when implemented, will solve the instructional problem;
- Providing teachers with release time to participate in essential and relatable professional development; and
- Permitting teachers the opportunity to make site visits to schools (local and distant) that are effectively implementing the required best practices.

Step 2: Quantitative or Hard/Outside Data and Information

Principals and site-based decision-making teams must examine "hard/outside" data sources by

- Deriving information from state and federal agencies in the form of statutes and reports, to include:
  - The State Education Agency codes, statutes, or official rulings;
  - The United States Department of Education regulations;
  - The Office of Civil Rights directives;
  - The No Child Left Behind (NCLB) Act of 2011 qualifiers;
  - Adequate Yearly Progress (AYP) measurements;
  - Academic Excellence Indicator System (AEIS) or state education agency reports and/or assessments; and
  - Individuals with Disabilities Education Improvement Act of 2004 (IDEIA) parameters.

Step 3: Qualitative or Soft/Inside Data and Information

Principals and site-based decision-making teams must examine "soft/inside" data sources by

- Analyzing survey results;
- Initiating focus groups and gathering relevant information;
- Conducting interviews of teachers, parents, and students;
- Initiating observations of effective teaching practices;
- Surveying organizational climate and culture;
- Examining student profiles;
- Seeking teacher opinions; and
- Conducting brainstorming sessions with members of the learning community.

Step 4: Quantitative or Hard/Inside Data and Information

Principals and site-based decision-making teams must examine "hard/inside" data sources by

- Reviewing records, such as:
  - Student academic records, to include cumulative folders;
  - State assessment and accountability records;
  - Fiscal education information management system (FEIMS) records;
  - School board policies;
  - Administrative regulations and procedures;
  - School district attorney opinions;
  - Attendance records of school meetings; and
  - Classroom assessments and other benchmarking reports.

Conducting a Needs Assessment

A needs assessment must be initiated prior to the development of a campus action or improvement plan and the development of a school budget (see Figure 4.1, page 81). Such an assessment requires a principal and team to ultimately prioritize school needs to positively impact the instructional program. To do so, the authors of this text—as former principals—strongly recommend that four essential phases be addressed in the assessment process. These phases are addressed in Table 5.2.

Generated Income Sources

"If you can conceive it, you can achieve it!" Do you recall this old adage? School leaders are designated many responsibilities, the budgetary process being obviously one, and as a result are often called upon to put

Table 5.2   Conducting a Needs Assessment

Phase	*Work to Accomplish*
I. Initiating the inquiry process 1. What needs improvement? 2. Why is improvement needed? 3. What data support the need to improve? 4. Do additional data need to be gathered to support areas in need of improvement?	1. Review the district's and school's mission or visionary statement to determine if the campus vision meets the "written" vision as well as the district's vision. 2. Analyze the current campus action or improvement plan. 3. Identify sources of data such as previously conducted studies and district and statewide test results, along with teacher, student, and parent surveys. 4. Identify other needed sources of data that may not be readily available, such as a longitudinal analysis of state indictor systems reports. This is a relevant approach to identifying instructional area(s) in need of improvement. Then, determine what methods or procedures are needed to collect any particular data.
II. Deriving consensus 1. Can consensus or agreement be reached regarding the needs or problems that must be addressed?	1. Review all pertinent sources of data in a transparent manner whereby all parties are collaboratively involved in the consensus-building process. Such a procedure better ensures "buy-in" within the site-based team and across the learning community.

(Continued)

Table 5.2   (Continued)

Phase	Work to Accomplish
2. Does the needs assessment process find areas that are important to bringing about organizational change and improvement? 3. Consider the following: Have the principal and site-based decision-making team overlooked any programmatic concerns, issues, or problems?	2. Consider all instructional and curricular concerns, problems, and targeted needs that have been identified. 3. Arrive at a high level of consensus and then narrow down the list of needs. This is a priority-driven process.
III. Organizing and analyzing the data 1. What data need to be collected and why? 2. From where will the data be collected? 3. What do the data reveal?	1. Following any analysis of data and an initial prioritization of perceived needs, principal and team must discuss each area of concern, note problems, and then outline specific actions to be initiated. This particular phase is all about answering the question "why do we do this?" 2. Principals must be prepared to share action or initiation proposals of data collection with members of the learning community. 3. Never avoid or ignore initiating a careful review of the research literature. Do not consider, and never implement, any organizational initiative that cannot be validated in the research literature or by empirical studies.
IV. Focusing on priorities 1. What is the greatest priority? The second greatest? The third greatest, etc.? 2. Priorities must be determined in accordance to the following criteria: • What human, fiscal, and/or material resources (including release time) are required? • Are internal or external or both levels of expertise available and/or required?	1. Conduct a full examination of instructional priorities and hold open, collaborative, and transparent discussions with the site-based decision-making team. These discussions must address each priority consideration proposed. 2. Present team-determined recommendations to the district administrative leader (superintendent or designee) along with the priority rankings of each identified need.

Table 5.2   (Continued)

Phase	Work to Accomplish
• By what means will the priorities be addressed, solved, and/or resolved? 3. Is there a sound research base in the professional literature for addressing each prioritized concern/problem/need and for supporting the proposed actions and/or implementations?	3. Most important—work together as a team in a most transparent and collaborative manner, reaching a fair and equitable consensus. Always remember: Students come first and foremost!

SOURCE: R. D. Sorenson, L. M. Goldsmith, Z. Y. Méndez, and K. T. Maxwell, *The Principal's Guide to Curriculum Leadership* (Thousand Oaks, CA: Corwin, 2011), and D. Tanner and L. Tanner, *Curriculum Development: Theory Into Practice* (Englewood Cliffs, NJ: Prentice Hall, 2006).

such adages to work. The effective school administrator quickly learns to generate additional sources of income for the school beyond those funds already allocated by district administration. The district allocation is just one of numerous income sources that must be generated if a school is to establish a comprehensive, high-quality, and cost-effective program.

Brimley et al. (2012) report that tax limitation efforts in many states, along with funding reduction at federal and state levels as a result of the Great Recession, have threatened to reduce local revenue. As a result, school officials must increasingly seek nontraditional sources of funding for schools. Such nontraditional income sources include grants from governmental entities and private foundations and gifts from business (adopt-a-school) partnerships, individuals within the community, and various corporations that are most interested in maintaining their commitment to education and to educational organizations. Income from many of these sources can be generated locally when a school administrator and team actively seek to make contact with these potential contributors.

Grants

Grants often provide an additional source of income for schools but are typically obtained on a competitive basis. This practice becomes even more intense and competitive during periods of economic setback. Grant funds are generally tied to a Request for Application (RFA) process whereby a great deal of time and effort, not to mention tedious research and data collection, must occur for an application to be seriously considered. Most grants are categorical in nature, as noted in Chapter 1. As a reminder, *categorical* refers to funds that are restricted to certain "categories" or activities such as technology, science, mathematics, or accelerated instruction. These funds can only be utilized within the particular category in which they were awarded and must further be monitored and accounted for by the local school and district. Just as important, the instructional program funded must be frequently evaluated, often by outside sources (evaluators) or agencies, to ensure that the grant dollars are appropriately allotted, utilized, and expended. Listed below are a number of important attributes associated with grant funding.

- Grants are generally time sensitive—funded dollars must be appropriated and spent within a specific period of time.
- Grants are generally available from state or federal agencies and are often related to certain educational acts or initiatives—NCLB, for example.
- Grants and funding information can be identified and located by accessing governmental, commercial, nonprofit, and educational organization websites or home pages. Three excellent resources for educators seeking grant funding are:
  - *The Grantwriter's Internet Companion: A Resource for Educators and Others Seeking Grants and Funding* by S. L. Peterson (2001);
  - *Finding Funding: Grant Writing From Start to Finish, Including Project Management and Internet Use* by E. W. Brewer and C. M. Achilles (2008); and
  - *Show Me the Money: Tips and Resources for Successful Grant Writing* by L. Starr (2008).
- Grants are generally restrictive—"in-kind" funds, for example, may be required whereby the funding agency expects the school or district to match the granted allotment with either dollars or services—transportation, custodial, equipment, or facilities usage are typical examples. Often the granted funds are further restricted and may not be used for furniture or travel or, in some cases, salaries. Such restrictions must be adhered to, or a school or district risks losing the grant and thus the badly needed dollars.

One example of grant funding is the *Teacher Quality Enhancement Grants* (http://www2.ed.gov/programs/heatqp/index.html). This NCLB–related grant program provides opportunities for faculty development in the area of math and science. Schools collaborate with universities and other entities to provide staff training in support of systematic change and development at a fraction of the cost to a school district in comparison to the cost associated with a district providing the training independent of the contributing entities.

A second example is the *National Professional Development Program* grant (http://www2.ed.gov/programs/nfdp/index.html). This grant provides funding to ensure that school personnel are well prepared to provide services to English language learner (ELL) students.

A third example is the *21st Century Community Learning Centers* grant (http://www.ed.gov/21stcclc/). This funding initiative aids with the formation of school–community partnerships to help keep local schools open after hours and during the summer.

Finally, one of the best sources for locating grant funding is the Internet. The Internet provides hundreds, if not thousands, of sites containing excellent information regarding grants. Such information ranges from daily announcements to useful statistics to tips and techniques for writing grants to current programs that are funded by grant dollars. Brewer and Achilles (2008) identify 101 Hot Sites for Grantwriters (p. 108), several of which are listed below. The following 10 Internet sites and their corresponding URLs could very well provide the school leader and team with the funding necessary to initiate a program or programs that could impact student success and achievement. Review this listing and bookmark your favorite site(s). A tidbit of advice for the grant seeker: The numerous sites identified and recommended often undergo changes and, as a result, the term "Under Construction" can very well indicate that a particular site may not be available. If so, move on to another site and source, and, as always, best of luck in your search for additional school funds!

1. National Science Foundation—http://www.nsf.gov/home/grants.htm

   This is an excellent site for grant writers interested in science and mathematics funding.

2. Apply for a Grant—http://www.ed.gov/fund/grants-apply.html

3. U.S. Department of Education Grants for Teachers—http://www.ed.gov/news/press-releases/education-department-awards-246-million-grants-support-teacher-and-principal-dev

   Bookmark the two sites noted above if you are a novice grant writer seeking direct information to education grants.

4. (The) Foundation Center—http://foundationcenter.org/

This site links grant writers to hundreds of private foundations and corporations that provide funding.

5. The Grants Library—http://researchguides.library.wisc.edu/content.php?pid=16143&sid=108666

This writing guide site houses the world's largest compilation of grant-oriented Web resources.

6. Amherst Grant Seeking Resource Packet—http://www.amherst.edu/offices/FCR/ac_grantseeking_packet

This is an excellent site worth visiting, with Web links to major grant-making organizations.

7. FEDSTATS—http://www.fedstats.gov/

Statistics are provided by more than 70 federal agencies, and the site also includes a wealth of information for the grant seeker.

8. Fundsnet Services ONLINE—http://www.fundsnetservices.com

This extensive website provides 1,500 links to grants and fundraising resources.

9. Grants and Related Resources—http://staff.lib.msu.edu/harris23/grants/index.htm

This website is great for providing the grant writer with a significant listing of grants and funding sources for nonprofit organizations.

10. National Agricultural Library—http://www.nal.usda.gov/ric/ricpubs/fundguide.html

The "Internet Resources" section of *A Guide to Funding Resources* includes links to searchable databases offering funding opportunities from government and/or private sources that are available to local governments, community organizations, and individuals. It provides Web links to more than 60 full-text online guides, manuals, and tips to assist grant writers prepare successful proposals. The section entitled "Additional Resources" is a bibliographic listing of published grant-writing resources and funding directories.

Fundraising

Additional school-site income is frequently generated through the fundraising efforts of school-sponsored groups such as parent–teacher organizations and booster clubs, to name a couple. Parental involvement is essential for most school fundraising efforts. Parent groups and organizations provide a wide range of valuable services and activities, both inside and outside the school. However, the role of parents and parent–teacher organizations is seldom specifically defined and, as a result, problems—especially in the fundraising arena—often arise. What we do know and appreciate as school leaders is that the involvement of parents in schools can result in support for obtaining additional resources. The importance of parent organizations most often relates to their desire to obtain quality services and resources for their schools. These efforts are typically "reactive" rather than "proactive;" thus, proper training and guidance from school leaders is essential to ensure parental efforts do not become administrative burdens or problems (Fullan, 2007).

Fundraising events typically involve the sale of merchandise ranging from consumable items (candy, cookies, pizzas, or Thanksgiving turkeys, for example) to nonperishable items such as Christmas gift wrap, t-shirts, raffles, candles, senior rings, yearbooks, school picture sales, and just about anything else the fertile mind can imagine.

Fundraisers can generate significant income for a school, income above and beyond the standard district allocation. Fundraisers can also serve as monetary sources for purchasing items such as stage curtains, playground equipment, instructional supplies, and even air conditioning for the school gym. However, if fundraising efforts are not properly planned and organized, schools can be faced with numerous financial pitfalls (Mutter & Parker, 2004). For example, fundraising—while financially compelling and potentially rewarding—can quickly turn sour with lost, missing, or stolen merchandise and/or generated funds. This can publicly tarnish a school or embarrass an administrator in the eyes of the community, not to mention the district superintendent or school board.

To avoid such problems, the effective school leader must either carefully follow designated district policies and procedures or proactively establish guidelines and regulations that allow for the proper management of fundraising merchandise, the selection of merchandise vendors, the designated responsibilities of those individuals involved, and the necessary bookkeeping systems. Such policies, procedures, and/or guidelines must be in place to protect a school's generated income, potential profit, and reputation. By neglecting to do so, a school administrator is breaking one of the cardinal rules of school budgeting: safeguarding school interests through the responsible stewardship of public funds and setting and adhering to internal fiscal controls, both of which are best business practices necessary to protect school assets and personnel.

Expenditure Accountability and Control

One of the most important aspects of the school budgetary process is the accounting for and control of school expenditures. While expenditure accountability and control vary from state to state and from district to district, three closely related factors must be followed with strict and complete propriety: appropriate visionary planning, careful budgeting, and effective expenditure of school funds. Each is crucial to ensuring that students benefit from a school's instructional program (Guthrie, Hart, Hack, & Candoli, 2007). District and school-site expenditure accountability and control are aided by the use of a fiscal education and information management system, appropriate accounting procedures, campus activity income collection, deposit guidelines, timely payment of bills, and budget amendment practices. These factors will be examined, and further consideration will be given to how the interweaving combinations of all factors contribute to effective and efficient school budgeting.

Fiscal Education and Information Management System

The fiscal education and information management system is an accounting and auditing process that is implemented in most states to control school and district budgets by utilizing a classification or codified structure (Governmental Accounting Standards Board [GASB], 2011). School districts as well as state departments of education need easy access to information directly related to the resources required to provide a fiscal infrastructure to support student learning. This codified information and management system electronically links revenues and expenditures, for example, from school to district office to state departments of education through an accounting process that traces and audits funding, examines programmatic considerations, and even reviews student achievement and accountability standards, as well as other important issues related to individual schools and districts. FEIMS can also detect material errors in the fiscal data of a school district and can further recognize and analyze the state-adopted fiscal accounting system that is required by state education code. Again, while certain aspects of a fiscal education and information management system may be utilized at local option, the overall structure is to be uniformly applied to all school districts in accordance with the Generally Accepted Accounting Principles (GAAP) as directed by the United States Department of Education and the Governmental Accounting Standards Board (GASB, 2011) in an effort to monitor and control expenditure accountability.

Accounting Procedures

The responsibility for wisely spending school funds to provide for a high-quality education for all students is further challenged by the precept that school dollars must also be actively and accurately accounted for and protected. The term *accounting* can be readily described as the process by which the effectiveness, legality, quality, and efficiency of budgeting procedures must be measured by the documented stewardship of all public funds (Thompson, Wood, & Crampton, 2008). While such a notion may have once been considered simply "good business" by schools and school districts, this same consideration, by today's budgetary standards, is a practical—if not essential—fiscal imperative.

Accounting procedures are defined as the "fiscal imperative" method of determining whether a school has provided a fiscally valued and educationally valuable service to its clientele by emphasizing that school accounting procedures must serve to:

1. Monitor all incoming funds and outgoing expenditures in relation to the attainment of the school's vision, goals, and objectives.

2. Protect public dollars from any potential loss attributable to irresponsibility, wrongful utilization, theft, and/or embezzlement by any individual associated with the school or school district.

3. Provide for an assurance that public funds are being used to better ensure the academic achievement of all students.

4. Ensure that all legal requirements are followed implicitly.

5. Inform the general community of any and all facts and information regarding the fiscal solvency of the school site and district.

In an effort to meet these accountability standards, the Governmental Accounting Standards Board (2011) issued a statement that emphasizes that accountability is the paramount objective of any budgetary process and, as such, all fiscal accountability reports must include information that (a) compares actual financial results with the legally adopted budget, (b) assesses the financial condition of a school or system, (c) complies with finance-related laws, rules, and regulations, and (d) assists in evaluating the efficiency and effectiveness of a school's or district's fiscal budget and educational program.

Finally, the National Center for Education Statistics (2009b) identifies four standard accounting practices that guide schools and districts in their common goal of accounting for public funds in relation to the budgetary process.

1. Define and utilize account classifications and codes that provide meaningful financial management information.

2. Comply with the Generally Accepted Accounting Principles as established by the Governmental Accounting Standards Board.

3. Recognize and utilize accounting technology and safety and security procedures.

4. Comply with all state and federal laws and fiscal accountability reporting requirements.

By adopting and following these standards, school leaders allow for the continuous monitoring of expenditures as well as accountability and control of budgeting procedures—all of which are most definitely considered to be "best practices" for further ensuring that students are benefiting from school appropriations. Equally important, all school personnel are protected from any potential legal entanglements that are often associated with the mishandling of district dollars.

Collection and Deposit Structures

The school leader, as budget manager, quickly realizes that the basis for effective budgeting is not only the planning aspect of the budgetary process but also the proper accounting of revenue collected and deposited. Good budgeting must be based on a structure of collections and deposits that further establishes an accounting control mechanism to preclude any monetary mistakes and possible theft or embezzlement.

Such a structure is imperative, since most schools have activity accounts that are based on the collection of funds from school clubs, booster organizations, general fees, and numerous other dollar-generating initiatives.

The School Activity Account

The school activity account is one important area of the budgetary process in which sound financial practice must be exercised. Many administrators will confide that there are two problematic areas that can get a school leader in serious trouble—sex is one, and money is the other—especially when an activity account is involved (Sorenson, 2007). The school activity account is one budgetary consideration that poses the most serious financial complications and implications. For example, the activity account at many schools (high schools in particular) can generate significant income from revenue sources such as fundraisers, vending machines, school pictures, athletic receipts, library and textbook fines, student clubs and organizations, numerous student fees, school store operations, field trip receipts, appropriated district funds, and the list can go on and on.

In most states, thousands of dollars flow through a school's activity account. As a result, administrators have the primary fiscal responsibility of not only managing such a budget but also complying with federal and state laws and district policies and procedures (Brimley et al., 2012). School activity funds must be safeguarded, and prudent verification of all accounts within the activity fund must be monitored and audited for the purpose of ensuring that such monies are appropriately utilized for student benefit.

School administrators must understand the school activity account can quickly become a nightmare if appropriate bookkeeping practices are not in place, followed, and maintained. Funds collected from various school-related activities must be accounted for as money received and spent in relation to the different activity accounts in which said dollars have been allocated. For example, money collected from ticket sales related to the school athletic banquet must be placed in the athletic account; money collected from the sale of school pictures for the purpose of postal services must be placed in the postal account. Now, let's return to bookkeeping practices and the development of an income collection and deposit structure.

Components of the Collection and Deposit Structure

The purpose of any collection and deposit structure is to establish budgetary controls to prevent general accounting mistakes, blatant theft, and/or embezzlement of funds. This structure is composed of several components that identify key personnel who should be bonded prior to collecting, accounting for, and depositing funds. The term *bonded* relates to a legal process known as *surety bonding*, which is frequently defined as a guarantee of performance. In other words, a bonding agency will reimburse a school district for any financial loss related to fraud, theft, or embezzlement that might occur as a result of an individual who has been entrusted with the handling of funds (Brimley et al., 2012). Returning to the components of collection and deposit, a carefully crafted budgetary structure should include and ensure:

Cash Receipts Collections—When generated dollars, typically in small denominations, are brought into the school office by an activity sponsor, at least two bonded individuals should collect, count, and account for the funds. In this manner, the total amount of cash and checks submitted should accurately match the receipts presented and also match the amount listed on the receipt given to the sponsor.

Activity Account Postings—Following the cash receipts collection, the monetary amount should be counted and double counted, again by bonded personnel, and then entered into the bookkeeping system. If the system is electronic, a summary cash receipts report is automatically generated and provides the bookkeeping staff and school leader with a listing of the receipt entries, as designated by date, along with the dollar amount of said receipts and the specified activity account (athletics, school pictures, library fund, for example) into which the collected receipts are to be entered.

Bank Deposit Procedures—Following any account posting, a bank deposit slip must be prepared immediately. Then, a third bonded individual (someone different than the two individuals who are collecting, accounting, and preparing the deposit slip) should be selected to place the funds in a deposit bag and promptly directed to make the bank deposit. Many school districts require that two individuals take any deposits to the bank. Other districts contract the bank depositing process with an armored collection and transport service. While such procedures are not absolutely necessary, each is a wise practice. Proper bank depository procedures help ensure that the amount of money received totals the daily deposit. Furthermore, such procedures reduce the possibility of human error, theft, and/or embezzlement.

Bank Reconciliation Processes—The bank reconciliation process reveals much about the management of a school's budgetary practices. Proper reconciliation of bank statements and records is considered one of the most important fiscal safeguards available to a school leader. Bank reconciliation is nothing more than a check-and-balance system that ensures that the school's bank statement matches the data recorded in the school's financial records. This process, while tedious and time-consuming, provides an opportunity for the school leader to identify differences that may exist between bank records and school records. This process goes beyond the trust factor to a method of verification by providing for a monthly analysis of the school's financial records. School leaders should be cognizant of the possibility that problems associated with the school's bank statement could very well signal financial problems elsewhere—in other school accounts, for example, or with the school's accounting procedures. Mutter and Parker (2004) have noted that "repeated, irreconcilable differences between a bank statement and the school's books may indicate incompetence or fraud" (p. 17). Nothing could come closer to the truth, and every school leader must recognize that such possibilities can and do exist in schools, and, as a result, the administrator, as the budgetary manager, should be ever vigilant. Applicable to today's school budgetary accounting process, and a motto every principal should adopt, is a quote attributed to President Ronald Reagan when speaking about the U.S. relationship with the Soviet Union and intermediate-range nuclear missiles during the 1980s: "Trust but verify" (Reagan, 1987). Exactly! Avoiding any political connection, the authors highly recommend that a principal must "trust but verify" all accounting procedures. Again, this makes good business sense!

Understanding each of the specified components as well as the need for income collection and deposit is an essential element of the budgetary process and one that must be mastered by the school administrator to prevent fiscal problems that could lead to the ending of what may very well have been a successful and most satisfying administrative career.

Timely Payment of Bills

One of the most overlooked aspects of expenditure control is the timely payment of bills. Timely payment of bills can be a source of revenue, as this practice often translates to the collection of a discount. In other words, vendors often offer discounts for early payment. For example, many vendors provide for a 15% discount if the bill is paid within 30 days or a 10% discount if the bill is paid within 60 days. For any school administrator to avoid or ignore the possibility of early payment of bills is to neglect the potential of controlling expenditures and, more important, keeping school money in school pockets. When a vendor discount is earned, that is money saved, and money saved is simply ensuring that there are funds for further allocation to meet other important educational needs.

Some administrators might suggest that the payment of bills accrued by each school is the responsibility of the district's business office and that there is little that can be done beyond the school site. We beg to differ! The effective school administrator must work to ensure that his or her bookkeeping clerk regularly contacts the business office department in charge of payment of bills. This method of reminder can very well encourage business department personnel to speed up the payment process, and, as a result, a discount is collected, an additional expenditure is controlled, and the money saved remains at the school level.

Budget Amendments

Flexibility is an operative term associated with school budgeting. Those administrators who carefully manage and monitor the school budget realize all purposeful planning combined with the best of intentions can go by the wayside when academic goals and objectives change for the betterment of the students served. For example, consider the following scenario.

When amendments or transfers are necessary, the school administrator must move funds from one account to another to correct a previous posting by transferring a portion, if not all, of a balance from one account to another. Again, consider the previous technology-oriented

THE ABOVE-BASIC ALLOTMENT ARRIVES AT BROADWAY SCHOOL

During the second semester of the recent school year at Broadway School, Principal Whitten Van Horn appreciated the fact that additional funds were allocated to the school due to a significant increase in unexpected student enrollment. An "above-basic" allotment of $50,000 was transferred to the school by district administration at the conclusion of the first semester to make up for the financial strain the increased enrollment was imposing on the educational program, most notably in the area of technology. The computer lab had been abandoned last school year, as each student was being provided with his/her own e-tablet. Due to the increased student enrollment, funding for the e-tablets feel short by about 33 students. This equaled to approximately a $16,500 shortfall in necessary funds. Therefore, Dr. Van Horn was ecstatic in recognizing that he and his team could use the "above-basic" allotment to supplement the technology account to purchase the additional e-tablets. Subsequently, he made an amendment or transfer within the school budget, as such was needed to facilitate the incoming new dollars and to further account for the new funds.

scenario and note that an "above-basic" allotment was provided to the school to adjust for the unexpected increase in student enrollment. This allotment was transferred from the district level to the school and placed in the technology, over $10,000 line item account. At the school-site level, the funds were needed for e-tablets for each student. Therefore, an adjustment or amendment had to be submitted, with the funds being transferred to the proper accounts—Technology Equipment/Software. To facilitate the transfer of any funds and to further amend the school budget, administrators utilize either standardized forms or memoranda that have been approved by the school district (see Forms 5.1 and 5.2). These forms, typically completed online, serve as a method of budgetary accountability and provide the necessary documentation, ensuring that the adjustment and/or transfer will occur.

Budget amendments are an essential part of the budgetary process and are utilized in an effort to move funds from one account to another and, at times, to correct an accounting error that has been made. It is recommended that the school leader follow district budget amendment instructions and procedures by making wise decisions with regard to income and expenditure adjustments and transfers and by completing the appropriate paperwork involved in the budget-amendment process. While budget amendments are sometimes necessary, the effective school administrator readily learns that the overuse of the adjustment and transfer process can send questionable signals to and raise serious inquiries from business department personnel, district-level administrators, and even school board members, who in many systems have final approval over budgetary changes.

Budgetary Systems

Chapter 1 outlined the differences between school finance and school budgeting. School finance is often associated with stringent fiscal policies and accountability procedures. School finance, simply put, is the process by which funding to support public schools is raised and distributed (Guthrie et al., 2007). On the other hand, budgeting has been defined by Brimley et al. (2012) as a process that involves planning, allocation, and expenditure of funds, and a continuous monitoring and evaluation of each of the pieces within the process. This working definition correlates effectively with *The Budget Plan* section previously examined in this chapter.

The school budget serves numerous functions, often depending on which system of budget administration a school district uses. The

Form 5.1   Sample Budget Amendment Request (Standardized Form)

STAR Independent School District

Budget Amendment Form

School or Department: Star Middle School

From Account #	Amount	Previous Budget	Current Budget
199-11-6399.00-041-11	$50,000.00	$78,055.00	$28,055.00
To Account #	Amount	Previous Budget	Current Budget
199-11-6636.00-041-11	$50,000.00	$2200.00	$52,200.00
From Account #	Amount	Amount	Current Budget
199-11-6636.00-041-11	$16,500.00	$52,200.00	$35,700.00
To Account #	Amount	Amount	Current Budget
199-11-6693.00-041-11	$16,500.00	$1000.00	$17,500.00

Campus Action Plan Goal/Objective/Activity or Need Addressed

Goal IV: Provide an intensive, technology-centered curriculum that emphasizes the learning and application of technological communicative skills at all grade levels.

Objective 1.6: Explore and implement a technologically oriented instructional program with the utilization of e-tablets to better increase student achievement.

Activity 2.3: Upgrade the technological equipment by abandoning the computer lab and providing each student with a personal e-tablet.

Justification for Budget Amendment

Star Middle School plans to amend a portion of its allocated funds from the Supplies and Materials account and transfer said funds to the Computer Lab account to purchase desktop computers, and to the Furniture and Equipment account to purchase computer stations to better meet the campus need for additional technology equipment as related to the recent increase in student enrollment. Consequences of nonapproval would hinder our ability to increase student achievement in the area of language arts and language development because the current computer hardware and furnishings are inadequate, again due to the significant increase in student enrollment. Implementation would begin immediately during the second semester of the current school year.

_____   _____
Originator   Date Requested

_____   _____
Principal   Date Approved

_____   _____
Director of Budgeting   Date Approved

Form 5.2   Sample Budget Amendment Request (Letterhead Correspondence)

STAR Middle School

"Committed to Excellence"

TO: Director of Budgeting, STAR ISD

FROM: Dr. Whitten Van Horn, Principal

DATE: January 12, _____

SUBJECT: Budget Amendment Request

The following transfer of funds is being requested:

Amount	From Account Number	To Account Number
$50,000	199-11-6399.00-041-11	199-11-6636.00-041-11
$16,000	199-11-6636.00-041-11	199-11-6395.00-041-11

Campus Action Plan Goal/Objective/Activity or Need Addressed

Goal IV: Provide an intensive, technology-centered curriculum that emphasizes the learning and application of technological communicative skills at all grade levels.

Objective 1.6: Explore and implement a technologically-oriented instructional program with the utilization of e-tablets to better increase student achievement.

Activity 2.3: Upgrade the technological equipment by abandoning the computer lab and providing each student with a personal e-tablet.

Budget Amendment Justification

Broadway School plans to amend a portion of its allocated funds from the Supplies and Materials account and transfer said funds to the Technology Equipment/Software more than $5,000 (per unit cost) for extensive classroom technological updates. Additionally, funding from the Technology Equipment/Software more than $5,000 (per unit cost) will be transferred to the Technology Equipment/Software less than $5,000 (per unit cost) account to purchase e-tablets to better meet the campus need for additional technology equipment as related to the recent increase in student enrollment. Consequences of nonapproval would hinder our ability to increase student achievement as well as technologically oriented communication and learning, as the current number of e-tablets is inadequate, again due to the significant increase in student enrollment. Implementation would begin immediately during the second semester of the current school year.

Approved by: _____

Budgeting Director, STAR Independent School District

most common budgetary systems, which are typically prescribed by state education code or local board policy, include function/object budgeting, zero-based budgeting, and school-based budgeting. Each system has particular strengths and weaknesses, but all are intended to serve important functions, including a projection of proposed sources, allocations, and expenditures of funds for the next fiscal year. While budgetary administration and budget systems go hand in hand, it must be noted that each varies from state to state and all must be appropriately administered and evaluated within the confines of standard accounting practices as defined by the National Center for Educational Statistics in the *Financial Accounting for Local and State Systems Handbook* (2009b) and correlated with the Generally Accepted Accounting Principles, as established by the Governmental Accounting Standards Board.

Function/Object Budgeting

This particular administrative system of budgeting is based on a process whereby anticipated expenditures are entered into the budget ledgers through a codified and electronic process. Funds within this administrative system are budgeted according to *function* (instruction or administration or health services, for example) and *object* (supplies and materials or payroll or professional and contracted services, for example). This system is used by many school districts across the nation since it is the required format of most state and federal education agencies (see Table 5.3). The function/object budgetary system also closely aligns with the fiscal education and information management system of each state.

Table 5.3   Function/Object Budgeting and Coding

199 – 11 – 6395.00—041 – Current Year – 30

The *function code* is an accounting entity that identifies the purpose of any school or district transaction.	The *object code* identifies the nature and object of an account or transactions. For example: payroll, supplies and materials, capital outlay.
Function **11** refers to *instruction.* Thus, this particular code represents a transaction that will impact the instructional program of a school or district.	Object **6395** *refers to technology equipment/software under $5000.00 (per unit cost).* This particular object code is found under the main object heading (6300) entitled: *Supplies and Materials.*

The strength of function/object budgeting correlates with the administrative need of schools and districts to exercise the maximum amount of fiscal control over funds, especially when numerous individuals are responsible and accountable for the budgeted dollars. The function/object budgetary system readily provides for quick and easy administration of the school budget and further allows for sensible decision making in relation to the general analysis of cost and benefit factors associated with evaluating specific instructional programs and programmatic expenditures relative to student academic gains and achievement.

A weakness frequently attributed to the function/object budgeting system is the system's strongest point. Function/object budgeting, while providing for analysis and assessment of programs and expenditures, unfortunately lacks specificity as well as depth and detail necessary to aid with the often essential and ongoing analysis that is so critical in mandated evaluations of differing instructional programs.

Zero-Based Budgeting

Following the 1977 U.S. Supreme Court ruling *Serrano v. Priest*, a budgetary system known as zero-based budgeting gained popularity in states such as California, New Mexico, Texas, and others where educational inequities existed in state funding formulas, processes, and procedures (Alexander & Alexander, 2011; Dayton, 2002; LaMorte, 2011). This system of budgeting is based on the most advantageous concept of involving all parties in the budgetary decision-making process, with school administrators and teams carefully analyzing budgeted line items, whether each is currently in place or is being newly proposed. Beginning the budget-development process with zero dollars, the learning community, with administrative guidance, is charged with ranking all budgetary considerations in priority order, then choosing potential alternatives based upon funding allocations and further annually evaluating all programs that are associated with the accompanying budget.

The downside to zero-based budgeting is the significant amount of time, effort, and paperwork associated with the process as well as the fact that there are only so many dollars appropriated by the school district. Many school districts and administrators—often to the dismay of the learning community—decide that this particular budgetary system is too cumbersome and complicated, especially when compared to other budgetary preparation systems.

School-Based Budgeting

School- or site-based budgeting is a system similar in concept to the zero-based budgetary system. It, too, incorporates the idea of involving all parties in the budgeting effort for the betterment of student achievement and school reform. This system of budgeting gained credible recognition during the late 1980s and early 1990s. The system provided the learning community—especially faculty and staff—with serious and legitimate input into the school budgeting process. School-based budgeting has been described as a decentralized system of providing appropriations for all aspects of the school program (Brimley et al., 2012; Guthrie, Springer, Rolle, & Houck, 2007; Wohlstetter & Buffett, 1992). For example, school staff can often impact the final decision as to what areas of the school budget will be funded and for what amount. Such areas can include the instructional program, instructional supplies, technology equipment, textbooks, library books, travel, professional development, and, in some instances, the distribution of school personnel salaries.

One potential benefit of the school- or site-based budgeting system is the ongoing analysis of student needs in relation to teaching resources and budgeted dollars. The effectiveness and efficiency of this system relates to the essential planning and recognition, by all parties, of those educational factors (socioeconomic status or ethnicity, for example) that can impact or influence student achievement (Sorenson & Cortez, 2010). Such a budgetary system is advantageous because it enables the school-site team to exert significant influence not only on the budget development process but also on school policy and programmatic decisions. In addition, this particular system is considered to positively impact the morale and climate of a school, since many individuals within the learning community are actively involved in the decision-making process. Finally, school- or site-based budgeting, much like site-based decision making, can very well serve to increase the academic achievement of students (Baker, Green, & Richards, 2008; Sorenson, Cortez, & Negrete, 2010; Ubben, Hughes, & Norris, 2011; Yukl, 2010). One can only be reminded of a most correlating quote from Guthrie et al. (2007, p. 235): "The dead and heavy hand of centralized, tightly drawn decision making stifles innovation and results in a one-size-fits-all instructional mentality." The authors of this text agree!

Another important consideration associated with the school- or site-based budgeting system relates to an understanding that district administrators must rethink the top-down approach to school budgeting and decision making and assume a more facilitative or collaborative role at the school level in the budget-preparation and decision-making processes (Sorenson, 2008). Typically, district administration continues to determine, monitor, and evaluate allocated dollars associated with maintenance, cafeteria, and transportation services. Responsibility for these areas of educational management often requires additional and more specified expertise that extends beyond that of the instructional leader and site-based team.

The downside to the school- or site-based budgetary system relates to three considerations: (1) The addition of parents and community members in the budgetary decision-making process requires significant training and learning for all constituents involved; (2) equity among differing schools may be endangered, as some schools' budgetary decision-making process reflects greater participation and advocacy of the constituents; and (3) certain budgetary decision-making procedures as related to personnel, for example, can bring potential legal entanglements.

The advantage of any or all of the budgeting systems identified within this chapter relates most importantly to the implementation and utilization of the site-based decision-making model and process and to an understanding that while each budgetary system can be effective, no single system is necessarily better than the other. The bottom line: School systems should never settle for one of the budgetary approaches when a combination of fiscal practices can be incorporated for a more systematic and comprehensive evaluation, on a cost and benefit basis, to best enhance the instructional programs and learning activities offered students at each campus (Herman & Herman, 2001).

Accounting and Auditing Procedures

Proper accounting and auditing procedures have been described by Thompson et al. (2008) as a protective process for school district administrators and personnel. Such an assessment is absolutely correct since the two terms, *accounting* and *auditing*, go hand in hand and serve as the critical elements in best safeguarding individuals and organizations from financial wrongdoing, suspicion, accusation, and even innuendo (Sorenson & Goldsmith, 2006). Auditing serves four functions:

1. Auditing makes good business sense—audit investigations are essential to determining if appropriate and legal expenditure of funds has occurred.

2. Auditing and the accompanying regular investigations provide written documentation to school administrators, superintendents, and board members who must be kept abreast of the financial dealings of the district and schools. Such documentation provides proof to the educational constituency (parents, taxpayers, state and federal governmental agencies) that the fiscal integrity of a school or district is sound, intact, and following the dictates of law.

3. Auditing helps to detect human and technical error in the accounting process. In any school system, large or small, errors will occur, and the audit investigations delineate between accidental and intentional errors.

4. Auditing can be the guiding force that brings about necessary change to accounting procedures and financial operations in need of improvement.

Several types of auditing procedures have been developed to provide a system of checks and balances to an educational organization. The two most common are internal and external auditing.

Internal auditing is a self-checking process that typically provides for monthly reports to the school board. These reports detail the financial status of the school district and, in most instances, reveal expenditures of the differing schools within a district. Internal auditing is generally a continuous examination of a school's and district's accounting system in which a multiple-approval process is incorporated to safeguard against error or fraudulent practices.

External auditing is the formal accounting process by which a school's financial records are examined by a qualified and independent accountant—typically a Certified Public Accountant. External audits are generally ordered on an annual basis, with an accounting firm spending anywhere from 3 to 9 weeks conducting an extensive and exhaustive investigation that checks revenues and expenditures and further compares cash balances against encumbrances. External auditing ensures that all statutory and legal requirements are in good order. External audits provide reports and findings in written and presentation formats, as well as fiscal and accounting recommendations to superintendents and school boards. Audits serve as a measurement of the trust factor in any educational organization by validating the fiscal management (good or bad) of a school system. The auditing process is more than good business, it is money well spent to better ensure the sound fiscal stewardship of a school and school system.

Fraudulent Practices

Fraudulent practice in the education business may not be an everyday occurrence. However, newspaper accounts regularly reveal that dishonest and unethical employees manage to divert thousands of dollars from a school's activity account into the pockets of the unscrupulous embezzler. When school personnel hear district gossip about such capers but realize that these types of dealings are not making the local newspaper or evening newscast, this is usually associated with the fact that school systems do not want to provide unsolicited attention and unsettling fodder for community consumption. However, if you are a school leader of any tenure, you quickly recognize that embezzling can very well happen during your watch. Therefore, the possible advent of such fraudulent actions makes it worthwhile to learn about the subject. School leaders would be well advised to examine the school's recordkeeping and auditing procedures to best negate any tempting prospects and looming loopholes.

Fraudulent practices are closely akin to an individual's ethical decision-making process as revealed in Chapter 2 and Chapter 3. Beckner (2004), for example, examines the topic of responsibility and two relatable considerations: discretion and accountability. Johnson (2009) examines character and integrity. Both note that a school leader must exhibit discretion and accountability by exemplifying levels of honesty, trustworthiness, and responsibility that appropriately and discretely follow school policies and procedures.

Accountability standards, exemplifying the highest levels of ethical conduct, must also be maintained. A perfect example was unfortunately showcased in a school district in which an associate superintendent for business and financial affairs entertained colleagues at a local men's club and subsequently charged lap-dancing expenses, to the tune of $2,000 in a single visit, to the school district's credit card. The expectation for responsible behavior and personal ethical standards quickly went by the wayside. The cost for such a personal indiscretion: the loss of the associate superintendent's professional reputation and the subsequent public humiliation of the individual and his family. The district also suffered both internal turmoil and external criticism. This, in turn, negatively affected the public's confidence in the school district's leadership team and several school board members. Ultimately, the community outcry resulted in numerous administrative resignations, and several school board members who ran for re-election went down in defeat (Osborne, Barbee, & Suydam, 1999). A second example involved the superintendent of an urban southwestern school district. Conspiring to defraud the school district by securing a $450,000 sole-source contract under false pretenses, the superintendent was arrested at his office, handcuffed, and subsequently escorted by FBI agents to a federal courthouse, where he was charged with conspiracy to commit mail fraud and aiding and abetting theft from instructional programs receiving federal funds. Charges called for up to 20 years in a federal prison. The superintendent resigned in disgrace to await federal prosecution and sentencing (KFOX 14 Television, 2011; Schladen & Kappes, 2012).

Embezzlement

Embezzlement has been defined as the fraudulent appropriation of property by an individual to whom it has been entrusted (Office of Management and Budget, 2005; Sorenson & Goldsmith, 2006). The operative term within this definition is *entrusted*. The embezzler is usually a trusted employee who is taking advantage of a school leader's confidence or a school leader's lack of attention to detail. Embezzlers have a method of operation, a thinking process that is frequently thrust upon unsuspecting schools and school systems. Embezzlers often believe they are smarter than the school leader, and they generally perceive themselves as being someone who can outwit a less-than-sterling school business department. Embezzlers are more likely to be:

1. Female (64% of the time);
2. Employed as clerks in a business, finance, budgeting, bookkeeping, or accounting office or department;
3. Acting alone (84% of the time);
4. Well dressed; and
5. Hidden in a single office or cubicle (Worrell, 2011).

Common schemes are typically quite simple to employ because the trusted employee has generally won the confidence of a school leader. In fact, the best embezzlers are often the individuals who are given more authority than a position dictates. These same individuals have also realized that the ability to embezzle is only limited by their own imagination. Most embezzlement at the school level involves the pocketing of cash received through activity fund–related dollars coming into the school office—especially in relation to fundraising programs and efforts.

The theft of cash is quick and easy, and it is often difficult to detect. An act of embezzlement is accomplished by a trusted employee who simply doesn't enter the cash receipt in the accounts-receivable records. A perfect example involves cash received from a school activity or from a club sponsor who is less interested in the details associated with recordkeeping and thus simply trusts the administrative office clerical staff to "count this for me please, I've got to get back to class—my students are taking a test!" To prevent this scenario and the associated monetary temptation, a school principal should insist, if not demand, that all cash received be accompanied by a written receipt of the calculated dollar amount, and a cash receipt must be provided by the "trusted" employee to the club or activity sponsor immediately upon receipt of the cash funds.

Another preventive step is the "spot-check" process instituted by the school leader. This process further assures that cash received is cash recorded. In other words, the school leader needs to purposefully check on a regular basis with differing school activity or club sponsors to determine when funds are coming into the school and, most notably, into the school office. The school leader should also carefully monitor the bookkeeping records, always looking for suspicious signs of fraud and theft. The school leader should also understand that unexpected internal audits by district business office personnel can often prevent employee embezzlement efforts.

Finally, never underestimate the vulnerability of a school or district to an act of embezzlement. An ounce of prevention may very well be the cure for the common scheme. Effective school leaders must recognize the following 10 precautionary practices that can inhibit and discourage embezzlement.

1. Ensure that the individuals who expend monies are not the custodians of accounting for said monies.

2. Review all bank statement reconciliation procedures.

3. Keep two separate and independently maintained sets of bookkeeping records as related to receipts and expenditures.

4. Provide for effective and appropriate reconciliation of receipts and accounts.

5. Never sign blank checks before leaving for a conference or vacation.

6. Develop and utilize bookkeeping policies or regulations.

7. Utilize bonded employees only.

8. Cross-train office personnel to perform bookkeeping responsibilities.

9. Utilize an independent accountant to conduct regular internal and external audits.

10. Review on a regular basis with office staff the detailed expectations for appropriate and ethical office bookkeeping standards and procedures.

Other Risk Factors

While an incident of monetary theft or embezzlement may not be directly tied to the school administrator, a public perception will definitely exist that such a fraudulent practice occurred on the administrators' watch and therefore the administrators share responsibility. Some school leaders take a lax approach to the budgeting process by delegating all or part of the budget process and accompanying tasks to others or simply deciding "instruction is my bag" and, as a result, either neglecting or ignoring important budget details. Such thinking or action can very well be considered a costly risk factor, if not an ultimate criminal mistake.

Hughes and colleagues (2009) examined a Center for Creative Leadership report that studied the topic of career derailment; in other words, how leaders fall short of the personal success predicted earlier in their careers. Three different but quite compelling causes of career derailment quickly came to light when examined in relation to fraudulent practices at school: (1) failure to constructively face an obvious problem, issue, or circumstance; (2) mismanagement; and (3) inability to select trustworthy subordinates. Reflect upon the three noted causes for career derailment, and then consider three interesting questions related to the risk factor of monetary theft or embezzlement: (1) Do you perceive the fraudulent problem as being the result of the leader's actions or inactions? (2) Do you perceive the leader was aware of the consequences of his or her actions or inactions? (3) Which of the three causes do you perceive would most likely lead to the career derailment of an educational leader from the perspective of a fraudulent practice at school?

Appropriate auditing and accounting procedures, while never completely foolproof in eliminating the potential for fraud and embezzlement, do serve to assure the educational clientele of the fiscal state of a school and district, and such procedures further discourage unethical practices. Effective school leaders understand that any misuse or misappropriation of school funds can quickly destroy the public trust. Most important, the effective school leader acknowledges that any and all unethical and fraudulent activities can very well derail, if not promptly conclude, a career that was once perceived to be most promising and long lasting.

The Leadership Role: Ethical and Moral Behaviors

Research conducted by O'Donnell and Sorenson (2005) revealed educational leaders face numerous dilemmas of differing dimensions on a regular basis. The best of leaders recognize these dilemmas as opportunities for doing what is right, not necessarily what is expedient. School leaders have an obligation to set ethical and moral examples for the organizations they serve. Those leaders who do not honor integrity, those who fail to establish truth and who further negate moral reasoning, are the same leaders who fail to inspire honesty and ethical practice in others. Such inappropriate behaviors in the education business lead to moral abandonment, pure selfishness, and the ultimate in career derailment.

Several years ago, a Harris poll reported that 89% of workers and leaders surveyed believed it was important for leaders to be upright, honest, and ethical in their behaviors. However, only 41% indicated their current leader had such characteristics (Vamos & Jackson, 1989). Such an indictment serves to underscore the need for strong character and ethical behavior in the school leadership business. Followers place their trust in a leader who models integrity, and when leaders compromise their moral and ethical values, they risk losing the respect they so readily deserve (Nelson & Toler, 2002). Recently, in a school district in an urban center in the United States Southwest, four ethically and morally oriented misbehaviors on the part of a district leader allowed for a culture of corruption, manipulation, arrogance, and rule (policy) exemptions. The four behaviors were: (1) inappropriate sexual conduct, (2) fiscal mismanagement, (3) forged documentation, and (4) data manipulation. The interim superintendent of the district noted that the days of playing fast and loose were over!

What is known about ethics is striking: "Ethics has to do with what leaders do and who leaders are" (Northouse, 2013, p. 378). "Fast and loose" behaviors frequently lead to devastating professional and personal consequences. While the daily pressures of life and career are often overwhelming, the effective school leader must remain an individual of committed character, integrity, and personal ethics. Leaders can ill afford to ignore strong moral and ethical margins, because the aforementioned stresses can compromise the decision-making processes. When such occurs, a leader's character is terribly strained, revealing flaws, cracks, and defects that in turn allow a leader to be susceptible to deception (lying and cheating), inappropriate behaviors (sexual affairs), questionable or illegal actions (embezzlement), and a general lack of personal accountability (Goldsmith & Sorenson, 2005; Nelson & Toler, 2002; Sorenson, 2007). See the end-of-chapter case study application *Sex, Money, and a Tangled Web Woven* (pp. 147–149) for a real-life account. Remember, truth is stranger than fiction!

Professional behavior, personal integrity, and appropriate ethical conduct must be the defining qualities of any leader. Nothing less will do. If trust and integrity serve as the paramount bond between school administration and faculty, what guidelines or principles should serve as the focal point to better ensure ethical conduct and moral leadership? Here are five targeted areas for serious leadership consideration.

1. *Show Respect*—True leaders earn respect by showing respect for others. When leaders fail to respect followers, they fail to understand the main goal of leadership, which is leading. This may seem quaint, but effective leaders epitomize affirmation, listening, esteem, care, and concern—all inherently related to respect. Respect has been described by Northouse (2013) as granting credibility to the ideas of others and treating others in a way that makes them feel valued and competent.

2. *Demonstrate Integrity*—Whatever qualities, skills, or talents a leader may possess, lacking integrity is an absolute flaw. Yukl (2010) advances the theory that leaders who demonstrate high levels of integrity are more credible, more open, more collaborative, more receptive to receiving bad news or negative feedback, and are less likely to be consumed with impressing their superiors at the expense of others.

3. *Exhibit Honesty*—Honesty is best defined in relation to what it is not, what an effective leader cannot be: deceitful, untrustworthy, and fraudulent. The leader who exhibits honesty reveals a genuine honorableness in character and action.

4. *Resist Temptations*—The moral and ethical strength of any school leader is often tested by the many temptations in life. Resistance is often accompanied by endurance. When a leader is close to temptation, a loss of perspective has occurred. Resisting temptation serves to make a school leader more respected, honest, and endearing to others who furthermore perceive the leader to be an individual who possesses the highest level of integrity.

5. *Provide Service*—The effective school leader is one who is involved in servant leadership. The servant leader is one who is willing to empathize and understand by listening, by observing, and by assisting others within the learning community (Greenleaf, 2002). Servant leadership provides for a level of tolerance by recognizing the strengths and talents of others when their weaknesses and mistakes may be more than obvious (DePree, 2003). Servant leadership can help others overcome their own weaknesses and mistakes by targeting those areas for personal and professional growth while at the same time emphasizing their not-so-apparent strengths and talents. In turn, followers are more likely to be just as tolerant of a leader when mistakes are made and when weaknesses are exhibited (Beckner, 2004; Shapiro & Stefkovich, 2011).

Now, some serious advice for the educational leader: The best of school leaders always make appropriate decisions by upholding legal, moral, and ethical behaviors, even in an era in which a general cynicism exists regarding the integrity of individuals in leadership positions, especially those leaders who actually espouse personal ethics and moral values. All school leaders would be wise to consider and remember the following adage, as no words of advice could ring truer:

> *It's important that people know what you stand for. It's equally important that they know what you won't stand for.*
>
> —Mary Waldrop

Final Thoughts

The budget development process, with its numerous components, is a legal mandate in most states. Effective and efficient budgeting practices are dependent upon skillful school leaders who know more than budgetary management. School leaders must not only understand fiscal accountability and control, they must also be aware of collection and deposit structures, budgetary systems, and accounting and auditing procedures. Moreover, school leaders must realize how the visionary component of school-based planning integrates with the budget development process and how each collaboratively functions to build a stronger academic program that, in turn, positively impacts student achievement.

The budget development process is more than implementing and utilizing effective and efficient fiscal practices. The budget development process is an integral part of visioning and planning from which all members of the learning community have a voice, a stake, and a right to impact the academic success of students. Many years ago, long before the concept of school-based budgeting gained popular acceptance in schools, Roe (1961) revealed that the school budget is the translating of "educational needs into a financial plan which is interpreted to the public in such a way that when formally adopted it expresses the kind of educational program the community is willing to support, financially and morally, for a one-year period" (p. 81). Such sentiment couldn't be expressed any better half a century later, except to say: Unlike J. Paul Getty, as noted in the introductory quote, it is hoped that educational leaders find allocating money to support academic goals and student achievement to be a considerable pleasure!

Discussion Questions

1. What is the purpose of a budget plan and how does it interact in relation to the school action or improvement plan?

2. Identify at least two sources of income that a school leader and team can generate; discuss the pros and cons of each; and further explain how these sources relate to the visioning and planning aspects of the school budgeting process.

3. Which of the components of the collection and deposit structure are essential to the budgetary handling of the school activity account? Support your answer.

4. Consider the purposes of accounting procedures and explain how such practices can assist schools in their quest of accounting for the expenditure of public funds.

5. Which budgetary system has your school or district adopted? Discuss how this particular system further commits your school or district to the site-based decision-making and management approach.

6. What precautions should a school leader take with regard to the possibility of embezzlement? In what ways is your

school vulnerable to this budgetary risk factor and how would you as a school leader address the identified vulnerabilities?

7. Fraudulent practices have been described as being "closely akin to an individual's ethical decision-making process." How does ISLLC Standard 5, identified in Chapter 2, support this statement?

8. You have recently been named a new school leader. Outline your responsibilities as related to effective and efficient budgetary practices, and further explain how the learning community (faculty, students, parents, external patrons, etc.) should be involved in the development of the school budget.

Case Study Application: Sex, Money, and a Tangled Web Woven

Dr. Edgar Buchannen was principal at Fullerton Peak High School in the suburban community of Gibsonville. He had been in this position of instructional leadership for nearly 5 years. Previously, he had experienced a very successful principalship at Woodson Middle School in a major metropolitan area just north of the state capital. Dr. Buchannen had worked diligently with his new faculty to raise student academic achievement from low performing to a significantly higher state department standard of accountability. Such a task had not been easy, but Dr. Buchannen was convinced that he and his team—along with the students at Fullerton Peak High—had jumped a most difficult hurdle.

In the interim, Dr. Buchannen had developed a great working relationship with Lisa Nicoles, the school's bookkeeping and attendance clerk. The two had "clicked" from their first day together, and they really appreciated each other's work ethic. One Saturday morning, Eddie—as he had asked Lisa to call him—came in early to catch up on some budgeting issues while Lisa was completing the student demographic information needed for the next scheduled round of statewide testing. Both were pleased to see one another working on the important tasks at hand, and soon they took a break to enjoy a morning doughnut and cup of coffee. Lisa complained of a neck ache from working all morning to enter the demographic data into the computer system, and Eddie quickly offered to massage her neck. Lisa did not object or complain.

Well, you've heard the story before—all too common in our business—and we need not go any further other than to reveal that such an act quickly led to serious complications. Over the next few months, a steamy affair developed, although the two tried to keep any suggestion of impropriety away from the office.

Unfortunately, Lisa's marriage was falling apart, and although Eddie was married with three children of his own, the two carried on their secret romance. With Lisa's failing marriage, she had developed—along with her husband, who had a serious gambling problem—credit card debts to the tune of $125,000. She was in deep trouble, since these financial complications were in her name, and the collectors were demanding payment or repossession of tangible assets. What she needed was cash, and she needed it fast. While the romance grew, so did a little problem that Lisa had at work—she was regularly taking money from the school's differing activity accounts such as athletics, drama, band, choir, and even the "cola wagon," which took in hundreds of dollars at the varsity football game each Friday night.

Dr. Edgar Buchannen had no idea of these embezzlement efforts until one evening when Lisa broke down in tears and told him that he needed to help her get out of this financial predicament. He grew furious and stated: "Help you! Wait a minute, aren't you the one stealing from the district? Don't involve me in your petty theft crimes!" Lisa, with a steely-eyed stare, retorted: "Don't play games with me, Mr. Self-Righteous. You're the one cheating on your wife, you two-faced fraud. You help me or else!"

Thus began a criminal partnership conceived in a mutual distrust of one another and based on some very questionable ethical and moral standards. From that point forward, a dangerous game of "borrowing" money, with every intention of paying back the stolen funds, escalated to a point of no return. The "borrowed" dollars never found their way back into the accounts, and the cover-up only lasted until someone in the district business office caught on to a scheme built on lies, deceit, misjudgment, and unethical practices.

Application Questions

1. What probable repercussions will Dr. Edgar Buchannen and Lisa Nicoles face as a result of their actions? Explain the risk factors associated with their behaviors.

2. Cooper (1998) examines two approaches to maintaining responsible conduct in organizations: internal and external controls. External control has been described as responding to an unethical situation by developing new rules or rearranging the organizational structure or establishing more cautious monitoring procedures. Internal control is often described as increasing preservice and inservice training programs or placing ethical leadership discussions on local meeting agendas. Which of these two policy perspectives would best be associated with this case study and why?

3. What legal implications are at issue in this case study? Which laws, education codes, or board policies have been broken or infringed upon? Give specific examples and explanations.

4. From the perspective of a school leader, how could the act of embezzlement presented in this case study have been prevented? Identify specific precautionary practices you would incorporate.

5. Northouse (2013) defines ethics as a "system of rules or principles that guide us in making decisions about what is 'right or wrong' and 'good or bad' in a particular situation." He further stipulates that ethics provide "a basis for understanding what it means to be a morally decent human being" (p. 424). Is Dr. Buchannen a morally decent human being? Support your answer.

6. What is the possible impact of such actions, as described in the case study, in relation to the school district? Support your response from both a budgetary and political perspective.

Chapter 6

Building the School Budget

All of us are smarter than any one of us!

—Japanese Proverb attributed to W. Edwards
Deming, *Out of Crisis* (2000, p. 114)

Site-Based Decision Making

Norton (2005) relates that leaders of the 21st century must be expected to be knowledgeable of how to work within the political functions of organizations and, moreover, highly skilled in operating in arenas of competition, conflict, problem solving, and decision making. Such thinking exemplifies the parameters by which school leaders utilize differing strategies for working with the learning community and readily correlate with the collaborative statement attributed to W. Edwards Deming in the introductory quote. Deming identified personnel as the key to program quality. He believed working collaboratively with employees to help them perform better, making decisions and solving problems as a team, and placing importance on the gathering of data were the essential keys to organizational and individual improvement (Razik & Swanson, 2010).

One of the most effective strategies to be incorporated by a school leader is the site-based decision-making (SBDM) process, as this approach to school leadership is superior to the autocratic process (followers do not play a role in defining the problem or in generating a solution or decision), exceeds the consultative process (followers are consulted but the leader makes the decision), yet is reflective of the group process (followers in collaboration with the leader reach a consensus relative to a solution to the dilemma or decision presented). What we do know about decision making relates to the concept that a high-quality decision has a direct and measurable impact on an organization (Hoy & Miskel, 2012). When the SBDM process is properly implemented, there is a total quality component to a decision—generally one in which the decision made has improved services to the clientele—the students, parents, faculty and staff, and the overall learning community. Visioning, planning, developing, implementing, and continuously evaluating a school budget must be an extension of the leader–follower collaborative decision-making dimension. Recall the words of Edward L. Bernays: "I must follow the people. Am I not their leader?" (*Columbia*, 1996). He might have added: "I must lead the people. Am I not their servant?"

During the 1980s, public schools began to shift to a business-purpose approach, incorporating business principles into program planning, daily operations, and an overall reform movement in response to concerns about the quality of education in America (Webb, 2006). This paradigm shift, as applied to school fiscal matters, was associated with the decentralization of district budgets. During the late 1980s and early 1990s, W. Edwards Deming's "total quality" principles were infused into the mainstream of public school reform efforts. The term *quality*, like integrity, fairness, and ethics—as discussed in Chapter 2—was then, and often continues to be, difficult to define, although everyone claims to know quality when they see it. John M. Loh states that the definition of quality is quite simple: "It is a leadership philosophy which creates throughout the entire enterprise a working environment which inspires trust, teamwork, and the quest for continuous, measurable improvement" (*Columbia*, 1996). While Loh's definition serves as a start for understanding the school budgeting process, a more practical and working definition of quality might be identified as a continuous process that is achieved through a change in organizational culture. In other words, a school leader must ensure that the budgeting process, in collaboration with site-based decision making, is never ending (continuous) by transforming the shared norms, values, or beliefs (culture) of a school into one in which the leader becomes a facilitator and the followers become active participants. Therefore, the school leader, for the betterment of the organization, must place emphasis on total quality through the empowerment of others by utilizing participative decision making, by articulating a vision, and by involving many in the planning and development stages of a school budget. Hence, "all of us are smarter than any one of us." This change process is one that makes the work of schools more intrinsically motivating and, thus, more appealing, rather than one of a controlling nature in which the members of the learning community are extrinsically motivated as a result of a top-down attitude and approach (Hughes et al., 2009).

Why Site-Based Decision Making?

The site-based decision-making process is crucial to building an effective school budget. First, all actions regarding the budgetary process are considered, assessed, evaluated, and approved in a public forum with all stakeholders involved. Site-based decision making is essential in an era of intense scrutiny, transparency, accountability, and fiscal conservatism. Effective school leaders welcome the opportunity to showcase the sensitive subject of public fund expenditures and the overall school budget in an open forum. Second, when utilizing site-based decision making, the budgetary process is "above board" or "transparent." In other words, there are no hidden funds or secret accounts. Third, all stakeholders are involved, and thus private and personal agendas meet with little merit and have a tendency to go by the wayside. Fourth, current research reveals that decentralizing four key resources (power, information, knowledge, and rewards) will enhance organizational effectiveness and productivity (Hadderman, 2002). Hadderman further stipulates,

> highly involved schools need real power over the budget to decide how and where to allocate resources; they need fiscal and performance data for making informed decisions about the budget; their staff needs professional development and training to participate in the budget process; and the school must have control over compensation to reward performance. (p. 27)

Finally, and perhaps most importantly, budgetary decisions must be made on a "student-first" basis. For these reasons alone, it only makes sense to incorporate the site-based decision-making model into the budget development process.

Who Builds the School Budget?

The authors of this text strongly support the idea of all stakeholders being actively involved in the development of a school budget. This requires a collaborative process involving the school leader doing more than calling a group of representatives together for the purpose of reviewing the already completed school budget. Appropriate training, supervision, guidance, and direction—in a most confident, energetic, intelligent, creative, tolerant, adjustable, dependable, and social manner—must be the leadership norm in a systematic budget development process. Note the words of Alex Cornell: "The real world is a messy place—yet, even a messy place should be attacked systematically" (*Columbia*, 1996). Building a school budget must involve all parties who, working collaboratively, develop the budget from a more specific, systematic, and decision-making perspective.

Recall from Chapter 4 and Chapter 5 that the academic action or improvement plan is useless unless it is directly integrated with the budget plan. Working collaboratively with the school leader, representatives of the learning community begin determining the educational needs of an organization in relation to the allocated funds. Sound budgeting theory dictates the involvement of all stakeholders serving in a representative capacity. Unfortunately, the active participation of members of the learning community in the budgetary process has been given significant lip service by far too many school leaders when, in fact, such collaboration is often minimal in practice. Considering this assessment, examine which stakeholders should be involved in the budget development process and further identify their respective roles and responsibilities.

The School Leader

The school leader at the site level is the most important individual in the budgeting process. School leaders today can be described as having considerably more years of teaching experience prior to assuming their first administrative position (NAESP, 2008) and are increasingly female at both the elementary and secondary levels— making up to 20% of high school principals, compared with 12% in 1988 and 7% in 1978 (NASSP, 2001). Administrators of color continue to be underrepresented in our public schools, with only 2.6% Black and less than 1% Hispanic (Banks, 2000; Matthews & Crow, 2010).

Today, school leaders view their role as being hurried, overburdened, and frustrating with more responsibility, less authority, and increasing stress (Sergiovanni, Kelleher, McCarthy, & Fowler, 2009). Specifically, principals today are leaders in the middle, caught between high expectations, constant pressures, managing a daily barrage of administrative and instructional demands, and handling unremitting stressors.

What is needed in terms of school leadership reform is a distributed leadership model as described by Elmore (2002), as well as The Change Leadership Group at the Harvard School of Education (2006). This model closely correlates with the SBDM process in which leadership does not reside in specific roles or with specific persons but in the relationships that develop between the differing individuals in social, cultural, and instructional roles and responsibilities. In other words, leadership at the school level must be collaborative, participative, and shared. Keeping these descriptors in mind, the school leader, as well as the campus team, plays a very important role in the budgeting process. Delving deeper into the differing roles and responsibilities as related to the development of the school budget is now required.

School-Site Administrators

Differing administrators, with differing titles and responsibilities—principal, assistant principal, site specialist, campus facilitator, or coach—often make budgetary decisions. These individuals may very well serve as the school's budget manager. As previously noted within this chapter, budgetary decision making can occur as follows:

1. By autocratic method and manner ("My way or the highway!")

2. By involving a select group of individuals (those who understand best!)

3. By working in collaboration with a site-based decision-making team (again, "all of us are smarter than any one of us!")

The latter is the best approach to building a school budget because those who have worked collaboratively in developing an academic action or improvement plan must be responsible, along with the school leader, for determining the budgetary needs of the organization. In this process, the school leader or designated leader provides the SBDM group with the necessary forms and figures indicating previous and current year budget allotments and expenditures. Budget histories are very useful in providing fiscal information to all stakeholders. This information is essential in understanding how budgetary allotments and expenditures influence and impact student achievement over time.

Next, the school leader must seek teacher and staff input by asking for the submission of inventory requests for specific supplies, materials, and other educational needs that are essential to the establishment of an exceptional instructional program. Faculty and staff who have been accustomed to an autocratic approach to the school budgeting process may not initially be thrilled about this new approach to building the school budget because it may seem to be a waste of valuable time, since their ideas and suggestions have never been sought or implemented before. However, with the passage of time and with proper guidance, the team will begin to realize that the process is worthwhile, that their input is actually being sought, valued, and utilized to determine what expenditures are important in providing the best possible learning environment. Moreover, the team soon learns the school leader is genuinely interested in their ideas and input.

Interestingly, as time goes by, the school leader realizes the faculty and staff are in many respects the best persons to evaluate optimal considerations for the teaching and learning process. Again, with proper training, guidance, and leadership, budgeting team "buy-in" comes quite easily. The days when the budgeting process was described as too complex or a time when a chosen few were the only ones able to develop a budget or the "tight-ship" era when authoritarian rule was the norm must be over. A new era of collaborative decision making and participative leadership and teamwork becomes boldly institutionalized within an organization's culture.

Finally, once the necessary input has been collected, a budget meeting is scheduled, and the process of bringing recommendations for budgetary expenditures begins in earnest. Building a school budget, from a school leader's perspective, is a step-by-step process that ultimately culminates in a document that has been developed in collaboration with representatives of the learning community. This document, when properly prepared, contains more than just the budgeted dollars. It is a document that allocates funds for the best instructional methods and programs that further ensure the academic success of all students.

Other Committee Members

Question: What is the one question often posed by school leaders in relation to the budgetary process? Answer: Which individuals should serve as stakeholders on the budget development team? Such a determination varies from school to school. Some states and school districts define the parameters of the site-based decision-making process and the stakeholders who will serve on the budget development team. For the sake of further discussion, the site-based decision-making/budget development team membership is defined as those individuals (elected and/or appointed and voting and/or nonvoting members) who are representative of the learning community. Such contributing members could be teachers representing grade levels or departments, as well as band, choir, orchestra, drama, and athletic directors, paraprofessionals, custodians, parent–teacher organization representatives, parents, military liaisons, community members (chief of police, for example), school administrators, central office administrators (directors of curriculum, special education, bilingual education, gifted and talented education, maintenance and transportation, and business operations, for example) as well as comptrollers or business managers, and even the superintendent of schools. The key to identifying committee members is inclusive representation of the learning community. A closer examination of the differing members and their roles is required.

School-Site Directors

Band, choir, orchestra, and drama directors should be automatically represented on the budget development team, since these individuals often serve as budget managers with responsibilities related to instruction, extracurricular issues, purchasing musical instruments and materials, uniforms, costumes, and the cost of transportation. The building-level athletic director can very well serve on the team to help coordinate expenditures related to the athletic program and to further supervise costs associated with transportation, coaches' salaries and stipends, officials, uniforms, ticket-takers, police, ambulance, doctors, and meal and lodging expenses (Herman & Herman, 2001).

Teachers and Grade-Level or Department Chairs

Teachers and other certified personnel should be an integral part of the school committee because these individuals know and understand the students and the instructional programs, and they are the professionals who most affect a school's culture and climate, which directly impacts students' ability to excel and achieve. Grade-level or department chairs are generally the most informed and best prepared to lead the instructional program, and thus, their areas of expertise qualify them to effectively make budgetary decisions.

Central Office Administrators

Administrators may be required at times to serve on the school committee when their particular area of expertise and advice is needed. Central Office administrators are generally nonvoting members who can provide helpful advice when certain topics outside the committee's level of expertise are being discussed and examined.

Students

Often overlooked, students (typically Grades 6 and above) can provide legitimate advice and consideration as related to the budgetary process. Who knows better what is most relevant, timely, and workable in relation to student issues and, in some instances, programmatic considerations?

Community Members

Community members often provide the insight that only an "outsider" can visualize. Many times, school administrators and faculty are myopic when it comes to school and programmatic issues. Sometimes, whether educators like it or not, the "outsiders"—the community members—can present a long-overlooked or often ignored perspective that, when addressed, can have a positive and long-lasting impact on school reform, improvement, and most important, student achievement.

School Budget Applications

Ovsiew and Castetter (1960), in their classic text *Budgeting for Better Schools,* suggest there are several integrating aspects of a school budget that ensure better budgets for better schools. Their book—while more than half a century old—may be dated; however, their message is not. Examine the budgetary components and applications essential to building an effective school-based budget. By following this prescribed and step-by-step process, the school leader can experience a sense of security that the proposed budget will meet with appropriate recognition and approval at the district-level budget hearing and defense session.

Descriptive Narrative—A detailed description of the school (years of operation, location, demographic information such as percentage of free and reduced-price lunch population, federal program eligibilities and identifiers, and other important descriptors such as socioeconomic backgrounds and poverty status of the student population) identifies in narrative form the areas of budgetary need and consideration.

Programmatic Identifiers—Identifiers relating the grades of the school, total students enrolled, ethnic distribution, and other programmatic considerations (special education, gifted and talented, bilingual education, vocational education, etc.) along with the number of faculty employed—teachers, counselors, nurses, administrators, librarians, paraprofessionals, clerks, secretaries, and so on—are detailed in this narrative.

Mission Statement—A statement of introduction as related to the school's goal or philosophy about the nature of learners, learning, and the purpose of the school serves to explain the rationale of the organization and how it impacts the decision-making and budgetary process.

Student Enrollment Projections—A chart or table utilizing the Cohort Survival Method (see *Projecting Student Enrollment* in this chapter) is used to project student populations critical to any school budget as future student enrollment increases or decreases. Increases or decreases in student enrollment are indicative of the funding necessities essential for a school's success. Many school districts, especially in urban areas, will project student enrollment as much as 30 years. The reason: districts must know the locations of potential population growth patterns to purchase land for the building of future schools or to make decisions regarding school closures.

Analysis of Academic Action or Improvement Plan—When analyzing the academic action or improvement plan of a school, consider the following questions:

1. What aspects of the instructional program need improvement?

2. What pertinent sources of data verify any areas of improvement?

3. Which of the concerns, problems, or needs are most significant for improving the overall instructional program?

4. Which of the proposed improvement efforts are within the school's budgetary scope and capability for effective action and implementation?

5. Which of the concerns, problems, or needs are of the highest priority, and is there a sound research base for addressing each prioritized concern, problem, or need?

Additionally, numerous states identify components to be addressed in campus action or improvement plans. For example, as previously identified in Chapter 5, the state of Texas has 13 essential campus action or improvement plan components as stipulated by law (TEC §11.252 and §11.253—Texas Education Agency, 2012c):

1. Student performance
2. Special education
3. Violence prevention
4. Parental involvement
5. Staff development
6. Suicide prevention
7. Conflict resolution
8. Dyslexia treatment programs
9. Dropout reduction
10. Technology
11. Discipline management
12. Accelerated instruction
13. Career education

A careful analysis of a campus action or improvement plan should reflect the inclusion of these and/or other important components as identified by a state or school district. Such components are essential to a campus action or improvement plan serving as the vehicle that drives the direction of a school's instructional program, positively impacting student academic achievement.

Needs Assessment—A needs assessment serves to identify what areas or aspects of the school program need improvement after a review of all pertinent sources of data (e.g., academic action plan, previous studies, local and statewide test results, and surveys of teachers, students, and parents). In addition, a review of the research literature, along with collaborative team discussions regarding each area of instructional and/or programmatic concerns, is particularly useful and beneficial.

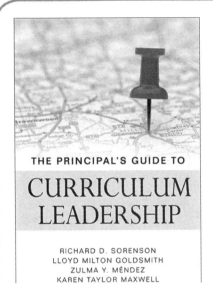

The Principal's Guide to Curriculum Leadership (2011) is an excellent source and reliable desk reference for the practicing or prospective school leader. Chapter 3, pages 54–83, of this text provides a step-by-step, expectation-oriented guide to the identification of a site-based team, vision development, quality analysis, needs assessment, and the needs prioritization process, as well as instructional enhancements and a "how-to" approach to conflict polarization.

THE PRINCIPAL'S GUIDE TO

CURRICULUM LEADERSHIP

RICHARD D. SORENSON
LLOYD MILTON GOLDSMITH
ZULMA Y. MÉNDEZ
KAREN TAYLOR MAXWELL

Priority Analysis—A priority analysis immediately follows a needs assessment. Principal and team interacting collaboratively determine the campus instructional and student-centered priorities and then ordinate the priorities. In other words, list in order what is the most important need, followed by the second most, then third most, and so forth. The funding of needs must be in priority order. Listed below are several examples of identified priorities from a needs assessment recently conducted at a public school in an urban center located in the southwestern United States:

• Staff development will be initiated with all faculty, with a concentration in research-based strategies proven to be effective in assisting English language learners (ELLs) to acquire the language and skills needed to be successful in all content areas. Forms of assessment must be empirically researched and utilized to monitor the progress of this particular subgroup in order to best determine if the implementation of instructional strategies is effective relative to increasing student test scores and improving academic achievement. This training will be conducted and facilitated by the Hispanic Educational Learning Program (HELP) initiative.

• Staff development will be initiated with all faculty, with a concentration in research-based strategies proven to be effective in assisting and motivating male Hispanic students to best experience academic success in the classroom in all core areas. Teachers must be provided additional training regarding the analysis of student data to determine the academic progress of this subgroup. Consultants from the Southwestern Regional Research Laboratory (SWRL) will conduct this training.

• To increase special education (SPED) test scores to 80% > and English language learners' (ELLs) test scores to 90% > in mathematics, seventh- and eighth-grade mathematics teachers will continue to utilize the "Closing the Gap" academic initiative to best provide SPED and ELL students with academic achievement-oriented instruction. Teachers will also utilize district-determined best teaching and learning practices and strategies during classroom instruction to target programmatic objectives in which SPED and ELL students are at risk of failing.

• To further increase SPED and ELL student test scores and to improve the teaching and learning of students in these subgroups, teachers will incorporate differentiated instructional techniques utilizing the research-based EdScope-At-Risk Student Analysis program, to be purchased by the school.

• Student attendance rates, most notably of ELL students, must be increased by implementing the empirically, research-based, and more efficient student attendance monitoring system (StudentTrak) to be purchased by the school. Research reveals that this particular tracking system of student attendance provides for a more efficient collaboration with parents and guardians, community members, assistant principals, attendance clerks, teachers, and counselors.

Teacher/Student Distribution Table—Table 6.1 indicates the distribution of students by grade level or subject area (secondary schools) in relation to the number of staff dedicated to serving students from a programmatic consideration (e.g., bilingual classrooms, inclusion-monolingual classrooms, and monolingual-only classrooms). This table provides a visual understanding of why and how an increase or decrease in student enrollment impacts the budgetary allotment for teacher salaries, paraprofessional assistance, and program development.

Faculty Apportionment Table—This table (see Table 6.2) reveals the apportionment or distribution of the entire faculty in relation to the number of assigned personnel to a school. This table allows the school leader and team, as well as central office and business department administrators, to visualize areas of need in relation to the student enrollment projections.

Table 6.1   Teacher/Student Distribution Table

	Bilingual		Inclusion-Monolingual		Monolingual Only	
Pre-K	15 t & ta		15 t & ta			
Grade K	22 t	5 + 10 t & ta	21 t	22 t	22 t	22 t
Grade 1	21 t	5 + 10 t & ta	22 t	22 t	20 t	21 t
Grade 2	20 t	5 + 10 t & ta	21 t	22 t	22 t	
Grade 3	22 t	5 + 10 t & ta	22 t	22 t	20 t	21 t
Grade 4	20 t	4 + 10 t & ta	22 t	21 t	22 t	
Grade 5	28 t	5 + 15 t & ta	31 t	35 t	33 t	32 t
Spec Ed			43 2 t & 5 ta			
# Students	148	29 + 65	197	144	139	96
# Staff	7 t 1 ta	6 t 6 ta	9 t 6 ta	6 t	6 t	4 t

NOTE: t = teacher; ta = teacher aide or assistant

Table 6.2   Faculty Apportionment Table

Position	No. Assigned to Campus
Principal	1
Assistant principal	1
School secretary	1
FEIMS clerk	1
Instructional facilitator	1
Counselor	1
Nurse	1
Nurse assistant	1
Librarian	1
Total faculty	**9**

Position	No. Assigned to Campus
G/T teacher	½
Speech therapist	½
PE teacher	1
Music teacher	1
Office aides	2
Title VI aides	1
Custodians	4
Food services	5
Total faculty	**15**

Above Basic Personnel Request and Justification—The Above Basic Personnel Request narrative is a necessary component of the budgetary process, as this particular section of the school budget justifies the need for increased faculty and staff. Furthermore, this narrative seeks those critical funds for additional personnel that may be above the basic school allotment.

Allocation Statement—The allocation statement serves to provide in tabular form (see Table 6.3) a brief but descriptive distribution of funds. Within this statement, the total student population count is noted along with the average daily attendance (ADA) or average daily membership (ADM) rate. In addition, the statement identifies the ADA or ADM funding on a per-pupil basis along with the special education, gifted and talented, bilingual/ESL, Title I, and state compensatory funding allocations. Finally, a total allocation is listed. This total allocation is the basis for building the school budget.

Table 6.3   Allocation Statement

		State Allocation			Campus Allotment
Student Population	=	818			
Average Daily Attendance	=	90%	818 × 0.90	=	736.2 = 736
ADA Funding	=	736	× $2,537.00	=	$1,867,323.00
Special Education	=	72	× $7,125.00	=	$513,000.00
Gifted and Talented	=	45	× $285.00	=	$12,825.00
Bilingual/ESL	=	148	× $237.50	=	$35,150.00
Title I (82%)	=	671	× $262.50	=	$176,137.00
State Compensatory	=	671	× $475.00	=	$318,725.00
Total Allocation				=	**$2,803,837.00**

Salaries for Personnel Table—This section of the school budget details in tabular form (see Table 6.4) the exact identification and distribution of salaries for personnel.

Table 6.4   Salaries for Personnel

Personnel Salaries		
Teachers, nurse, librarian	=	$47,500
Principal	=	$101,000
Assistant principal	=	$87,000
Counselor	=	$55,000
Diagnostician	=	$57,000
Instructional facilitator	=	$60,000
Speech therapist	=	$52,000
Testing coordinator	=	$49,000
Security officer	=	$41,000
Secretary	=	$35,000
Instructional/clerical aides	=	$31,000
Nurse assistant	=	$31,000
Custodian (head)	=	$37,000

(Continued)

Table 6.4   (Continued)

Personnel Salaries

Custodian	=	$30,000
Food services	=	$12,100
Consultant(s)	=	$2,500
		per day

Supplements (Stipends) = $2,000

Resource (Special Education)	Head nurse
Bilingual	Head counselor
Math	Head custodian
Science	Department chairs
Librarian	Diagnostician
Home Economics	

Salary Distribution Table—This table reflects salaries and supplements (stipends) of all school personnel, incorporating the appropriate payroll descriptions and budgetary coding. While most school districts across the United States do not require principals to be responsible for payroll budgetary allotments and management of personnel salaries, some smaller districts, in fact, do so. The compiling of a payroll analysis via the *Salary Distribution Table* (see Table 6.5) also provides for a better understanding of how payroll (personnel salaries) can significantly impact district and campus budgetary costs. Recall from previous chapters that upward of 75% to 85% of a school district's revenue is typically required for payroll expenditure. This means the majority of a school's budgetary funding allocation is expended even before a principal and campus site-based team examines the campus budgetary allotment. This enormous expenditure requires principals to be effective financial stewards of the funding allotment they do receive. To coin an old phrase: *Money does not grow on trees*, or in the case of a school, in the principal's office!

Final Budget Compilation—The final budget compilation is to be completed in a tabular format as dictated by the school district and on the forms (typically in electronic format) provided by the district business department. If the school district does not specify the format or provide the necessary budget compilation forms, the use of the Microsoft® Excel software program is a recommended method, although other marketed versions are readily available. The final budget compilation must utilize the fund, function, object, subobject, organization, fiscal year, and program intent codes (see Chapter 1 or Table 6.6 in this chapter for examples).

Table 6.5 Salary Distribution Table

Fund	Function	Object. Subobject	Organization	Year	Program	Description		Total
199	11	6119	103	13	11	Payroll -- Regular Education Teachers (24)	$	1,140,000.00
199	11	6119	103	13	11	Payroll -- Math/Science Stipends	$	24,000.00
199	11	6119	103	13	23	Payroll -- Special Education Aides (4)	$	116,000.00
199	11	6129	103	13	11	Payroll -- Secretary	$	35,000.00
199	11	6129	103	13	11	Payroll -- Support Personnel (PEIMS)	$	29,000.00
199	11	6129	103	13	11	Payroll -- Support Personnel (Attendance)	$	29,000.00
199	11	6129	103	13	11	Payroll -- Support Personnel (Budget)	$	29,000.00
199	11	6129	103	13	11	Payroll -- Support Personnel (Receptionist)	$	29,000.00
199	11	6129	103	13	11	Payroll -- Support Personnel (At-Risk)	$	29,000.00
199	11	6129	103	13	11	Payroll -- Support Personnel (Discipline)	$	29,000.00
199	11	6129	103	13	24	Payroll -- Tutors (8)	$	232,000.00
						SUBTOTAL -- FUNCTION 11: INSTRUCTION	$	1,721,000.00
199	12	6119	103	13	11	Payroll -- Librarian	$	47,500.00
199	12	6119	103	13	11	Payroll -- Librarian Stipend	$	2,000.00
						SUBTOTAL -- FUNCTION 12: INSTR. RES. & MEDIA SRVC.	$	49,500.00
199	23	6119	103	13	11	Payroll -- Principal	$	90,000.00
199	23	6119	103	13	11	Payroll -- Asst. Principal	$	74,000.00

(Continued)

Table 6.5 (Continued)

Fund	Function	Object. Subobject	Organization	Year	Program	Description	Total
						SUBTOTAL -- FUNCTION 23: SCHOOL LEADERSHIP	$ 164,000.00
199	31	6119	103	13	11	Payroll -- Counselor	$ 110,000.00
199	31	6119	103	13	11	Payroll -- Head Counselor Stipend	$ 2,000.00
199	31	6119	103	13	23	Payroll -- Diagnostician (.5)	$ 28,500.00
199	31	6119	103	13	23	Payroll -- Diagnostician Stipend	$ 2,000.00
						SUBTOTAL -- FUNCTION 31: GUIDANCE, COUNSELING	$ 1,132,500.00
199	33	6119	103	13	11	Payroll - Nurse	$ 47,500.00
199	33	6119	103	13	11	Payroll - Nurse Stipend	$ 2,000.00
						SUBTOTAL - FUNCT 33: HEALTH SERVICES	$ 49,500.00
199	35	6129	103	13	11	Payroll - Food Services (Cafeteria Manager)	$ 22,000.00
199	35	6129	103	13	11	Payroll - Food Services (7)	$ 84,700.00
						SUBTOTAL - FUNCTION 35: FOOD SERVICES	$ 106,700.00
199	51	6129	103	13	11	Payroll - Head Custodian	$ 37,000.00
199	51	6129	103	13	11	Payroll - Head Custodian Stipend	$ 2,000.00
199	51	6129	103	13	11	Payroll - Custodians (6)	$ 180,000.00
						SUBTOTAL - FUNCTION 51: PLANT MAINT. & OPERATION	$ 219,000.00

(Continued)

Table 6.5 (Continued)

Fund	Function	Object. Subobject	Organization	Year	Program	Description		Total
199	52	6129	103	13	11	Payroll - Security	$	41,000.00
199	52	6129	103	13	11	Payroll - Security Clerk	$	29,000.00
						SUBTOTAL - FUNCTION 52: SECURITY SERVICES	$	70,000.00
219	11	6119	103	13	25	Payroll - Bilingual Teachers (5)	$	237,500.00
219	11	6119	103	13	25	Payroll - Bilingual Stipend	$	10,000.00
						SUBTOTAL - FUNCTION 11: INSTRUCTION (BILINGUAL)	$	247,500.00
224	11	6119	103	13	23	Payroll - Special Education Teachers (5)	$	237,500.00
224	11	6119	103	13	23	Payroll - SPED Stipend	$	10,000.00
224	11	6119	103	13	23	Payroll - Speech Teacher (.5)	$	26,000.00
						SUBTOTAL - FUNCTION 11: INSTRUCTION (SP. ED.)	$	273,500.00
243	11	6119	103	13	22	Payroll - Career/Technology Teacher	$	47,500.00
						SUBTOTAL - FUNCTION 11: INSTRUCTION (CAR. TECH.)	$	47,500.00
		6100				TOTAL PAYROLL COSTS	$	4,080,700.00
						GRAND TOTAL	$	4,080,700.00

Budget Allocations

Budgetary allocations are derived from a variety of revenue sources. These sources—federal, state, and local—provide funding dollars associated with budgetary allocations and are generally identified as governmental fund types with descriptors such as General, Special Revenue, Capital Projects, and Debt Services. The two most important governmental fund types insofar as the school budget allocation is concerned are General and Special Revenue. General funds are typically available for school allocations with minimal planned expenditure and purchasing restrictions. General funds are needed to sustain the normal operations, administration, and counseling expenditures of a school. Special Revenue funds are governmental funds used to account for the proceeds of specific revenue sources that are legally restricted to expenditures for specified purposes. Examples include Title I (Improving Basic Programs), Vocational Education, and Food Services. Dollars from these funding sources are then utilized as the basis for budgetary allocations at the school level.

School budget allocations are typically based on an average daily attendance or an average daily membership formulation. ADA versus ADM is a school finance issue regarding the relationship between student attendance and financial support. Determining the allocation by ADA benefits school districts with higher attendance and penalizes those with lower levels of attendance. More students in attendance equates to more money for districts. In addition, more students in attendance equates to more learning taking place, a fact supported by test scores. Proponents of ADM, as the basis for school funding, cite whether a student is in attendance on any particular day, the costs of district operations (salaries, utilities, transportation, other services, etc.) remain constant, and thus, the allocation of funds should recognize such (Brimley et al., 2012). Nevertheless, the allotment (based on either of the formulations)—along with additional dollars that may be appropriated as a result of the number of identified ELLs, gifted and talented, special education, and at-risk students—serves as the initial basis for school allocated funds. Additional allotted monies for the school can come from grant dollars, technology funds, maintenance funds, staff-development allocations, and other miscellaneous allotments. While most of these allotted dollars allow for administrators to implement and control activities authorized by the budget, certain limitations or restrictions can be placed on the budget for the following reasons:

- The budget limits the type, quantity, and quality of instruction provided at the school level, especially in an era of fiscal conservatism, often a result of an economic downturn.
- The public is critically interested in education and, more specifically, instruction.
- School operations are often diverse and broad in scope and, thus, important budgetary planning is necessary for effective and efficient expenditure of funds.
- School allocations provide direction for the school's future.

Restricted Funds

While budget allotments are used for a variety of services and expenditures at the school level, some are more restrictive than others. Once basic school allotments are appropriated to particular areas within the budget, function restrictions limit their use unless district approval is obtained in the form of a budget amendment or transfer.

Restricted funds are often associated with Title I, bilingual education, and special education dollars and programs. For example, many school districts carefully restrict the expenditure of funds appropriated to these particular programs on the basis of federal and state guidelines that often stipulate that funded dollars within these particular budgeted categories can only be utilized for the purpose of student-related instruction. Consider the following scenario.

The concept of restricted funds brings a school leader full circle in terms of understanding the need for accounting code structures that have been determined and designated by the Governmental Accounting Standards Board. These accounting code structures

HEY, I FOUND THE MONEY!

The office secretary at Sandy Cypress Middle School needed a new file cabinet, desk, and carpet but recognized that the general funds allocated had already been appropriated and encumbered within the budget. However, Sam Nachin, the school administrator, thought to himself: "Hey, I found the money," noting that the Title I accounts had just enough funds to be appropriated for office upgrades. Thus, in an electronic instant, the Title I dollars were encumbered and plans were made for a quick purchase of office items. No doubt, creative thinking

(Continued)

(Continued)

on the part of Mr. Nachin occurred. His actions are a reminder of the old adage: "Necessity is the mother of invention." However, the Title I funds were specifically and categorically designated for Title I–eligible students. Chances are the justification for incorporating Title I funds for the purchase of new office equipment for the school secretary would be a real stretch of the imagination in relation to the budgeted funds utilized.

Pause and Consider

- Check with school administration to determine the specific guidelines regarding the expenditure of Title I funds.
- Can Mr. Nachin purchase office furniture, equipment, and carpet for his school secretary? What do district guidelines dictate? If no, why are such stringent guidelines in place?

ensure a sequence of coding is uniformly applied to all schools and school districts to account for the proper appropriation and expenditure of public funds (GASB, 2011).

Coding Applications

States require a standard fiscal accounting code system. State coding systems are implemented and uniformly utilized by all local school districts in accordance with generally accepted accounting principles. States require a standard fiscal accounting code system be adopted by each school district. The system must meet the minimum requirements prescribed by state boards of education and is subject to review and comment by state auditors. In addition, the accounting system utilized by states and school districts must conform to the Generally Accepted Accounting Principles (GAAP) as identified by the Governmental Accounting Standards Board (2011). The fiscal accounting code system ensures that the sequence of codes is uniformly applied to all school districts across a state. The budgetary accounting code system is a labeling method designed to ensure the accuracy and legality of expenditures. School budgets are tracked by state education agencies via the budgetary accounting code system.

School district accounting systems are organized and operated on a fund basis. A fund is an accounting entity with a self-balancing set of accounts recording financial resources and liabilities. A school district designates the fund's financial resources for a distinct purpose. State or federal governments, as well as the local school district, may establish the fund's purpose. Previously identified in Chapter 1 and shown again in Table 6.6 is an example of a state's operating accounting code structure as well as explanations that describe the specifics of each code. Table 6.7 through Table 6.11 provide examples of categories for fund codes, function codes, object codes, organization codes, and program intent codes.

Fund codes **(1)** contain three digits with the first digit identifying regular, special, and vocational programs. A second digit denotes either the grade level or particular program area or category such as the local operating fund. The third digit further defines program type in relation to student classifications, type of services, and/or student population. For example, the number 211 identifies the Title I federal fund group.

Function codes **(2)** are typically two- to four-digit numbers that further designate budget program areas (see Table 6.8). Function codes represent as many as nine different categories. For example, the

Table 6.6   Example of a State's Operating Accounting Code Structure

199 — 11 — 6399.00 — 001 — Current Year — 11

1	2	3 4	5	6	7

Table 6.7   Categories for Fund Codes

Fund Codes—1st Digit (Nine Categories)	
100 –	Regular programs
200 –	Special programs
300 –	Vocational programs
400 –	Other instructional programs
500 –	Nonpublic school programs
600 –	Adult and continuing education programs
700 –	Debt service
800 –	Community service programs
900 –	Enterprise programs
000 –	Undistributed expenditures

most commonly used function code category within a school budget is instruction, although other areas including school leadership, guidance counseling, and health services are frequently incorporated.

Object codes **(3)** are three- to four-digit numbers used to further describe program allocations and expenditures. Object codes represent seven different categories (see Table 6.9). The object codes represent the nature or object of an account, a transaction, or a source.

Subobject codes **(4)** are used as accounting entries to delineate, for example, secondary-level departments such as English, mathematics, science, physical education, and history.

Organization codes **(5)** are three-digit numbers that identify accounting entries as being high school, middle school, elementary school, superintendent's office, or school board (see Table 6.10). This

Table 6.8   Categories for Function Codes

Function Codes—Nine Categories	
10 –	Instruction and instructional-related services
20 –	Instructional and school leadership
30 –	Support services—student (pupil)
40 –	Administrative support services
50 –	Support services—nonstudent-based
60 –	Ancillary services
70 –	Debt service
80 –	Capital outlay
90 –	Intergovernmental charges

Table 6.9   Categories for Object Codes

Object Codes—Seven Categories	
6000 –	Expenditure/expense control accounts
6100 –	Payroll costs
6200 –	Professional and contract services
6300 –	Supplies and materials
6400 –	Other operating costs
6500 –	Debt service
6600 –	Capital outlay—land, buildings, and equipment

Table 6.10   Categories for Organization Codes

Organization Codes—Two Categories	
001–699 –	Organization units—schools
700 –	Organization units—administrative

code readily notes which high schools in a district are the oldest or the newest. For example, Elm High School (001) is the first or oldest high school, followed by Birch High School (002), Oak High School (003), and Hickory High School (004), and so forth. The same coding designation is true for middle and elementary schools as well.

Fiscal year codes **(6)** identify the fiscal year of budgetary transactions.

The program intent code **(7)** is frequently represented by two digits and designates the rationale of a program provided to students. This code accounts for the cost of instruction and other services directed toward a particular need or a specific student population. The 11 program intent codes are identified in Table 6.11.

Table 6.11   Categories for Program Intent Codes

Program Intent Codes—Eleven Categories	
11 –	Basic educational services
21 –	Gifted and talented
22 –	Career and technology
23 –	Special education
24 –	Accelerated instruction (at-risk programs)
25 –	Bilingual education
26/27 –	Nondisciplinary alternative education programs
28/29 –	Disciplinary alternative education programs
30 –	Title I

Activity 1: Utilizing Accounting Codes

Using Tables 6.7 through 6.11, and the *Accounting Codes Reference Sheet* found in Resource B (pp. 219–222), determine the accounting code to be utilized to complete a school requisition form relative to the following situation. Write your answer in the blanks provided.

_____—____—_____—_____—____

The Special Services department has requested additional mathematics manipulatives to be utilized in several classrooms at Maple High School. These needed supplies could very well help increase the overall mathematic test scores at the second oldest high school in Mapletown Independent School District, as the statewide accountability system now holds all schools accountable for the academic achievement of special education students. (Answer provided at the conclusion of this chapter.)

Activity 2: Utilizing Accounting Codes

Carefully read and assess the scenario presented and then apply the proper accounting codes by referring to *Accounting Codes Reference Sheet* found in Resource B.

_____ _ ___ _ _____ _ ___ _ ___

Kit Monami, assistant principal at Eagletown High School, the third oldest high school in the district, was designated as the budget manager by her principal this school year. Kit was quite competent in her new role and found working with the school budget and budget team to be quite challenging yet most interesting. In her role as budget manager, she interacted with the high school departments and their many demanding personalities. Most recently, Steven Johnson, the head football coach at Eagletown High, had asked Kit if his request for additional athletic supply funds had been included in the budget for the upcoming school year. He was particularly concerned about the need for a new digital recorder for filming the defensive line during afterschool practice. "How else does the district expect us to win if I can't film the weekly progress of the team?" the coach inquired. Kit explained that she needed Coach Johnson to calculate the cost of the digital recorder, complete the necessary requisition form, and then she would determine if there were additional funds available in the specified account within the school budget.

In this scenario, as Coach Johnson completes the budget requisition form, consider the proper coding for each category—fund, function, object, organization code, and program intent code—and then fill in the Budget Accounting Code found on the requisition form as noted in Form 6.1. (Answer is provided at the conclusion of the chapter.)

Form 6.1   Sample Requisition Form

Eagletown Independent School District

"Home of the Soaring Eagles"
100 Eagle Nest Drive
Eagletown, USA

Requisition Form

Requisition No. _____

Purchase Order No. _____

School _____   Originator _____

Budget Accounting Code _____ – _____ – _____ . _____ – _____

Stock #	*Qty.*	*Qty. shipped*	*Description*	*Unit Cost*	*Total Cost*

Merchandise Received by _____

Total Amount $_____

Approved by _____   Date _____

Projecting Student Enrollment

Student enrollment information is important to schools and districts in relation to declining or increasing enrollments and the corollary, revenue generation. The effects of declining enrollments can be detrimental to a school's budget. Consider the following in relation to a decline in a school or district enrollment: reduced state aid; hiring freezes or a reduction in force (RIF); smaller class sizes, thus creating the need for fewer teachers; and redistricting of school boundaries and the possible closing of school facilities. Increasing enrollments can create overcrowded classrooms, and a need for rapid staff and facilities expansion (Ubben, Hughes, & Norris, 2011).

Therefore, accurate enrollment projections are vital to budgetary allotments, staff planning, and facilities utilization. Over the years, numerous methods have been incorporated by school districts to project student enrollment. The most common model to date remains the *ratio retention* or *cohort survival method*, which provides sufficiently accurate results. Today, the cohort survival method is frequently utilized by schools in the form of computer software programs developed by companies such as Ecotran Systems, Inc., of Beachwood, Ohio, Educational Data Systems of San Jose, California, and Education Logistics, Inc., of Missoula, Montana (Webb & Norton, 2008).

School leaders must recognize that most central office administrators prefer to underestimate enrollment projections because the potential negative impact on cost to a school district is less (Seyfarth, 2007). This is important to know since underprojections can equate to less than an appropriate and necessary allocation to the school. Moreover, underprojecting student enrollment equates to understaffing a school.

Table 6.12 describes the cohort survival method. It is important to note that procedures required to project student enrollments are of three types: gathering demographic data, analyzing the data for possible trends, and then projecting student enrollment on the basis of the evaluated findings. In addition, a careful review and examination of all external environment information is critical to ensure accurate enrollment projections. Listed below are several considerations as related to external environment information:

- Emerging communities, to include the building of new homes, rental properties such as apartment complexes, and the development of mobile home parks
- Changing population patterns

- Nonpublic school enrollments
- Open school enrollment policies
- Initiation of voucher plans
- A significant public event such as the loss of a major community employer
- Mobility rate

The cohort survival method accounts for the number of students enrolled in each grade level in a school or across a district over a specified number of years. Moreover, it requires a school to account for the number of students expected to enroll in kindergarten over the next 5 years. This accounting of potential kindergarten students is based on census data or housing surveys of children between the ages of 0 and 4 who reside in the school or district attendance zone. This information drives an average ratio calculation for each class from year to year. This average allows for future-year enrollment projections.

Table 6.12   Projecting Student Enrollment (Cohort Survival Method)

Directions: Review the list of procedures for utilizing the cohort survival method to better understand the process of projecting student enrollment. Following these procedures, and noted in Table 6.13, is a partially completed worksheet that can be utilized for the purpose of practice.

1. Begin the cohort survival method by incorporating previous school year data. For the purpose of initiating this activity, as noted in Table 6.13, utilize the current school year. In figuring the formula, set your calculator to round up (> 0.5) or down.

2. Recognize that the kindergarten enrollment for the current school year is 88. The first-grade student enrollment for the next school year is 115.

3. Now, using your calculator, divide the next school year first-grade student enrollment (115) by the current school year kindergarten student enrollment (88). This calculation will reveal a ratio of 1.31.

4. Use the worksheet noted in Table 6.13 to calculate the ratio for the remaining set of numbers.

5. Following the calculation of ratios, add each ratio in each column in Table 6.13 and divide by 4 to determine the average ratio. The average ratio for the first column is 1.12.

Table 6.12   (Continued)

6. Again, multiply the future school year #3 kindergarten enrollment (90) by the average ratio (1.12) that equates to a first-grade student enrollment projection of (101) for the future school year #4.

7. Continue your calculations for each grade level for the future school year #4.

8. Now, continue to calculate student enrollment projections for the future school year #5 by multiplying the kindergarten enrollment by the average ratio. Remember to not calculate ratios for years starting with future school year #3.

9. Further project student enrollments by adding across the *Projecting Student Enrollment Worksheet* (Table 6.13) to obtain the total student enrollment for each school year.

10. While there is no one method of projecting student enrollment to provide an absolute calculation, the cohort survival method has proven to be one of the most accurate formulas since the early 1950s.

NOTE: The information utilized in Table 6.12 was adapted in part from *Human Resource Leadership for Effective Schools* (2007) by John T. Seyfarth and from the author's personal experiences utilizing the cohort survival method at the school district level.

Table 6.13   Projecting Student Enrollment Worksheet

Enrollments by Grade Levels							
School Year	*K*	*1*	*2*	*3*	*4*	*5*	*Total*
Current Year	88	110	99	91	96	101	585
Ratio	*1.31*	*1.00*					
Next Year	93	115	110	96	99	109	622
Ratio	*1.06*	*.90*					
Future Year #1	91	99	103	112	109	115	629
Ratio	*.99*	*.97*					
Future Year #2	85	90	96	89	95	107	562
Ratio	*1.11*	*.97*					
Future Year #3	90	94	87	91	98	104	564
Average Ratio	*1.12*	*.96*					

Table 6.12

Enrollments by Grade Levels							
School Year	K	1	2	3	4	5	Total
Future Year #4	82	101	90				
	× 1.12	×.96					
Future Year #5	84	92	97				
	× 1.12						
Future Year #6	77	94					
	× 1.12						
Future Year #7	72	86					
	× 1.12						
Future Year #8	75	81					

Finally, it is important that all enrollment projections follow the guidelines below:

- Two separate projection models or methods should be utilized: one at the district level and one at the school level.
- Incorporate at the district level the cohort survival method to better account for student enrollment trends and community variables.
- Develop enrollment projections at the school level as well.
- Always monitor at the school level any enrollment changes. Monitoring means doing a student enrollment survey, for example, just prior to the close of the school year. Monitoring also suggests conducting housing surveys—especially if new construction projects, such as apartment complexes, are being built. One-bedroom apartments, for example, are typically designed for single dwellers with no children, while two- and three-bedroom units represent family dwellings and are indicative of a potential increase in student enrollment.

Important Budget Considerations

Barbara Hutton once stated what is obvious in life and in the practice of effective and efficient budgeting: "So, you want to take it with you—well, I've never seen a Brink's truck follow a hearse to the cemetery" (*Columbia*, 1996)! While an individual can save as much money as possible, at some point in time those saved dollars must be spent, given away, or inherited by someone because, as Hutton said, "You can't take it with you!" The same holds true in school budgeting—spend it or give it back. The authors suggest effective school leaders spend all the campus allocated funds, but do so in the most accurate, effective, and efficient manner possible. In other words, spend wisely! With this thought in mind, consider the following top 10 school budgeting priority listing. At the conclusion of each of the 10 statements, the identification (in parentheses) of district or school site responsibility is denoted.

1. *Utilize a Budget Calendar*—The purpose of the budget calendar is to ensure that the budget development process is continuous. The school leader who follows the guidelines and dates associated with a budget calendar maximizes the possibility that nothing interferes with budgetary preparation requirements or the best interest of the school and school system. (District)

2. *Identify Budgetary Allocations and Restricted Funds*—Know and understand the revenue sources and how such impact the school budgetary allotment. Recognize that allotments can be based on an average daily attendance formulation, and know how critical it is for the school leader to continuously monitor the enrollment of all students as well as those students served in special programs, for example, bilingual education, Title I, special education, and gifted and talented. Realize certain funds have specified restrictions associated with appropriateness of expenditures and student services. (District and school site)

3. *Project Incoming and Exiting Student Populations*—The effective school leader regularly monitors incoming and exiting student populations, as the student enrollment of a school can significantly impact the budget allocation. In addition, accomplished school leaders learn to utilize the cohort survival method as a process of projecting student population 5 years into the future. (District and school site)

4. *Project Faculty and Staff Increases and Reductions*—Any increase or reduction in faculty and staff strongly correlates to student enrollment. By utilizing the cohort survival method to forecast into the future, the school leader can assess how many faculty and staff will be needed to ensure a strong educational program. (District and school site)

5. *Conduct a Needs Assessment*—Efficient needs assessments allow school leaders to recognize which interventions were most effective in increasing student achievement and cost the least. (School site)

6. *Receive Input From All Stakeholders*—Effective school leadership incorporates collaborative strategies, which in turn generate the involvement and input from organizational followers. When collaborative decision making is implemented, visioning, planning, evaluating, and the overall budgeting process generate measurable improvements, all of which ultimately benefit students, faculty, and the organization. (School site)

7. *Project and Prioritize Expenditures*—Consider all line-item accounts within the budget, including supplies and materials, salaries, and capital outlay, for example, when analyzing and prioritizing budgetary expenditures. The school leader who actively monitors and regularly evaluates the budget is able to project and prioritize expenditures that focus on specified objectives, which are correlated with the instructional program, the school action plan, and the overall vision of the learning community. (School site)

8. *Build the Budget*—Exceptional budgetary leaders regularly meet with the budget development team to create a school vision, develop a plan of action, and build a budget. This level of quality leadership demonstrates the following outcomes essential in the budget development process:

- Knowledge of the complete budgetary process
- Knowledge of the amount of funding available and where the budgetary allotment is derived
- Knowledge of collaborative decision-making procedures, as well as proper protocols involving the input of all stakeholders
- Knowledge of accounting codes (School site)

9. *Defend the School Budget*—Skilled leadership and knowledge of the school budget permits an administrator to exercise ingenuity and competence in addressing questions, suggestions, and criticisms of the school budget at a budget defense hearing. Effectively defending the budget is an act of elucidating clear points and explicating proper justifications for budgetary decisions. Such actions in the formal budget defense hearing reveal leadership traits of credibility, transparency, and expertise. (District and school site)

10. *Amend and Adjust the School Budget*—Even with all the purposeful budgetary planning and careful monitoring and evaluation,

no administrator can expect the school budget to remain on target without certain adjustments being made during the course of a fiscal year. Budget amendments and transfers are necessary when unexpected circumstances and situations inevitably arise. Having a working knowledge of the amendment and transfer processes will facilitate the need to move funds from one account to another without leaving an impression of budgetary incompetence or mismanagement. (District and school site)

The Budget Calendar

School administrators recognize that effective budget development is based on continuous evaluation. This recognition also brings about the need for the development of a detailed budget calendar. The budget calendar lists critical dates for the preparation, submission, review, and approval of the school budget. A variety of straightforward techniques are generally used in developing a budget calendar. While the details involved in developing a school budget are not the same in all districts, it is recommended that the following steps be considered and incorporated when preparing a budget calendar:

1. Develop a master district calendar to ensure that all budgetary actions and activities are consistent and compatible across the district and from school to school.

2. Identify specified budgetary actions and activities for inclusion in the calendar and arrange them in chronological order.

3. Assign completion dates for each action and activity and note them on the budget calendar. Completion dates should be assigned by working backward through the actions and activities from legally mandated dates as stipulated by state law and local district policy.

4. Assign dates and space accordingly to ensure sufficient time is allowed for the completion of each action and activity listed on the budget calendar.

5. Identify on the budget calendar the person(s) specifically responsible for each action or activity listed. This procedure is particularly useful to school administrators because it identifies their own detailed responsibilities and task completion dates.

Again, the budget development process and proposed calendar will vary from state to state and district to district as fiscal year beginning dates typically start anywhere from July 1 to September 1. School officials who fail to establish a budget calendar or who procrastinate the budget-development process are making a serious mistake, because the avoidance of approaching deadlines will definitely interfere with conscientious budget-building efforts (Brimley et al., 2012).

Outlined in Table 6.14 is a proposed budget calendar with specified considerations as related to the budget development process.

Table 6.14   Proposed Budget Calendar

Schedule	Procedure
Prior to February 1	The superintendent of schools establishes the budget planning format and schedule for preparation of the next fiscal year budget.
	Person Responsible: Superintendent
February 1	A Budget Request by Function and Object form should be distributed to school administrators for completion by March 1. Columns for "Actual Previous Year" and "Estimated Current Year" should be completed prior to the form being disseminated to the administrators responsible.
	Person Responsible: Associate superintendent for finance
February 15	Projected student enrollments should be developed.
	Person Responsible: Associate Superintendent for Administration in collaboration with school leaders
March 1	School administrators should return the completed Budget Request by Function and Object form to the district administrator responsible for the initial review and consideration of school needs.
	The school budget preparation process begins with the involvement of the budget development team.
	Person Responsible: School leaders and site-based decision-making team members.

(Continued)

Table 6.14   (Continued)

Schedule	Procedure
April 1	Completed school budgets should be submitted to the district administrator responsible for the consolidation of the organizational budget.
	Person Responsible: School leaders
April 15	The district administrator should submit the overall organizational budget to the superintendent of schools for review, along with suggested revisions prior to consolidation into a total district budget.
	Person Responsible: Associate superintendent for finance
May 15	The accepted budget for the entire school district should be prepared and ready for adoption in its final form.
	Person Responsible: Associate superintendent for finance and superintendent
June 1	The superintendent of schools should have completed the review of the accepted budget in its final form.
	Person Responsible: Superintendent
Months of June/July	Budget workshops are scheduled for school board members.
	Person Responsible: Superintendent and school board
No later than August 15	The district budget should be submitted to the local school board for public hearings and final approval. This final date will vary from district to district. However, the final approval date is typically prescribed by state law, as any district and school budget must be approved prior to the expenditure of public funds.
	Person Responsible: School board, superintendent, and associate superintendent for finance
No later than August 31	Budget adopted
	Person Responsible: School board

The development and utilization of a budget calendar assists in the formulation of an integrated plan of fiscal operations and further provides a means of communication between the various levels of the organization. Finally, the budget calendar effectively provides each administrator within the organization with appropriate information and deadlines necessary to perform specified budget development duties and responsibilities.

The Budget Hearing and Defense

Many districts require school administrators, department directors, and other school personnel responsible for the development of budgets to formally meet and independently defend their budgets. This process can be quite stressful if the administrator has not properly prepared the budget. Preparation for the budget hearing and defense requires the school administrator to devise an interesting and informative manner of presenting the fiscal and budgetary facts. This is often accomplished with visual aids presenting the necessary budgetary points and justifications. The school administrator must comprehend the budgetary components (accounting codes and descriptors), have been intimately involved in the budget development process, and understand the rationale for the monetary requests accompanying the proposed budget. Some districts require the school administrator to meet with the superintendent or a designee, and, in some instances, a committee of supervisors or peers. In any case, the process typically includes the necessary justification of questioned budgetary items, with final approval coming only after adjustments or revisions have been made to the proposed budget.

Finally, it is advised that the school administrator follow this useful adage: The best defense is a good offense. In other words, work hard at developing an effective budget, do the necessary homework associated with the budgetary tasks, and be prepared to expect the unexpected when defending the budget.

Final Thoughts

The effective school leader understands the importance of budgeting, especially as schools and school districts realize that the function of a budget is more than mechanics and mathematics. The development of a school budget today, especially in eras of fiscal constraint and accountability, requires strong leadership skills, a vision with a purpose, and an action plan for the future. The development of an effective school budget necessitates teamwork, dedicated efforts, and proper coding. Budget development demands budgetary applications whereby major budgeting considerations increase opportunities for all stakeholders to play an active role in defining school issues and addressing problems. This process generates appropriate decisions and solutions.

Effective leadership enables a school administrator to develop a budget that projects the school's vision and academic action plan. Moreover, the effective school leader informs the general public regarding the direction of the school program and provides the framework for appropriate accounting and wise expenditure of educational dollars—all for the benefit of students. While no budget is ever perfect, proper visioning, regular planning, and continuous evaluation transform a common ledger of revenue and expenditures into a supporting document leading students to academic success and fulfilling the campus and district visions or missions.

Building a school budget is never an easy task. Budgeting provides the necessary framework to help make a school's vision a reality. With the institutionalization of site-based decision making in schools today, educational leaders have the opportunity and the obligation to engage the learning community in the budget development process by working collaboratively with all stakeholders to incorporate visioning and planning as necessary components in better budgets for better schools. By applying proven budgetary theory and techniques, administrators today—working with an attitude of "all of us are smarter than any one of us"—can utilize budgeting applications whereby the final budget compilation can positively impact the overall educational program and, most important, increase achievement.

Discussion Questions

1. What is the purpose of the accounting code system?

2. How have the total quality movement and the site-based decision-making process impacted the development of budgets in public schools?

3. Identify "stakeholders" in the budget development process and explain how the concept of "all of us are smarter than any one of us" can serve to ensure better budgets for better schools.

4. Who must be responsible for student enrollment projections—school district administration or school principals? Explain your answer.

5. How might the school budget applications detailed within this chapter serve the school administrator at the budget defense hearing?

6. Why are certain budget allotments more restrictive than others? Explain your answer by providing examples.

7. You are in the second semester of your first year as a school administrator, and the budget season is hastily approaching. You know your school enrollment has been rapidly growing over the past 3 years. The associate superintendent for fiscal administration informs you that your budget allotment will be less for the upcoming fiscal year because the school district needs extra funds for a new facilities improvement effort. Your current enrollment is 815 students. Last school year, the campus enrollment was 796. The year prior, the enrollment was 779. Three years ago, the enrollment was 761. For previous years 4, 5, and 6, student enrollment was 761, 757, and 752, respectively. How should you address the possibility of a decrease in your budgetary allotment? What methods would you apply and specifically utilize to resolve this budgetary issue at the upcoming budget defense hearing? Apply your answer(s) in writing.

8. Why is the incorporation and utilization of a budget calendar important to building an effective school budget?

Case Study Application 1: Shifting Paradigms With Changing Times

Note: This case study is a continuation of the one introduced in Chapter 4. The reader will recognize the characters portrayed and will further apply accounting codes to the budgetary allotments designated in Table 4.4 on pages 106–107 of Chapter 4 within the *PBHS Nonprioritized Identified Needs* chart.

Part IV: The Budget—Coding the Budgetary Allotments

The Situation

Dr. Hector Avila, principal, and Ms. Abigail Grayson, assistant principal, at Pecan Bay High School sat down the next Tuesday afternoon with the

SBDM committee to review the prioritized needs listing as related to the next fiscal year school budget. It was obvious there were more needs than dollars at Pecan Bay High School. Dr. Avila thought to himself, "Isn't that always the case!" Nevertheless, the decisions had been made in the best interests of the students at PBHS. Dr. Avila was proud of the committee's efforts. Ms. Grayson was more than impressed with the progress that had been made and with how much she had learned from an outstanding instructional leader. While funding every need would be impossible based on the $100,000 allotment, the next step in the visioning, planning, and budgeting process was to integrate the needs with budgetary descriptors and accounting codes. This would be a learning experience for not only Ms. Grayson but also the entire SBDM committee. What Dr. Avila really appreciated about the site-based decision-making initiative was the fact that every aspect of the budget was being considered, assessed, evaluated, and approved in a public forum where all would recognize there were no hidden agendas or secret principal "slush" funds.

Following a short period of greetings and welcoming committee members to the conference room, the business of coding the differing needs began in earnest. Troy Allens, one of the initial opponents to the SBDM process and good friend of Ed Feeney, was present, smile on his face, and excited to be a part of a group who had bought into the concept of "all of us are smarter than any one of us!" Even old Ed was slowly but surely coming along and had even sat in on a SBDM meeting for Troy a few weeks ago when Troy had to take his daughter to a softball game.

Thinking It Through

Now that you have prioritized the differing needs at Pecan Bay High School and constructed an abridged action plan, it is time to consider all line-item accounts within the school budget in relation to the fund, function, object, sub-object (utilize .00 for this exercise), organization, fiscal year, and program intent codes. Review from Chapter 1 the *Ten Steps to Budgeting Success* and then determine what the committee has accomplished: (1) determine the allotment, (2) identify any fixed expenditures, (3) involve all parties, (4) identify potential expenditures, (5) cut back as is necessary, (6) avoid any debts, (7) develop a plan of action, (8) set goals, (9) evaluate the budget, and (10) abide by the budget.

Where are you and your team in the 10-step process?

Take an opportunity to turn to Resource B: *Accounting Codes Reference Sheet.* Use this document to complete the Budget Spreadsheet exhibited in Table 6.15 by listing the correct accounting codes as associated with the prioritized needs previously selected. To better assist, an example indicating the proper accounting code for Health Services (Nurse or Clinic) has been provided and listed on the first row of the Budget Spreadsheet. Note that the description category of the Budget Spread Sheet is associated with the Function and Object code descriptors. Remember, accounting codes may vary from state to state and from district to district. The process utilized in this text is simply an example. Seek your own state or school district version of the accounting code process to complete this task.

Table 6.15   Budget Development Spreadsheet

Fund	Function	Object Subobject	Year	Program Intent	Organization	Description	Total
199	33	6399.00	Current date	11	002	Health Services (Nurse)	$1000.00
						Grand Total	$

NOTE: This form also appears in Resource A.

Case Study Application 2: Requisition Season at Cover Elementary

Donna Arnold, assistant principal at Cover Elementary School, has been given the responsibility of serving as budget manager for the current school year. Donna has been an assistant principal at Cover for 3 years. She has really come to like the old school, the first one built in the school district well over 60 years ago. One of Donna's specified tasks associated with the role of budget manager is to review all campus requisitions and assign the appropriate accounting codes. This evening, after a long day at school, Donna sits down and begins analyzing a stack of requisitions placed on her desk earlier by her secretary. As she examines each requisition, she realizes how important it is to learn the differing accounting codes in order to save time. While Donna thumbs through the stack of requisitions, she notes out loud what is being ordered and then speculates as to the appropriate code for entry in the fund account blank.

Requisition #1: Janice Minsky orders the "director's cut" of the 1960 video production *Alamo*, starring John Wayne, to show to her Title I fourth-grade social studies class.

_____ __ ____ __ _____.____ __ ____ __ ____ __ _____

Requisition #2: Dolores Chavez needs one grand prize trophy and several ribbons for "placing," as well as certificates of achievement, for the gifted and talented students participating in the annual National Geography Bee.

_____ __ ____ __ _____.____ __ ____ __ ____ __ _____

Requisition #3: Henri Adams, librarian, requests several new book titles for the school library, as the bilingual teachers strongly desire books in the native languages of their English language learners.

_____ __ ____ __ _____.____ __ ____ __ ____ __ _____

Requisition #4: Betty Sanchez, the school nurse, is requesting she be permitted to attend the National Conference for Wellness Programs to be held in Chicago, Illinois.

_____ __ ____ __ _____.____ __ ____ __ ____ __ _____

Requisition #5: Julie Aikman requests a set of colored transparencies to aid her special education students with visual-reading perception problems.

_____ __ ____ __ _____.____ __ ____ __ ____ __ _____

Requisition #6: Larry Nolton, building principal, is seeking to renew the subscriptions to *The Journal of Principal Leadership* for all of his administrative team members.

_____ _ ____ _ _____.____ _ ____ _ ____ _ _____

Application Question

Using Tables 6.6 through 6.11 within the chapter, as well as Resource B: *Accounting Codes Reference Sheet,* indicate the fund, function, object, subobject (utilize .00 for this exercise), fiscal year, program intent, and organization codes for each of the requisition submissions noted above. Place your answer in the blanks below each requisition number. (Answers are provided at the conclusion of this chapter.)

Case Study Application 3: The Budget Development Project

The Budget Development Project provides the reader with a comprehensive examination of a fictitious school and school district. The school will be known as Mountain Vista Elementary School, and the district will be called Mesa Valley Independent School District.

Mesa Valley ISD serves a major suburban area just north of a large urban center. The school district has earned an outstanding reputation over the years for its strong academic and extracurricular programs, its effective school leadership, and its financial stability. The district's tax base, while more than adequate, remains most interestingly diverse, with local revenues generated from the agribusiness industry, which includes pecan growing, milk and dairy products, cotton farming, and cattle ranching, as well as an infusion of high-tech industries that ultimately attracted the now-famous computer software company, Styl-USA, Inc. With a diverse tax base also comes a diverse population with socioeconomic levels representative of the poor agribusiness workers, the medium-income urban-flight families, and the independently wealthy CEOs—all of whom now reside in what has become known as Technology Valley.

Mesa Valley Independent School District serves 25,502 students. The district has 3 high schools, 5 middle schools, and 15 elementary schools. Mountain Vista Elementary School is the fifth oldest elementary school in the district, with a population of 818 students enrolled for the current school year. Listed in Table 6.16 are total student enrollments over the previous 5 school years.

Table 6.16   Student Enrollment

School Year	Student Enrollment
Previous Year #1	831
Previous Year #2	845
Previous Year #3	850
Previous Year #4	826
Previous Year #5	808

The campus has a free and reduced-price lunch population of 87% and is thus considered a Title I schoolwide project. The average daily attendance is 90%. Mountain Vista has a unique student population ranging from high-socioeconomic-background to high-poverty status. The school is also home to a large English language learner (ELL) population, since many of the families living within the attendance zone are legalized farm workers employed by the numerous agribusinesses.

Mountain Vista Elementary School houses prekindergarten through Grade 5, with a student population of 80% Hispanic, 10% white, 5% African American, and 5% Asian American. Gifted and talented students make up 4% of the population, 5% of the student body is identified as special education, and 25% is served in the bilingual education program. Also, the school has 42 teachers, 1 counselor, 1 nurse, 1 nurse assistant, 1 assistant principal, 1 instructional facilitator, 1 librarian, 13 instructional aides, 2 clerical aides, 1 secretary, 1 attendance clerk, and 1 principal.

Each of the grade levels at Mountain Vista Elementary School has six sections of students with the exception of prekindergarten (two sections—one bilingual and one monolingual), Grade 2 (five sections), and Grade 4 (five sections). Every grade level has one section of bilingual students, one section of special education inclusion-monolingual students (excepting prekindergarten), with the remaining sections serving monolingual students. Each section of bilingual students at every grade level is served by one teacher and one instructional aide. The prekindergarten sections are served by one teacher and one instructional aide each. Finally, the special education students are served by two teachers and five instructional aides.

Mountain Vista Elementary School also employs, half time, one gifted and talented teacher and one speech therapist, as well as a full-time physical education teacher, music teacher, and Title VI aide. There are four custodians and five food services employees that serve the school. Finally, both faculty and administration agree that Mountain Vista Elementary School is in need of a full-time campus diagnostician and hope to convince the superintendent during the budget defense hearing of this educational need.

The Mesa Valley Independent School District associate superintendent for finance has indicated that each elementary school will be provided a per-pupil campus budget allocation of $2,537 for the next school year. This allocation is to support the school's academic programs, salaries, any supplemental stipends ($2,000) for special education teachers, bilingual teachers, math and science teachers, testing coordinators, and head librarian, counselor, nurse, custodian, and grade-level chairs. Table 6.17 lists the annual salaries of all school personnel.

Table 6.17 Salaries

Personnel Position	Salary per Year ($)
Teachers, nurse, librarian	47,500
Principal	101,000
Assistant principal	87,000
Counselor	55,000
Diagnostician	57,000
Instructional facilitator	60,000
Speech therapist	52,000
Testing coordinator	49,000
Security officer	41,000
Secretary	35,000
Instructional and clerical aides	31,000
Nurse assistant	31,000
Custodian (head)	37,000
Custodians	30,000
Food services	12,000
Consultant(s) per day	2,500

Mountain Vista Elementary School has been experiencing problems with reading achievement and, consequently, low problem-solving skills in the area of mathematics as measured by the State Assessment of Essential Skills (SAES). This problem encompasses most of the content areas since reading is the primary factor for academic success. The site-based committee believes that the promotion of literacy at school and within the community should be a campus priority. Other academic considerations are included within the proposed campus action plan for the next school year. However, a needs assessment and priority analysis have not been conducted in relation to the action plan. Identified on subsequent pages is the Mountain View Elementary School's Campus Action or Improvement Plan (CAP or CIP).

Finally, the school has recently experienced a turnover in campus leaders. The prior principal replaced a strong and effective instructional leader who had gained the trust, confidence, and respect of the learning community. However, this principal—Mr. Belton Dwanes—has since retired after leading the school to the highest accountability rating according to the State Education Agency. Mr. Dwanes's replacement for the previous 2 years had been a less-than-effective instructional leader, and both he and his assistant principal resigned to pursue other educational interests. During the 2 years after Mr. Dwanes's retirement, the instructional program at Mountain Vista Elementary School had suffered, and just this school year, Dr. Jenda Taft and her assistant, John Steven Leakey, assumed the roles of principal and assistant principal. Both realized they had their work cut out for them, but both are professionals with excellent credentials and reputations. Both leaders, after reviewing the campus Academic Achievement Indicator Report (AAIR), certainly understood the charge that had been issued to them by Dr. Leroy J. Thedson, the Mesa Valley ISD superintendent: "Turn Mountain Vista around and get those scores back on track. I expect all of your test groups and subpopulation scores to be at 90% and higher in the next 2 years!"

Directions: To best complete the *Budget Development Project,* the following format is suggested. Carefully read, in sequence, each information guideline along with supporting materials and then complete the noted tasks before moving on to the next set of instructions. Refer to, read, and follow Information Guideline #4 only after completing the first three directives and activities.

This particular project has been an extremely successful activity and is often considered the most popular aspect of our budget course teaching and learning, as it permits the prospective school leader to gain significant and practical insights and experiences into building a school budget.

While no clinical practicum can ever be as true to life as the on-site experience, the processes detailed within the *Budget Development Project* are intended to present the reader and student of the budgeting process with a meaningful and relevant perspective that is as close as possible to the actual budgetary practices of a real school and school district.

1. Follow the *Sorenson-Goldsmith Integrated Budget Model,* as identified in Chapter 4, which showcases the eight components necessary to define and select the appropriate stakeholders, conduct a needs assessment, analyze the data presented, prioritize needs, set goals and objectives, and develop an action or improvement plan.

2. Review all information and data provided (including the Mountain Vista Action Plan and Academic Achievement Indicator Report) to determine if the information and data are being appropriately, effectively, and efficiently utilized. If not, make any and all necessary changes.

3. Develop a campus budget for Mountain Vista Elementary School by reflecting upon the budgetary applications detailed in Chapter 6. Your completed budget project should include

a *descriptive narrative, programmatic identifiers,* a *mission statement, student enrollment projections,* an *analysis of the academic action plan,* a *needs assessment* and *priority analysis,* a *teacher/student distribution table,* a *faculty apportionment table,* a *forecast of population* trends utilizing the *cohort survival method,* any *above basic personnel requests and justifications,* an *allocation statement,* and a *salaries for personnel table,* along with the *final budget compilation* utilizing accounting codes, descriptors, and dollar totals.

—BEGIN THE BUDGET DEVELOPMENT PROJECT—

Good luck and good visioning, planning, and budgeting!

4. Now, after completing Information Guides 1, 2, and 3, you may turn to the *Mesa Valley Independent School District Memorandum* found at the conclusion of this case study. Remember, this memorandum is to be read and complied with only after you have completed the first three information guidelines.

Campus Action Plan

Mountain Vista Elementary School

Mesa Valley Independent School District

Campus Action Plan

SBDM Committee

Belinda Del Monte, preschool teacher	Jaye Minter, music teacher
Karla Billingsly, Grade 1 teacher	Phyllis Canton, instructional aide
Leslie Lovington, Grade 2 teacher	Suzan Rollins, PTA president
Dianna Sanchez, Grade 3 bilingual teacher	Molly Corlioni, parent
Barbara Axleson, Grade 4 Title I teacher	Flo Cortez, parent
Susie Wigington, Special Education teacher	Lisa Nachin, parent
Randy Woodson, Chief of Police, community member	John Steven Leakey, assistant principal

Dr. Jenda Taft, Principal

Mission Statement

Mountain View Elementary School will provide a safe environment for all students by fostering productive citizens for a better tomorrow.

Goal I: Increase student achievement after a review and analysis of SAES data.

Objective 1: By student population—gender, ethnicity, educationally disadvantaged (at risk), and instructional setting teacher—develop strategies that will increase student achievement.

Strategy 1: Target specific instructional objectives.

Action(s) Implementation(s)	Responsibility Staff Assigned	Timeline Start/End	Resources (Human, Material, Fiscal)	Audit (Formative)	Reported/ Documented
Identify instructional areas of strength; areas needing improvement; and areas of weakness with regard to specific SAES objectives.	Principal and teachers	August–May (current year)	SAES English Language Arts Reading Objectives and Measurement Specifications booklet; SAES Mathematics Objectives and Measurement Specifications booklet; MVISD Curriculum Guides; Instructional Resource Center materials; teacher-made materials; SAES disaggregated data Mountain Vista SAES Booklet Time on Target criterion-referenced pretests	Disaggregated Data Information Sheets, SAES ATTACK skills worksheets, diagnostic and screening results, and lesson plans	Principal's office

Evaluation (Summative): All disaggregated student groups will obtain 90% or greater mastery on SAES.

Goal II: Provide a curriculum that addresses higher-order thinking skills to increase student academic performance.

Objective 1: Explore and implement programs that will increase overall student achievement.

Strategy 1: Continue current instructional programs.

Action(s) Implementation(s)	Responsibility Staff Assigned	Timeline Start/ End	Resources (Human, Material, Fiscal)	Audit (Formative)	Reported/ Documented
Develop staff development programs for Grade 4 process writing. Enhance the reading program by implementing: ___ phonemic/phonetic instruction ___ increased reading time per day ___ learning centers ___ subgrouping ___ integrated units ___ reading styles inventories Continue cross grade-level planning during the first 6 weeks of school.	Principal and teachers Director of Elementary Education	August–May (current year)	*Integrated Reader* library books and software; *Phonetic Readers* teaching resources; *SOAR With Knowledge* instructional materials; *Maria Carlo Reading Styles Inventory;* and teacher-made resources	*Integrated Reader* participation charts and printout reports, as well as lesson plans, Teacher observation of student performance, Principal visitation and participation in classroom	Principal's office; lesson plans, and library circulation records

Evaluation (Summative): All disaggregated student groups will obtain 90% or greater mastery on SAES.

Goal II: Provide a curriculum that addresses higher-order thinking skills to increase student academic performance.

Objective 1: Explore and implement programs that will increase overall student achievement.

Strategy 1: Continue current instructional programs.

Action(s) Implementation(s)	Responsibility Staff Assigned	Timeline Start/End	Resources (Human, Material, Fiscal)	Audit (Formative)	Reported/ Documented
Continue the *On-To Math* program. Develop a math curriculum cross-referenced guide incorporating *On-To Math, Maxim Math,* and *Math This Way* instructional programs. Design math diagnostic tests to be administered in Grades 1–5. Integrate science and social studies into the math instructional program with the extensive implementation of *SOAR With Knowledge.* Plan lessons to incorporate the *Living Science Center* into the instructional program at least twice each 6 weeks throughout the school year.	Principal, teachers, Resource Center coordinator, and the Director of Elementary Education	August– May (current year)	*On-To Math* and *Maxim Math* teaching resources, MVISD curriculum guides, library books, classroom libraries and readers, periodicals, newspapers, other reading materials, and teacher-made resources	Software printout reports, as well as lesson plans, Teacher observation of student performance, Principal visitation and participation in classrooms	Principal's office and lesson plans; and library circulation records

Evaluation (Summative): All disaggregated student groups will obtain 90% or greater mastery on SAES.

Goal III: Develop methods and strategies to assist at-risk students to achieve academic success.

Objective 1: Identify and serve students in at-risk situations in order that they obtain 80% or greater mastery on SAES.

Strategy 1: Extend learning opportunities and intervention programs for at-risk students.

Action(s) Implementation(s)	Responsibility Staff Assigned	Timeline Start/ End	Resources (Human, Material, Fiscal)	Audit (Formative)	Reported/ Documented
Follow guidelines for identification of at-risk students as mandated by the State Education Agency and the MVISD At-Risk Plan. Continue tutoring, counseling, special education, and 504 referral programs, and interagency involvement referrals. Enhance the student mentoring program between Grades 3 and 4 at-risk students and Grades PreK–2 at-risk students. Implement Title I compacts to encourage parental involvement and awareness, as well as increase student achievement and teacher responsibility.	Principal, teachers, counselor, instructional aides, and security officer	August–May (current year)	Principal and counselor, At-Risk Coordinator, and the campus At-Risk committee	At-Risk Student Activity and Identification Sheets	Principal's office

Evaluation (Summative): All disaggregated student groups will obtain 90% or greater mastery on SAES.

Goal III: Develop methods and strategies to assist at-risk students to achieve academic success.

Objective 1: Identify and serve students in at-risk situations in order that they obtain 90% or greater mastery on SAES.

Strategy 2: Offer parent training and information sharing opportunities.

Action(s) Implementation(s)	Responsibility Staff Assigned	Timeline Start/End	Resources (Human, Material, Fiscal)	Audit (Formative)	Reported/ Documented
Conduct a parent classroom orientation program during the first 6 weeks of the school year. Provide for a *Parent University* each school year. Survey parents to determine needs to be addressed during the *Parent University* program.	Principal, counselor, At-Risk coordinator and committee, and teachers	August–May (current year)	Newsletters, meeting notices, and parent survey and evaluation forms; Child care, phone bank, and door prizes	Parent newsletters, parent training workshop notifications, parent classroom orientation sign-in sheets, and parent evaluation forms	Principal's office

Evaluation (Summative): Parent training opportunities and orientations will be held in order that all disaggregated student groups will obtain 90% or greater mastery on SAES.

ACADEMIC ACHIEVEMENT
INDICATOR REPORT

Campus Report

CAMPUS NAME: MOUNTAIN VISTA ES
DISTRICT NAME: MESA VALLEY ISD
CAMPUS NUMBER: 105
ACCOUNTABILITY RATING: ACCEPTABLE

Exemplary

Recognized

Acceptable

Low-Performing

State Education Agency

District Name: Mesa Valley ISD
Campus Name: MOUNTAIN VISTA ES Campus #: 105

Academic Achievement Indicator Report
Campus Performance Accountability Rating: Acceptable

Total Enrollment: 831 Grade Span PreK–5
School Type: Elementary

Indicator:	State, %	District, %	Campus, %	African American, %	Hispanic, %	White, %	Asian American, %	Econ. Disadv., %
SAES % Passing								
Grade 3								
Reading	71.3	78.9	74.2	75.6	69.7	80.5	83.2	67.4
Math	74.6	79.2	73.8	65.7	61.7	84.2	86.3	63.7
SAES % Passing								
Grade 4								
Reading	78.7	81.0	70.7	70.2	61.5	78.6	81.2	60.9
Math	68.3	71.6	62.3	58.4	57.7	66.0	71.3	40.0
Writing	78.6	84.7	75.2	70.7	69.6	80.6	83.2	60.7
SAES % Passing								
Grade 5								
Reading	75.5	77.2	60.1	57.6	52.9	69.3	72.4	40.0
Math	77.3	78.0	67.3	58.6	47.6	70.2	73.5	47.2
Attendance	94.5	95.6	90.1	88.5	85.3	95.4	98.7	82.3

Student Information

Total Students: 831

Students by Grade:	Prekindergarten	32
	Kindergarten	124
	Grade 1	121
	Grade 2	102
	Grade 3	123
	Grade 4	105
	Grade 5	181
	Special Education	43

Retention Rates by Grade, %:

	State	*District*	*Campus*
Kindergarten	1.7	0.7	2.2
Grade 1	4.7	3.9	5.1
Grade 2	1.7	0.7	1.9
Grade 3	1.1	0.6	1.3
Grade 4	0.9	0.7	1.2
Grade 5	0.8	0.3	0.9

Budgeted Operating Expenditure Information

Budgeted Operating Expenditure Information

	Campus	Pct.	District	Pct.	State	Pct.
Total Campus Budget	$2,108,247	100	$116,168,713	100	$12,711,996,407	100
By Function						
Instruction	$1,486,314	70.5	$88,520,559	76.2	$9,559,421,298	75.2
Administration	$215,041	10.2	$8,596,486	7.4	$953,399,731	7.5
Other Campus Costs	$406,892	19.3	$19,051,668	16.4	$2,199,175,378	17.3

Budgeted Instructional Operating Expenditures by Program

	Campus	Pct.	District	Pct.	State	Pct.
Regular Education	$1,142,975	76.9		86.9		86.8
Special Education	$84,720	5.7		11.4		11.2
Title I Education	$219,974	14.8		15.0		14.9
Bilingual Education	$11,891	0.8		4.7		3.6
Gifted/Talented Ed.	$26,754	1.8		1.3		0.6

Memorandum

Mesa Valley Independent School   *Committed to*
District   *Excellence in Education*

TO: Dr. Jenda Taft, Principal
             Mountain Vista Elementary School and
             The Budget Team Members
FROM: Dr. Leroy J. Thedson, Superintendent of Schools
DATE: Spring (Current Year)
SUBJECT: Budgetary Constraints and Reductions

Due to the recent closure of the Mountain Stream Manufacturing Plant, a significant loss of district revenue has occurred. To ensure that the district budget and reserves remain solvent, all schools and departments are being asked to include a nine percent (9%) reduction (see specified accounts) within their organizational budgets for the upcoming fiscal year.

Specified line item accounts by code/description:

199-11/13-6112.00	*Substitutes*
199-11/13-6118.00	Extra Duty Pay
199-11/23-6269.00	Rentals—Operating Leases (copiers)
199-11/13/23/31/33-6411	Travel

Please note that the school district, along with the board of trustees, remain genuinely concerned about this temporary financial setback. However, also know that all areas of the district budget are being reduced, and expected revenue to be generated from the Mesa Vista Valley Packing Company—which is scheduled to open within the next two years—will hopefully make up for this unexpected budgetary issue.

Your continued commitment to the students of this school district is most appreciated.

Chapter 6 Answers

Noted below are the answers to the activities in this chapter.

Answer to Form 6.1: Sample Requisition Form

199—36—6399.00—91

Answers to Activity 1 and Activity 2: Utilizing Accounting Codes

#1 200—10—6300—002—23
#2 199—36—6399—003—91

Answers to Application Questions

Requisition #1: 199—11—6399.00—Current School Year—11—101
Requisition #2: 461—11—6399.00—Current School Year—21—101
Requisition #3: 219—12—6669.00—Current School Year—25—101
Requisition #4: 199—33—6411.00—Current School Year—11—101
Requisition #5: 199—11—6329.00—Current School Year—23—101
Requisition #6: 199—23—6329.00—Current School Year—11—101

Resource A

Selected Forms

Budget Development Spreadsheet

Fund	Function	Object Subobject	Year	Program Intent	Organization	Description	Total
						Grand Total	$

Strategy Page

Goal 1:

Objective 1:

Strategy 1:

Actions	Responsibility	Timeline Start/End	Resources (Human, Material, Fiscal)	Reported/ Audit (Formative)	Documented

Evaluation (Summative):

Resource B

Experiential Exercises

Gladys Weatherspoon Case Study

Background

Gladys Weatherspoon (your mom) is an 83-year-old widowed schoolteacher who is experiencing declining health. She cannot continue to live independently in her long-time family residence. Gladys is a diabetic with poor vision, osteoporosis, and limited mobility.

Her Medicare insurance coverage necessitates that she have a supplemental Medicare insurance plan at a cost of $250 per month. Gladys's prescription drugs for diabetes and osteoporosis cost her $100 per month. In addition, she has credit card debt of $3,500 with a minimum monthly payment of $150.00.

You are concerned that your mother might be showing signs of depression and dementia. Sometimes, after talking with her on the phone, you think she is forgetting things that she should be remembering. Her long-time family physician, Dr. Coates, has your mom's complete confidence. However, when the doctor told Gladys that she cannot continue to live in her current arrangement, your mother called you to complain. She vehemently disagrees with Dr. Coates's assessment and wants no changes to be made in her current living condition.

Her minister, Mr. Paul, is concerned that Gladys appears to be withdrawing from her church family. She used to be a regular at the ladies' weekly Bible class and luncheon, but her attendance has become sporadic. She tells Mr. Paul that she just gets busy and forgets what day it is. Gladys's long-time friend and neighbor, Rosa, checks on her at least twice a day. Gladys's financial advisor, Cynthia Money, has been assisting Gladys with her investments for 20 years. You have no concerns about any advice Cynthia has been giving your mother. However, you are concerned that Cynthia has not engaged you or your siblings in the conversation about your mother's investment options.

Recently, Gladys went to her family attorney and gave her second oldest son, Walter, power of attorney over her estate and all of her financial and medical affairs. Since Walter lives in the same community, his selection is a logical choice. However, several of the siblings are concerned that only one child has the power of attorney. Sam Flowers, a widower and a member of Gladys's church, takes Gladys out for supper every Friday. Sam has approached Gladys on several occasions about investing in his nephew's new business. He says she can double her money in 1 year. Gladys has said "no" so far but is seriously considering this opportunity and does not want to talk about it with you or her other children. Even Cynthia has not been included in this potential decision.

Your brother, Walter, has helped her find a senior citizen sitting service that costs $7.00 per hour. The senior citizen sitting service can provide cleaning, cooking, transportation, medicine distribution, and so forth, and the service can be scheduled in 1-hour increments up to 24 hours per day based on the needs of the client. Walter's desire is that his mother can afford 210 hours of service per month.

The other siblings in the family do not agree with Walter's idea of a senior citizen sitting service. They believe their mother's health has deteriorated to the point that the family needs to consider other options:

a. An assisted-living center at $3,000 per month (all bills included)

b. In-home hospice care (short-term for 6 months) at $3,500 a month (all bills included)

c. A nursing home at $4,000 per month (all bills included)

d. Removing all of her financial resources/assets and placing her in a Medicare-eligible facility

The table below contains a basic financial balance sheet itemizing her monthly expenses, income, and assets.

Gladys's Fiscal Balance Sheet

Monthly Expenses	Monthly Income	Capital Assets
Utilities: $150	Social Security: $700	C.D.: $25,000
Medicine: $200	Retirement Pension: $1,000	IRA: $25,000
Medical: $100	Investment Income: $300	Home: $80,000
Medicare insurance: $250		Automobile: $10,000
Food: $300		
Housing (real estate taxes, insurance, and repairs): $300		
Transportation: $100		
Miscellaneous: $200		
Home water softener (3-year contract): $75.00		
Credit card: $150		
Total: $1,825	**$2,000**	**$140,000**

The Budgeting Codes Activity

Directions: Carefully read and assess each scenario presented and then refer to the Accounting Codes Reference Sheet, subsequently found within this resource, to complete the activity. Fill in the blanks with the proper accounting codes. For the purpose of this exercise, utilize the current school year for fiscal year coding and .00 for the subobject code.

Note: Accounting codes vary from state to state and from district to district. The codes utilized in Resource B are only one particular example.

1. Smyler Grogan, assistant principal at Desert Valley Elementary School, had been given the responsibility of budget manager and was working with the budget development team to prepare the school budget for the next fiscal year. In the course of the budget preparation process, Grogan was genuinely contemplating which accounting codes would best correlate with the budgetary decisions made by him and the team. He knew that the school's guidance counselor, Mrs. Vestal Umberger, needed a new filing

credenza for her office. Desert Valley was built in 1962 and was the third elementary school in the district at the time; and Mr. Grogan realized that much of the furniture in Mrs. Umberger's office had never been replaced.

Fill in the blanks with the proper coding:

_____ — ____ — _____ . ____ — ____ — ____ — _____

2. Consuelo Estringel, principal at the Mission Hills Alternative Center for Education, was reviewing the monthly budget report when she realized that she had not budgeted for the additional $2,000 that would be needed to pay for the honorarium to be provided to the staff development presenter who was coming next week. Quickly, she began completing a district budget amendment and transfer form to ensure that the budgeted dollars would be available in the correct account. The presenter was a known expert in the area of teaching methodologies as associated with effective alternative school settings. Dr. Estringel finished the budget amendment, thus making certain that the appropriate funds were budgeted for this summer school program. She then called the presenter to verify his acceptance of the district contract.

Fill in the blanks with the proper coding:

_____ — ____ — _____ . ____ — ____ — ____ — _____

3. Tim Spedman, site-based committee chair at Western Ridge Middle School, was just finishing his lunch when Letty Muñoz—the school secretary—came by and told Tim that he needed to provide her with an accounting code for a recent purchase he had made. Letty always had to track down Tim each time he spent money out of the school's activity account for items associated with the journalism department. She knew that Tim was an exceptional teacher, but he had to be more responsible when it came to keeping up with activity fund expenditures.

Letty, being quite frustrated at the moment, thought to herself: "This old school (the second middle school built in the district) is really getting to me!" She then told Tim that he needed to allocate funding for the copy machine that the department was leasing from the Whatacopy Shop. In fact, she bluntly told him to "finish that devilled-egg sandwich and get me those account codes right away!"

Fill in the blanks with the proper coding:

_____ — ____ — _____ . ____ — ____ — ____ — _____

_____ — ____ — _____ . ____ — ____ — ____ — _____

4. Bayou Elementary School was the newest elementary campus in Pecan Grove Independent School District. It had just opened 4 months ago to accommodate the growing population of students in the greater Hudston metropolitan area. The seven other elementary schools were highly rated according to the statewide accountability standards. Susan Dianes knew that she had a task on her hands as she assumed the role of the school's first principal. Nevertheless, Dr. Dianes had been a strong assistant principal for 4 years at Enchanted Path Elementary School and had been an outstanding special education teacher for 7 years in a nearby school district. However, today, she had to work with the site-based team, and some difficult decisions had to be made.

Dr. Dianes had received word earlier in the week that the school budget was about to be cut in the area of student field trips. Student travel had become a school board issue, and starting next semester, any new student travel requests would be denied. Dr. Dianes knew that the fourth-grade class always made a major end-of-the-year trip to Seaside Kingdom down on the coast. Monies must be encumbered now, or any attempt next semester to fund the trip would be met with stiff resistance from central office administration, not to mention the school board.

Later that afternoon, Dr. Dianes and the site-base team met, and all agreed that funds must be amended from other budgetary accounts. Thus, Dr. Dianes and the team reviewed the budget, determined where the cuts would come from, and then Dr. Dianes completed the necessary budget amendment/transfer forms.

Fill in the blanks with the proper coding:

___ — ___ — _____ . ___ — ___ — ___ — _____

Accounting Codes Reference Sheet

State education codes across the nation require that a standard fiscal accounting system be adopted by each school district. A major purpose of any accounting code structure is to ensure that the sequence of codes uniformly applies to all school districts. Utilize this coding structure when responding to the scenarios presented in Resource B: Experiential Exercises.

199—11—6399.00—001—Current Year—11

1   2   3 4   5   6   7

1. Fund Code (500+)*

185 = State Compensatory Education
199 = General Fund
211 = Title I
219 = Bilingual Education
224 = Special Education
235 = Title IV
243 = Vocational Education (TechPrep)
255 = Title II
461 = Campus Activity Fund

2. Function Code (27)

11 = Instruction
12 = Instructional Resources and Media Services
13 = Curriculum and Staff Development
21 = Instructional Leadership (Instructional Specialist)
23 = School Leadership (Administration)
31 = Guidance Counseling and Evaluation Services
32 = Social Work Services
33 = Health Services (Nurse)
36 = Extracurricular (Stipends and Travel—Athletics, Drama, Choir, Band)
51 = Maintenance and Operations (Custodial Supplies)
52 = Security
53 = Computers/Maintenance and Repair (Students/Teachers)
61 = Community Services

3. Object Code (35)

6100 = Payroll Costs
6112 = Salaries or Wages for Substitute Teachers
6117 = Extra Duty Pay—Professional (Expenditures for Professional Development/Curriculum Writing as related to Function 12)
6118 = Stipends
6119 = Salaries or Wages—Teachers and Other Professional Personnel
6121 = Paraprofessional Personnel/Extra Duty Pay
6129 = Salaries for Support Personnel
6219 = Professional and Contracted Services
6249 = Maintenance and Repair
6269 = Rentals/Operating Leases (copiers, etc.)
6300 = Supplies and Materials

6329 = Reading Materials

6339 = Testing Materials

6395 = Technology Supplies/Equipment Under $5,000 (per-unit cost)

6396 = Furniture and Equipment Under $5,000 (per-unit cost)

6399 = General Supplies

6400 = Other Operating Costs

6411 = Travel/Subsistence (Employees)

6412 = Travel/Subsistence (Students)

6494 = Transportation (Buses)

6498 = Hospitality Expenses

6600 = Capital Outlay—Equipment

6636 = Technology Equipment Over $5,000 (per-unit cost)

6637 = Computer Labs

6639 = Furniture and Equipment Over $5,000 (per-unit cost)

6669 = Library Books

4. Subobject Code

This code is often used to delineate, for example, secondary-level departments. (For the purpose of the exercises and activities within this book, utilize .00 for the subobject code.)

5. Organization Code (School) (900)

001–040 = High School Campuses

041–100 = Middle School Campuses

101–698 = Elementary School Campuses

699 = Summer School Organizations

6. Fiscal Year Code

13 = 2012–2013

14 = 2013–2014

15 = 2014–2015

16 = 2015–2016

17 = 2016–2017

18 = 2017–2018

19 = 2018–2019

20 = 2019–2020, etc.

7. Program Intent Code (13)

11 = Basic Educational Services

21 = Gifted and Talented

22 = Career and Technology
23 = Special Education
24 = Accelerated Instruction
25 = Bilingual Education
26 = Alternative Education Placement (AEP) Services
30 = Title I (Schoolwide Project)
91 = Athletics
99 = Undistributed (Charges not distributed to specific programs, i.e., Employee Allowance for Cell Phones)

* The number in parenthesis represents the total number of differing accounting codes that might be utilized when developing a school budget. The codes listed within the Accounting Codes Reference Sheet are the most commonly utilized at the site level.

Resource C

Budgeting Checklist for School Administrators

School administrators have numerous tasks and responsibilities that are related to the school budget and other bookkeeping procedures. This checklist is intended to assist the school leader in mastering those tasks and responsibilities. Furthermore, it is anticipated that each of these checklist items will further serve to ensure a successful budgetary year as well as the overall success of those individuals involved in a most demanding yet essential process.

Bookkeeping Tasks and Responsibilities

- ❑ Review all receipt books.
- ❑ Reconcile all bank statements on a monthly basis.
- ❑ Account for petty cash funds and reconcile on a monthly basis.
- ❑ Ensure each month that all checks have been signed with proper signatures.
- ❑ Visit on a regular (weekly) basis with the bookkeeping clerk regarding all budgetary considerations.
- ❑ Ensure that all bookkeeping personnel are bonded.
- ❑ Monitor all payments of bills and potential discounts for early or timely payments.
- ❑ Review any bookkeeping or budgetary issues that require your approval or signature. Examples include:
    - ❑ Checks
    - ❑ Purchase orders
    - ❑ Financial reports

❑ Fundraising requests
❑ Amendments
❑ Field-trip requests

Budget Manager Tasks and Responsibilities

❑ Examine and review the budget on a monthly basis.
❑ Ensure that all requisitions that are prepared specifically list and identify the quantity ordered, proper accounting code(s), description of item(s) ordered, unit cost per item(s) ordered, subtotals, and grand totals are reflected on the requisition, originator is identified, and that the approval signature is noted.
❑ During the requisition or budget season, ensure that all requisition forms are prepared by faculty and staff and submitted on a timely basis.
❑ Ensure that all accounts have been properly audited by authorized outside accounting firms.
❑ Update the faculty handbook annually regarding any fiscal and/or budgetary topics or issues.
❑ Hold a faculty meeting prior to the budget development and requisition season to ensure that all parties understand the allocations provided as well as the proper procedures associated with requisition supplies, materials, and all other budgetary considerations.
❑ Develop a school academic action or improvement plan and integrate the plan with the school budget.
❑ Review the different budget accounts each month. Do not allow for overexpenditures to roll forward from one month to the next.
❑ Amend the school budget as is necessary and in accordance with the school academic action or improvement plan.
❑ Be aware of all district guidelines and deadlines associated with the school budget.
❑ Spend all school funds wisely, appropriately, legally, timely, and with a student-centered approach/application.

Fundraising Considerations

❑ All fundraising must comply with local board policy and/or administrative regulations.
❑ All fundraising requests must be monitored and approved prior to initiating any student-focused efforts.

❑ What additional outside sources of revenue (adopt-a-school businesses, grants, foundation dollars, etc.) can further facilitate and enhance the budgetary allotment?

Site-Based Team and Budget Development

❑ The budget development season begins each January with a meeting with the site-based team to initiate discussions about issues and considerations that will impact the budget proposed for the next school year.

❑ Establish a budget calendar and begin regular meetings for the purpose of developing the school budget.

❑ Plan to spend the time necessary for proper budget development. In most cases, this will require several afterschool meetings, at least two half-day sessions, and at least one full-day meeting.

❑ Provide the site-based team with the proper accounting codes and categories to begin the school budget development process.

❑ Establish with the team all revenue and expenditure targets for the next fiscal-year budget. Enter all revenue and expenditure funds on the appropriate school form to be submitted to the district business department.

❑ Examine any budgetary concerns that might have been problematic during the previous year budget cycle. Review the budget on an account-by-account basis.

Important Budgetary Questions

❑ What is the budgetary allotment for the next fiscal year?

❑ What is the basis for the upcoming budgetary allotment?

❑ What is the projected student enrollment for next year and what is the per-pupil allotment?

❑ Are there any money or budgetary concerns or considerations to be aware of this week?

❑ Are any employees not following proper fiscal procedures as related to the budget or bookkeeping management, receipts, purchase orders, reimbursements, or financial reports, to include bank reconciliation?

❑ Do any checks or purchase orders need approval and/or authorized signature?

❑ Are daily bank deposits being made?

❑ Are there any other items related to the school budget or bookkeeping procedures that need to be discussed or examined?

❑ What bookkeeping or budgetary improvements need to be made?

❑ When do I get a well-deserved vacation?

Resource D

State Departments of Education Websites

State education department home pages provide a vast amount of information related to educational topics and issues. In the case of this text, information gathered from different state education department websites, along with pertinent data, templates, and other relevant examples and materials, are essential links to better understanding the school budgeting and planning processes. Each state department website can prove particularly useful when principals or other affected personnel are seeking specific accounting code formats as related to your state. In most instances, budgeting or school finance-oriented links should exist on the state education department home pages and, as a result, should present opportunities for the viewer to download useful information. The best method for seeking specific budgetary topics, as related to individual states, is to simply explore the home page of interest, and the relatable links.

Listed below for your convenience is each of the 50 state education department websites. Remember that state education department home pages vary greatly in design and also in the amount of information provided. The best sites make available to the viewer the most up-to-date information and easy links to school budgeting and finance topics. School leaders should regularly take time to visit their state education department's website to review essential, if not critical, information related not only to budgeting and finance but to other educational issues as well.

State	Website
Alabama	http://www.alsde.edu/
Alaska	http://www.eed.state.ak.us
Arizona	http://www.azed.gov/
Arkansas	http://arkansased.org/
California	http://www.cde.ca.gov/index.asp
Colorado	http://www.cde.state.co.us/
Connecticut	http://www.state.ct.us/sde/
Delaware	http://www.doe.state.de.us/
Florida	http://www.fldoe.org
Georgia	http://www.doe.k12.ga.us/Pages/Home/aspx
Hawaii	http://doe.k12.hi.us
Idaho	http://www.sde.idaho.gov/
Illinois	http://www.isbe.state.il.us/
Indiana	http://www.doe.in.gov/
Iowa	http://educateiowa.gov/
Kansas	http://www.ksde.org/
Kentucky	http://www.kde.state.ky.us/KDE/
Louisiana	http://doe.louisiana.gov/
Maine	http://www.maine.gov/education/sb/index.html
Maryland	http://marylandpublicschools.org/msde
Massachusetts	http://www.doe.mass.edu
Michigan	http://www.michigan.gov/mde
Minnesota	http://education.state.mn.us/mde/index.html
Mississippi	http://www.mde.k12.ms.us
Missouri	http://dese.mo.gov/
Montana	http://bpe.mt.gov/default.mcpx
Nebraska	http://www.education.ne.gov/
Nevada	http://www.doe.nv.gov
New Hampshire	http://www.education.nh.gov/
New Jersey	http://www.nj.gov/education/
New Mexico	http://www.ped.state.nm.us/

State	Website
New York	http://www.nysed.gov/
North Carolina	http://www.dpi.state.nc.us/
North Dakota	http://www.dpi.state.nd.us
Ohio	http://www.ode.state.oh.us
Oklahoma	http://sde.state.ok.us
Oregon	http://www.ode.state.or.us/
Pennsylvania	http://www.education.state.pa.us/portal/server. pt/community/pennsylvania_department_of_ education/7237
Rhode Island	http://www.ride.ri.gov/
South Carolina	http://ed.sc.gov/
South Dakota	http://www.doe.sd.gov
Tennessee	http://www.state.tn.us/education/
Texas	http://www.tea.state.tx.us/
Utah	http://www.utah.gov/education/k12.html
Vermont	http://education.vermont.gov/
Virginia	http://www.doe.virginia.gov/
Washington	http://www.educationdepartment.org/ department/WA
West Virginia	http://wvde.state.wv.us/
Wisconsin	http://www.wisconsin.gov/state/core/ education.html
Wyoming	http://edu.wyoming.gov/Default.aspx

References

Alexander, K., & Alexander, M. D. (2011). *American public school law* (8th ed.). Belmont, CA: Wadsworth, Cengage Learning.

American Association of School Administrators (AASA). (2002). *Using data to improve schools: What's working.* Alexandria, VA: AASA.

Anderson, L. (1997). *They smell like sheep.* West Monroe, LA: Howard.

Baker, B. D., Green, P., & Richards, C. E. (2008). *Financing education systems.* Upper Saddle River, NJ: Pearson Education.

Banks, C. M. (2000). Gender and race as factors in educational leadership. In *The Jossey-Bass reader on educational leadership* (pp. 217–256). San Francisco: Jossey-Bass.

Bannock, G., Baxter, R. E., & Davis, E. (2011). *Dictionary of economics* (8th ed.). New York: Penguin Global (USA).

Barth, R. S. (2001). *Learning by heart.* San Francisco: Jossey-Bass.

Beckner, W. (2004). *Ethics for educational leaders.* Boston: Pearson Education.

Blumberg, A., & Greenfield, W. D. (1986). *The effective principal.* Boston: Allyn & Bacon.

Borja, B. R. (2005). Ethics issues snare school leaders. *Education Week, 24*(18), 1–4.

Borman, G. D., Slavin, R. E., Cheung, A., Chamberlain, A., Madden, N. A., & Chambers, B. (2007). Final reading outcomes of the national randomized field trial of Success for All. *American Education Research Journal, 44*(3), 701–731.

Bracey, G. W. (2002). *The war against America's public schools: Privatizing schools, commercializing education.* Boston: Allyn & Bacon.

Brewer, E. W., & Achilles, C. M. (2008). *Finding funding: Grant writing from start to finish, including project management and Internet use.* Thousand Oaks, CA: Corwin.

Brimley, V., Jr., Verstegen, D. A., & Garfield, R. (2012). *Financing education in a climate of change* (11th ed.). Upper Saddle River, NJ: Pearson Education.

Bureau of Labor Statistics. (2011, May 4). *Education pays.* Retrieved from http://www.bls.gov/emp/ep_chart_001.htm

Carroll, L. (1993). *Alice's adventures in Wonderland.* (Dover Thrift ed.). New York: Dover Publications.

Cavanagh, S., & Hollingsworth, H. (2011). *Education budget cuts: Schools face *fiscal cliff as stimulus money runs out.* Retrieved on February 10, 2012, from http://www.huffingtonpost.com/2011/04/06education-budget-cuts_n_845620.html

Change Leadership Group, The. (2006). *Change leadership: A practical guide to transforming our schools.* San Francisco: Jossey-Bass.

Celio, M. B., & Harvey, J. (2005). *Buried treasure: Developing an effective guide from mountains of educational data.* Seattle, WA: Center on Reinventing Public Education.

Cizek, G. J. (1999). *Cheating on tests: How to do it, detect it, and prevent it.* Mahwah, NJ: Lawrence Erlbaum.

Clover, C., Jones, E., Bailey, W., & Griffin, B. (2004). Budget priorities of selected principals: Reallocation of state funds. *NASSP Bulletin, 88*(640), 69–79.

Columbia World of Quotations, The. (1996). New York: Columbia University Press. Retrieved May 15, 2005, from http://www.bartleby.com/66

Cooper, T. L. (1998). *The responsible administrator: An approach to ethics for the administrative role.* San Francisco: Jossey-Bass.

Council of Chief State School Officers. (1996). *Interstate School Leaders Licensure Consortium (ISLLC): Standards for school leaders.* Washington, DC: Author.

Council of Chief State School Officers. (2008). *Interstate School Leaders Licensure Consortium: Standards for school leaders.* Washington, DC: Author.

Covey, S. R. (2004). *The seven habits of highly effective people.* New York: Simon & Schuster.

Creighton, T. (2006). *School and data: The educator's guide to improve decision making* (2nd ed.). Thousand Oaks, CA: Corwin.

Data Quality Campaign. (2009). *The next step: Using longitudinal data systems to improve student success.* Retrieved June 19, 2009, from www.Dataqualitycampaign.org/files/nextstep.pdf

Dayton, J. (2002). Three decades of school funding litigation: Has it been worthwhile and when will it end? *School Business Affairs, May,* 7–9.

Deal, T. E., & Kennedy, A. A. (1982). *Corporate cultures: The rites and rituals of corporate life.* Reading, MA: Addison-Wesley.

Deal, T. E., & Peterson, K. D. (1998). How leaders influence the culture of schools. *Educational Leadership, 56*(1), 28–30.

Deal, T. E., & Peterson, K. D. (2009). *Shaping school culture: Pitfalls, paradoxes, and promises* (2nd ed.). San Francisco: Jossey-Bass.

Deming, W. E. (2000). *Out of crisis.* Cambridge: MIT Press.

DePree, M. (2003). *Leading without power: Finding hope in serving community.* San Francisco: Jossey-Bass.

Desimone, L. M., Porter, A. C., Garet, M. S., Yoon, K. S., & Briman, B. F. (2002). *Educational evaluation and policy analysis, 24*(2), 81–112.

Dove, M. K. (2004). Teacher attrition: A critical American and international education issue. *Delta Kappa Gamma Bulletin, 71*(1), 8–15.

Earl, L. (1995). Moving from the political to the practical: A hard look at assessment and accountability. *Orbit, 26*(2), 61–63.

Earl, L., & Katz, S. (2005). Painting a data-rich picture. *Principal Leadership, 5*(5), 16–20.

Edmonds, R. R. (1979). Effective schools for the urban poor. *Educational Leadership, 37*(2), 15–24.

Eliot, T. S. (1935). *Murder in the cathedral.* San Diego, CA: Harcourt Brace.

Elmore, R. F. (2002). *Bridging the gap between standards and achievement.* Washington, DC: Albert Shanker Institute.

Erekson, O. H., DeShano, K. M., Platt, G., & Zeigert, A. L. (2002). Fungibility of lottery revenues and support for public education. *Journal of Education Finance, 28*(2), 301–311.

Fullan, M. G., (2007). *The new meaning of educational change.* New York: Teachers College Press.

Fullan, M. G., & Miles, M. (1992). Getting reform right: What works and what doesn't. *Phi Delta Kappan, 73*(10), 745–752.

Fullan, M. G., with Stiegelbauer, S. (1991). *The new meaning of educational change.* New York: Teachers College Press.

Garrett, T. A. (2001). Earmarked lottery revenues for education: A new test of fungibility. *Journal of Education Finance, 26*(3), 219–238.

Garza, C. L. (2005, January 16). Test-score swings draw scrutiny. *Fort Worth Star-Telegram,* Retrieved February 10, 2005, from http://www.dfw .com/mld/startelegram/news/local/10660418.htm

Glatthorn, A. A., Boschee, F., Whitehead, B. M., & Boschee, B. F. (2012). *Curriculum leadership: Strategies for development and implementation.* Thousand Oaks, CA: Sage.

Godwords Theology and Other Good Stuff (n.d.). [Online]. *Is 99.9 percent good enough?* Retrieved Feb. 11, 2005, from www.godwords.org/ stories/99percent.html

Goldsmith, L. M., & Sorenson, R. D. (2005). Ethics, integrity and fairness: Three musts for school vision and budgeting. *Texas Study of Secondary Education, 15*(1), 7–9.

Gorton, R., Schneider, G., & Fisher, J. (1988). *Encyclopedia of school administration and supervision.* Phoenix, AZ: Oryx.

Governmental Accounting Standards Board (GASB). (2011). *Codification of governmental accounting and financial reporting standards.* Norwalk, CT: Author.

Green, R. L. (2013). *Practicing the art of leadership: A problem-based approach to implementing the ISLLC standards* (4th ed.). New York: Pearson.

Greenberg, E., Dunleavy, E., & Kutner, M. (2007). *Literacy behind bars: Results from the 2003 national assessment* (NCES 200-473). U.S. Department of Education, National Center for Education Statistics. Retrieved from ED Pubs website: nces.ed.gov/pubs2007/2007473.pdf

Greenleaf, R. K. (2002). *Servant leadership: A journey into the nature of legitimate power and greatness.* Mahwah, NJ: Paulist Press.

Guthrie, J. W., Hart, C., Hack, W. G., & Candoli, I. C. (2007). *Modern school business administration: A planning approach.* Boston: Allyn & Bacon.

Guthrie, J. W., Springer, M. G., Rolle, R. A., & Houck, E. A. (2007). *Modern education finance and policy*. Boston: Pearson Education.

Hadderman, M. (2002). School-based budgeting. *Teacher Librarian, 30*(1), 27–30.

Harris, S. (2004). Strategies to meet the challenge of the age of accountability. *Insight, 18*(3), 25–28.

Haveman, M., & Sexton, T. A. (2008). *Property tax assessment limits: Lesson from thirty years of experience*. Cambridge, MA: Lincoln Institute of Land Policy.

Henrichson, C., & Delaney, R. (2012). *The price of prisons: What incarceration costs taxpayers*. Vera Institute of Justice, Center on Sentencing and Corrections. Retrieved from http://www.vera.org/pubs/price-prisons

Herman, J. J., & Herman, J. L. (2001). *School-based budgets: Getting, spending, and accounting*. Lanham, MD: Scarecrow.

Holcomb, E. L. (2004). *Getting excited about data: Combining people, passion and proof to maximize student achievement* (2nd ed.). Thousand Oaks, CA: Corwin.

Hopkins, D., & West, M. (1994). Teacher development and school improvement: An account of improving the quality of education for all (IQEA) project. In D. R. Wallings (Ed.), *Teachers as leaders: Perspectives on the professional development of teachers* (pp. 179–199). Bloomington, IN: Phi Delta Kappa.

Hoy, W. K., & Miskel, C. G. (2012). *Educational administration: Theory, research, and practice*. Boston: McGraw-Hill Humanities/Social Sciences/Languages.

Hughes, R. L., Ginnett, R. C., & Curphy, G. J. (2009). *Leadership: Enhancing the lessons of experience*. Boston: McGraw-Hill/Irwin.

Hylbert, A. (2002). The effects of the property tax extension limitation law upon revenue growth, bonded debt, and school business leader perceptions. *Journal of School Business Management, 14*(2), 9–14.

Institute of Education Sciences. (2012). *National assessment of Title I final report*. Retrieved February 15, 2012, from http://ies.ed.gov/ncee/pdf/20084014_rev.pdf

Iger, A. L. (1998). *Music of the golden age, 1900–1950 and beyond: A guide to popular composers and lyricists*. Westport, CT: Greenwood.

Johnson, C. E. (2009). *Meeting the ethical challenges of leadership*. Thousand Oaks, CA: Sage.

Johnson, R. S. (2002). *Using data to close the achievement gap: How to measure equity in our schools* (2nd ed.). Thousand Oaks, CA: Corwin.

Jones, T. H., & Amalfitano, J. L. (1994). *America's gamble: Public school finance and state lotteries*. Lancaster, PA: Technomic.

KFOX Television. (2011, August 2). *Update: EPISD superintendent Lorenzo Garcia arrested*. Retrieved February 20, 2012, from http://www.kfoxtv.com/news/news/update-episd-superintendent-lorenzo-garcia-arreste/nDTLn/

Laffee, S. (2002, December). Data-driven districts. *The School Administrator, 59*, 6–15.

LaMorte, M. W. (2011). *School law: Cases and concepts.* Boston: Allyn & Bacon Educational Leadership.

Lazear, J. (1992). *Meditations for men who do too much.* New York: Fireside/Parkside, Simon & Schuster.

Learning Point Associates. (2004). *Guide to using data in school improvement efforts: A compilation of knowledge from data retreats and data use at Learning Points Associates.* Retrieved April 2, 2012, from http://www.learningpt.org/pdfs/datause/guidebook.pdf

Leithwood, K. (1990). The principal's role in teacher development. In B. Joyce (Ed.), *Changing school culture through staff development: 1990 yearbook of the Association for Supervision and Curriculum Development* (pp. 71–90). Alexandria, VA: ASCD.

Levin, H. M. (2011). Waiting for Godot: Cost-effectiveness analysis in education. *New Directions for Evaluation, 90,* Summer. San Francisco: Jossey-Bass.

Linder, D. (n.d.). *Regulation of obscenity and nudity.* Retrieved September 6, 2004, from Exploring Constitutional Conflicts website: http://law2.umkc.edu/faculty/projects/ftrials/conlaw/obscenity.htm

Loeb, S., & Plank, D. N. (2007). *Continuous improvement in California education: Data systems and policy learning.* Berkeley, CA: Policy Analysis for California Education (PACE), University of California, Berkeley.

Lunenburg, F. C., & Irby, B. J. (2006). *The principalship: Vision to action.* Belmont, CA: Wadsworth.

Maeroff, G. I. (1994). On matters of body and mind: Overcoming disincentives to a teaching career. In D. R. Walling (Ed.), *Teachers as leaders: Perspectives on the professional development of teachers* (pp. 45–57). Bloomington, IN: Phi Delta Kappa.

Mandinach, E., & Jackson, S. (2012). *Transforming teaching and learning through data-driven decision making.* Thousand Oaks: Corwin.

Matthews, J., & Crow, G. M. (2010). *The principalship: New roles in a professional learning community.* Boston: Allyn & Bacon.

McCloskey, W., Mikow-Porto, V., & Bingham, S. (1998). *Reflecting on progress: Site-based management and school improvement in North Carolina.* (ERIC Document Reproduction Service ED 421766)

McLuhan, M., & Fiore, Q. (2005). *The medium is the message: An inventory of effects.* Berkeley, CA: Gingko Press.

Murphy, J., & Shipman, N. J. (1998). *The interstate school leaders licensure consortium: A standards-based approach to strengthening educational leadership.* Paper presented to the annual conference of the American Educational Research Association, San Diego, CA.

Mutter, D. W., & Parker, P. J. (2004). *School money matters: A handbook for principals.* Alexandria, VA: Association for Supervision and Curriculum Development (ASCD).

Nash, R. J. (1996). *"Real world" ethics: Frameworks for educators and human service professionals.* New York: Teachers College Press.

National Association of Elementary School Principals (NAESP). (2008). *The K–8 principal in 2008: A 10-year study.* Retrieved April 15, 2012, from http://www.naesp.org/10-year-study

National Association of Secondary School Principals (NASSP). (2001). *Priorities and barriers in high school leadership: A survey of principals.* Reston, VA: National Association of Secondary School Principals.

National Center for Education Statistics. (2009a) [Online]. *Financial accounting for local and state school systems: 2009 edition.* Retrieved February 10, 2012, from http://nces.ed.gov/pubs2009/fin_acct/index.asp

National Center for Education Statistics. (2009b). *Financial accounting for local and state systems handbook: 2009 edition.* Retrieved February 20, 2012, from http://nces.ed.gov/pubsearch/pubsinfo.asp?pubid=2009325

National Conference of State Legislatures. (2012). *State budget update: Fall 2011.* Retrieved February 14, 2012, from http://ncsl.org

National Education Association. (2010). *Rankings and estimates: Rankings of the states and estimates of school statistics 2010.* Atlanta, GA: Author.

National Policy Board for Educational Administration (NPBA). (2002). *Instructions to implement standards for advanced programs in educational leadership for principals, superintendents, curriculum directors, and supervisors.* Arlington, VA: National Policy Board for Educational Administration.

National Staff Development Council. (2001). *Standards for staff development* (rev. ed.). Oxford, OH: Author. Available at www.nsdc.org/educator index.htm

Negron, S. (2006). *Kinky Friedman: A Texas twister of a candidate.* Retrieved February 14, 2012, from http://newspapertree.com/view_article.sstg?c=4caab8c666334633

Nelson, A., & Toler, S. (2002). *The five secrets to becoming a leader.* Ventura, CA: Regal Books.

New Jersey School Board Association. (2007). *Financing special education in New Jersey.* Retrieved April 17, 2012, from http://www.google.com/url?sa=t&rct=j&q=&esrc=s&source=web&cd=7&ved=0CFoQFjAG&url=http%3A%2F%2Fwww.njsba.org%2Fspecialeducation%2FExecutive-Summary.pdf&ei=TMCNT6PfMMbF2QXyjeH_Cw&usg=AFQjCNFiOTYoASaOvvIsKvJBox7v1ZGK1w

No Child Left Behind Act. (2011). *Action plan components.* Washington, DC: Author.

Northouse, P. G. (2013). *Leadership: Theory and practice.* Thousand Oaks, CA: Sage.

Norton, M. S. (2005). *Executive leadership for effective administration.* Boston: Pearson Education.

Odden, A., & Archibald, S. (2001). *Reallocating resources: How to boost student achievement without asking for more.* Thousand Oaks, CA: Corwin.

Odden, A., & Wohlsletter, P. (1995). Making school-based management work. *Educational Leadership, 52*(5), 32–36.

O'Donnell, L., & Sorenson, R. D. (2005). *How sex and money ruined Dr. Ed U. Kator's career.* Manuscript submitted for publication.

Office of Management and Budget. (2005). *Preventing embezzlement.* Washington, DC: Author.

Oliva, P. (2005). *Developing the curriculum* (6th ed.). Boston: Pearson.

Osborne, J., Barbee, D., & Suydam, J. A. (1999). FBI is asked to examine CCISD. *Corpus Christi Caller-Times.* Retrieved June 17, 2005, from http://www.caller2.com/1999/october/06/today/local_ne/1147.html

Ovsiew, L., & Castetter, W. B. (1960). *Budgeting for better schools.* Englewood Cliffs, NJ: Prentice Hall.

Owings, W. A., & Kaplan, L. S. (2006). *American public school finance.* Belmont, CA: Wadsworth, Cengage Learning.

Peterson, S. L. (2001). *The grantwriter's Internet companion: A resource for educators and others seeking grants and funding.* Thousand Oaks, CA: Corwin.

Poston, W. K., Jr. (2011). *School budgeting for hard times: Confronting cutbacks and critics.* Thousand Oaks, CA: Corwin.

Property Tax Division of the Texas Comptroller's Office. (2012). *Window on state government: More challenges facing Texas education today.* Retrieved on February 13, 2012, from http://www.window.state.tx.us/comptrol/wwstand/wws0512ed

Ramsey, R. D. (2001). *Fiscal fitness for school administrators: How to stretch resources and do even more with less.* Thousand Oaks, CA: Corwin.

Razik, T. A., & Swanson, A. D. (2010). *Fundamental concepts of educational leadership and management.* Boston: Allyn & Bacon.

Reagan, R. (1987). *Remarks on signing the intermediate-range nuclear forces treaty, December 8, 1987.* Retrieved February 20, 2012, from http://www.reagan.utexas.edu/archives/speeches/1987/120887c.htm

Roe, W. H. (1961). *School business management.* New York: McGraw-Hill.

Rosenthal, B. M. (2011). *How Mercer Middle School soared after struggling.* Retrieved on February 19, 2012, from http://seattletimes.nwsource.com/html/localnews/2016936142_mercer05m.html

Ryan, K., & Cooper, J. (2004). *Those who can teach* (10th ed.). Boston: Allyn & Bacon.

Schimmel, D., Stellman, L. R., & Fisher, L. (2010). *Teachers and the law.* Upper Saddle River, NJ: Prentice Hall.

Schladen, M., & Kappes, H. (2012, February 4). *El Paso ISD's former superintendent Lorenzo Garcia sets trial date of June 18.* Retrieved from http://www.elpasotimes.com/news/ci_19890821

Sergiovanni, T. J., Kelleher, P., McCarthy, M. M., & Fowler, F. C. (2009). *Educational governance and administration.* Boston: Allyn & Bacon.

Severson, K. (2011, July 6). Systematic cheating is found in Atlanta's school system. *New York Times.* Retrieved from http://www.nytimes.com/2011/07/06/education/06atlanta.html

Seyfarth, J. T. (2007). *Human resource leadership for effective schools.* Boston: Allyn & Bacon.

Shapiro, J. P., & Stefkovich, J. A. (2011). *Ethical leadership and decision making in education: Applying theoretical perspectives to complex dilemmas.* New York: Routledge.

Shaw, P. L. (2012). *Taking charge: Leading with passion and purpose in the principalship.* New York: Teachers College Press.

Shipman, N. J., Topps, B. W., & Murphy, J. (1998). *Linking the ISLLC standards to professional development and re-licensure.* Paper presented to the annual conference of the American Educational Research Association, San Diego, CA.

Sorenson, R. D. (2007). How sex and money ruined Dr. Ed U. Kator's career. *Leadership in Focus 6*(Winter), 6–10.

Sorenson, R. D. (2008). Principal effectiveness: A twelve-step approach to leadership success. *Principal Matters: Journal for Secondary School Leaders 75*(Winter), 6–8.

Sorenson, R. D. (2010). Making sense of dollars and cents. School management. *NAESP Principal, 90*(1), 10–15.

Sorenson, R. D., & Cortez, M. T. (2010). The principal's role and responsibility in analyzing the campus improvement plan and conducting a needs assessment. *Instructional Leader, 23,* 11–14.

Sorenson, R. D., Cortez, M. T., & Negrete, M. A. (2010). What makes for an ideal principal? A framework for leadership development and organizational success as perceived by lead teachers. *Leadership in Focus, 19*(Spring), 46–49.

Sorenson, R. D., & Goldsmith, L. M. (2004, July). *The budget–vision relationship: Understanding the interwoven process.* Paper presented at the annual Texas Association of Secondary School Principals New Principals Academy, Trinity University, San Antonio, Texas.

Sorenson, R. D., & Goldsmith, L. M. (2006). Auditing procedures and ethical behaviors: Cures for the common scheme. *TEPSA Journal* (Winter), 10–14.

Sorenson, R. D., & Goldsmith, L. M. (2007). The budget–vision relationship: Understanding the interwoven process. *Journal of School Business Management 19*(1), 27–29.

Sorenson, R. D., & Goldsmith, L. M. (2009). *The principal's guide to managing school personnel.* Thousand Oaks, CA: Corwin.

Sorenson, R. D., Goldsmith, L. M., Méndez, Z. Y., & Maxwell, K. T. (2011). *The principal's guide to curriculum leadership.* Thousand Oaks, CA: Corwin.

Starr, L. (2008). *Show me the money: Tips and resources for successful grant writing.* Retrieved February 19, 2012, from http://www.education-world.com/a_curr/profdev/profdev039.shtml

Stein, J. (Ed.). (1967). *The Random House dictionary of the English language* (Unabridged ed.). New York: Random House.

Stokes, B. (2011). *America's first deflationary depression: Is a bigger one ahead?* Retrieved on February 15, 2012, from http://www.elliottwave.com/freeupdates/archives/2011/11/01/America-s-First-Deflationary-Depression-Is-a-Bigger-One-Ahead.aspx

Swanson, A. D., & King, R. A. (1997). *School finance: Its economics and politics* (2nd ed.). New York: Longman.

Tanner, D., & Tanner, L. (2006). *Curriculum development: Theory into practice.* Englewood Cliffs, NJ: Prentice Hall.

Taylor, B. O. (2002, January). The effective schools process: Alive and well. *Phi Delta Kappan, 83*. Retrieved September 24, 2012, from http://www.kappanmagazine.org/content/83/5/375.abstract

Tempel, E., Seiler, T., & Aldrich, E. (Eds.). (2011). *Achieving excellence in fundraising*. San Francisco: John Wiley & Sons.

Texas Education Agency (TEA). (2012a). *TEA correspondence*. Retrieved on February 13, 2012, from http://ritter.tea.state.tx.us/taa/finances06282010.html

Texas Education Agency (TEA). (2012b). *Highly qualified teachers*. Retrieved April 17, 2012, from http://www.tea.state.tx.us/index4.aspx?id=4650

Texas Education Agency (TEA). (2012c). *13 components of the campus improvement plan*. Austin, TX: Author.

Texas Taxpayers and Research Association (TTARA). (2012). *An introduction to school finance in Texas*. Retrieved February 10, 2012, from http://www.ttara.org

The Center for Public Education. (2009). The challenges ahead. Retrieved September 24, 2012, from http://www.centerforpubliceducation.org/Main-Menu/Public-education/An-American-imperative-Public-education-/The-challenges-ahead-.html

The Samuel Johnson sound bite page. (1751). Quotation details. Retrieved from http://www.quotationspage.com/quote/27548.html

TeachingValues.com. (2012, February 12). The universality of the golden rule in world religions. Retrieved from http://teachingvalues.com/goldenrule.html

Thinkexist. (2012). Dwight Eisenhower. Retrieved September 24, 2012, from http://thinkexist.com/quotes/dwight_david_eisenhower/

Thompson, D. C., Wood, R. C., & Crampton, F. E. (2008). *Money and schools*. Larchmont, NY: Eye on Education.

Ubben, G. L., Hughes, L. W., & Norris, C. J. (2011). *The principal: Creative leadership for excellence in schools*. Boston: Pearson Education.

U.S. Census Bureau. (2009). *Public education finances: 2009* (G09-ASPEF). U.S. Department of Commerce, U.S. Census Bureau. Retrieved from http://www.census.gov/govs/school/

Vail, K. (1999, February). Insert coins in slot: School vending machines generate funds—and controversy. *American School Board Journal*, 28–31.

Vamos, M., & Jackson, S. (Eds.). (1989, May 29). The public is willing to take business on. *Business Week/Harris Poll, 3107*, 29.

Verstegen, D. A., & Jordan, T. S. (2008). *A quick glance at school finance: A 50 state survey of school finance policies and programs. Volume I: State by state descriptions*. Reno/Las Vegas, NV: University of Nevada. http://schoolfinances.info

Walsh, J., Kemerer, F., & Manitois, L. (2009). *The educator's guide to Texas school law*. Austin: University of Texas Press.

Walton, M. (1986). *The Deming management method*. New York: Perigee.

Webb, L. D. (2006). *The history of American education: A great American experience*. Upper Saddle River, NJ: Pearson Education.

Webb, L. D., & Norton, M. S. (2008). *Human resources administration: Personnel issues and needs in education.* Upper Saddle River, NJ: Prentice Hall.

Wells, J. T. (2002, September). Billing schemes, part 3: Pay-and-return invoicing. *Journal of Accountancy, 194*, 96–98.

Wilkins, A. L., & Patterson, K. J. (1985). Five steps for closing culture-gaps. In R. H. Kilmann, M. J. Saxton, & R. Serpa (Eds.), *Gaining control of the corporate culture* (pp. 351–369). San Francisco: Jossey-Bass.

Will, G. (2005, February 17). These bones protected by muscle. *Abilene Reporter-News*, p. 4AA.

Wohlstetter, P., & Buffett, T. M. (1992). Promoting school-based management: Are dollars decentralized too? In A. R. Odden (Ed.), *Rethinking school finance: An agenda for the 1990s* (pp. 128–165). San Francisco: Jossey-Bass.

Worrell, D. (2011). *Fraud: 5 simple steps to prevent embezzlement and theft.* Retrieved on February 20, 2012, from http://www.allbusiness.com/finance/accounting-budgeting/16653461-1.html

Yeagley, R. (2002). A forum for becoming data savvy. *The School Administrator, 59*(11), 13.

Yukl, G. A. (2010). *Leadership in organizations* (7th ed.). Englewood Cliffs, NJ: Prentice Hall.

Index